W9-BWQ-953

the
FOX
at bay

THE FOX AT BAY

*Martin Van Buren
and the Presidency,
1837-1841*

James C. Curtis

THE UNIVERSITY PRESS
OF KENTUCKY
Lexington 1970

Standard Book Number: 8131–1214–1

Library of Congress Catalog Card Number: 72–111507

Copyright © 1970 by The University Press of Kentucky

A statewide cooperative scholarly publishing agency serving
Berea College, Centre College of Kentucky, Eastern Kentucky
University, Kentucky State College, Morehead State Uni-
versity, Murray State University, University of Kentucky,
University of Louisville, and Western Kentucky University.

Editorial and Sales Offices: Lexington, Kentucky 40506

for Elisabeth

Preface

MARTIN VAN BUREN realized a lifetime ambition when he took the oath of office to become the eighth president of the United States. Ironically, the day did not belong to him; on that bright sunny afternoon in March 1837, he stood in the shadow of his illustrious predecessor Andrew Jackson. Few historians have tried to shed light on Van Buren's term, regarding it as a mere extension of the Jackson regime. Van Buren is remembered more for such nicknames as "The Red Fox of the Kinderhook" and "The Little Magician" than for his actions as a politician and chief executive. By examining this relatively neglected administration, this narrative hopes to provide new insights into the nature of the Democratic presidency and the party it served.

A study of Van Buren's years in the White House reveals the great gulf that exists between the nineteenth-century presidency and its twentieth-century counterpart. Despite the energy, vigor, and determination of Andrew Jackson, the office of chief executive was, by modern standards, comparatively weak. There was no mandate for a legislative program that would weld together diverse local interests. Van Buren and his predecessors regarded themselves as administrators, pledged to promote efficiency and simplicity, cautious lest they arouse latent fears of despotism. Even in the process of recommending a program of recovery in 1837, Van Buren denied that the chief executive should assume responsibility for the nation's economy. He was to discover the consequences of bold executive initiative.

The structure of the Democratic party required the president to limit the range of his activities. Reflecting the decentralization of American society, Jackson's Democracy focused on the state level. This was at once its greatest strength and its most serious weakness. By coordinating the efforts of powerful state organizations, Jackson built an effective electoral coalition that would serve the Democrats for decades to come. Since there was no need for a national platform, the party could adhere to a vague, negative program, satisfy local demands, and still win three successive presidential elections. The Jacksonians would continue to be successful so long as they avoided taking a stand on issues that could not be translated into local terms. Should the administration ever force its lieutenants to choose between allegiance to the states and to the national organization, the party might well destroy itself.

For the president to maintain party unity under such circumstances was no easy task. In Washington, he remained isolated, at the mercy of limited communications. He had to rely upon his state supporters to exercise discipline and carry out directives. In addition to maintaining contacts with these officials, the chief executive could make his wishes known through the party press. If he lost the services of either the local hierarchy or strategic newspapers, the president would have few means of preserving cohesion.

As a founder of the Democratic party, Van Buren was no stranger to this mode of political operation. He had long argued that the national administration must develop deep provincial roots. During his early career, he helped build a powerful machine in New York that brought political order to the Empire State. When he entered Congress, Van Buren found party leaders distracted by internal dissension and unable to devote attention to state developments. He resolved to remedy this defect by working to create a new and more responsive national coalition.

During his labors in the 1820's, Van Buren constantly reiterated his belief in Jeffersonian principles. Never an abstract thinker, he saw in the theories of state rights and limited government a practical solution to the overriding political problem of maintaining the Union. By recognizing local initiative, by protecting state interests, he felt that the party could achieve harmony and avoid sectional chaos. Van Buren realized that such a political philosophy severely limited the activities of the federal government, but he felt that this was a small price for holding the country together. During his years as a presidential adviser, Van Buren tried to keep the Jackson administration faithful to this creed.

When Van Buren took office in 1837, the Democratic alliance showed signs of serious weakness. The spirit of concord so prevalent in 1828 had worn thin. During the bank war and the nullification crisis, Andrew Jackson subjected the party to severe strains, caused in part by his dramatic deviation from Jeffersonian doctrine. Van Buren wanted to restore harmony and to repair relations with the South. The onset of an unprecedented financial depression prevented him from achieving this goal and brought him into conflict with the very system that he had labored so hard to perfect.

In seeking a solution to the Panic of 1837, Van Buren was torn by conflicting forces. Bound by the logic of previous Democratic fiscal policy, he desperately searched for a means to counter opposition demands for a new national bank. Yet in formulating his plans for an independent Treasury, Van Buren met stiff resistance from his own state supporters, who objected to a project that seemed to threaten their interests. Van Buren found himself in the dilemma of trying to decide what was best for the whole nation without offending the individual states. Neither his political upbringing nor his ideological beliefs equipped him to meet this challenge.

In examining the administration's response to the Panic of 1837, I have dealt at length with the special session of Congress. Debate during these crucial weeks in the fall of 1837 established a framework within which the president had to operate for the remainder of his term. Furthermore, this session revealed many of the obstacles Van Buren would have to overcome to establish an independent Treasury —a task that consumed most of his time in the White House. In focusing on this quest for a solution to the Panic, I have slighted such issues as public lands and creation of a ten-hour workday for federal employees. These matters commanded little of the president's attention, and the administration considered them of secondary importance.

While absorbed with the financial crisis, Van Buren faced several troublesome problems in foreign affairs. Key Southern supporters urged the new president to annex the Republic of Texas and thereby signify his devotion to the interests of the slave states. Van Buren resisted this pressure because he wanted to avoid a major political debate on so explosive an issue. As a diplomat, Van Buren hoped to maintain peaceful relations with other nations and to avoid controversies that might disrupt the Democratic party. In 1838 the activities of a few reckless Americans threatened to involve the country in a war on the northern frontier. Van Buren tried to keep the nation on a neutral course. Foreign diplomats appreciated the president's good intentions but regarded the United States as a weak, irresponsible power, incapable of curtailing the inflammatory activities of its citizens. In foreign policy, as in domestic affairs, Van Buren found himself at the mercy of the federal system that he so loudly praised.

Part of the measure of any president is his success at the polls. Van Buren faced serious problems in preparing for the campaign of 1840. In rising to the challenge of the Panic of 1837, he did what no other president in over a decade had done; he staked the success of his administration on a bid for congressional support. The Whigs had long been waiting for such an occasion. Joining disgruntled Democrats, they mounted an assault that frustrated administration discipline for over three years. Van Buren soon realized that he had no hope of winning the battle in Congress without local backing. Considering the needs of the nation paramount to the demands of the states, he tried to convince fellow Democrats to endorse the sub-Treasury scheme. Local leaders reacted violently to this pressure; since the formation of the alliance, they had not faced such a predicament. Unaccustomed to having the policies of the federal government become an issue in state politics, many of the president's followers refused to join the crusade to pass the sub-Treasury bill. In the crucial Democratic strongholds of New York and Virginia, Van Buren encountered serious opposition that disrupted the Albany-Richmond axis and demonstrated Democratic vulnerability. These defections prevented Van Buren from gaining the quick victory he so desperately needed; by the time he finally signed the sub-Treasury into law, the war was all but lost.

Preoccupied by the incessant struggle, Van Buren was not in a position to survey objectively the political scene. Although he appreciated the Whigs' efficiency and grassroots organization, he never understood their tactics. Van Buren assumed that all the excitement of 1840 was temporary and that calm would soon return. He shuddered to think that the voters might be permanently swayed by the log cabin and hard cider mania. The politician, once so keenly aware of change, had grown blind to the need for innovation.

I am grateful to a number of libraries and institutions for assisting my research on this project. Fellowship funds from Northwestern University enabled me to complete the dissertation on which this study is based. The trustees of the Newberry Library shared this financial burden, and Dr. Lawrence Towner made my stay at the Newberry a delight. His wit and wisdom proved a constant source of encouragement. The University of Texas Research Institute provided a summer grant that facilitated preparation of the manuscript. I wish to thank Mr. P. Blair Lee of Philadelphia for permission to examine the Blair-Lee Papers on deposit at Princeton. Mrs. J. Pat. O'Keefe graciously typed the final version and kept her sense of humor throughout.

During my work I received wise counsel and generous advice. Professor Robert V. Remini shared his extensive knowledge of Van Buren's career and guided me to several important source collections. Professor Robert Wiebe offered a fresh outlook, forcing me to re-think many of my basic assumptions about Jacksonian politics. Professors James Chase and George Nielsen enhanced my understanding of politics in the Era of Good Feelings. Professor William Shade allowed me to read his manuscript on banking in the Old Northwest, and my colleague Norman Brown permitted me access to a draft of his recently published book on Daniel Webster and Whig politics in the 1830's. I owe special thanks to Professor Richard H. Brown for reading an earlier version of the manuscript with care. Professors Richard R. Beeman and Lewis L. Gould both have stolen time from their own endeavors to struggle with various drafts and to comment on both style and substance.

Two debts I doubt that I shall be able to repay. Professor Richard W. Leopold first suggested this topic in a seminar on the American presidency. Since then, he has been unsparing of time and patience. His painstaking criticism, wise counsel, and sympathetic understanding have added immeasurably to my work. My wife Elisabeth helped in ways too numerous to recount.

Contents

the
FOX
at bay

Prologue

On March 4, 1837, it seemed as though even nature favored the Democrats. The nation's capital teemed with visitors, none of whom could remember a more beautiful inaugural setting. The day broke crisp and clear; a bright sun promised to melt away the traces of a late winter snowfall that had blanketed the city forty-eight hours earlier. By noon, spectators jammed the parade route along Pennsylvania Avenue, pushing and shoving to gain a choice vantage point. It was a grand day for a celebration, and Washington rose to the occasion.[1]

In front of the executive mansion, four magnificent gray horses pranced nervously, straining at the traces of a gleaming new carriage. At precisely twelve o'clock, the presidential party appeared. Many onlookers caught their first glimpse of the careworn chief executive; his appearance must have come as a shock. The years in Washington had treated Andrew Jackson harshly. The loss of his wife, Rachel, unending battles with a stubborn political opposition, frequent periods of debilitating illness—each had exacted its price. Only that morning, Jackson's personal physician pleaded with the president not to take part in the ceremonies but to remain in seclusion as he had most of the winter. To no one's surprise, Jackson flatly refused. He would let nothing stand in the way of his participation in the inaugural. For him it was a moment of personal triumph, a final victory over his enemies. Within the hour he would witness the elevation of his adviser and confidant, Martin Van Buren, a man once rejected by the Senate as minister to England. Van Buren would take the oath from Chief Justice Roger B. Taney, whom the Senate had refused to confirm as secretary of the treasury. Thus the very first act of the new administration would repay two debts left over from the old; Jackson relished this revenge.[2]

For the man taking his seat next to Andrew Jackson, this also was a day of fulfillment. Veteran of countless political campaigns, Martin Van Buren bore none of the scars of battle. Life had been good to him and he showed it. No longer could he pride himself on a neat, trim figure. His once reddish hair had receded and turned to gray. At fifty-four he looked to all the world a calm, unruffled statesman, obviously enjoying his new position. A congressional colleague once characterized Van Buren as a "man of great suavity and gentleness of deportment, and, to those who associated the idea of violence with firmness, might be supposed deficient in that quality."[3] What a contrast the plump president-elect must have been to the gaunt old soldier seated beside him.

The carriage drew away from the White House preceded by a military honor guard. Band music filled the crisp, clear air. Along the entire length of Pennsylvania Avenue, spectators craned for a look at the coach, and broke into wild cheering as it passed. Finally the procession reached the entrance to the Capitol. Here the carriage stopped; Jackson and Van Buren alighted, following a welcoming committee up the steps and inside to the Senate chamber. They paused long enough to gather cabinet members, senators, and officials of the diplomatic corps before moving slowly to the eastern portico where the inaugural platform was constructed. The appearance of the entourage sent the crowd of 20,000 into an uproar. Van Buren stepped forward and in a clear, firm voice began to read his address. The multitude fell silent.

Van Buren began by stating his feelings at assuming the burdens of office. Like his predecessors, he was filled with a sense of inadequacy at undertaking such a heavy burden. Yet unlike them, he was not of the revolutionary generation. "I feel that I belong to a later age and that I may not expect my countrymen to weigh my actions with the same kind and partial hand." Although humble in tone, these opening observations reveal Van Buren's conscious identification with a new breed of statesman.

After this brief introspective introduction, the president-elect launched into the body of his remarks. He assured his listeners that the nation was prosperous and secure, united by an ingenious Consti-

[1] Washington *Globe*, March 6, 1837.

[2] Jackson to Nicholas P. Trist, March 2, 1837, in John Spencer Bassett and J. Franklin Jameson, eds., *The Correspondence of Andrew Jackson*, 7 vols. (Washington, D.C., 1926–1935), 5: 462–63; hereafter cited as Jackson, *Correspondence*; Richmond *Enquirer*, March 9, 1837.

[3] Thomas Hart Benton, *Thirty Years View*, 2 vols. (New York, 1854–1856), 2: 15.

tution and a remarkable system of federalism. To maintain this security, Americans must ever obey the dictates of the Constitution and respect the rights of the states. Only once during the course of his remarks did Van Buren descend from this lofty plane. Near the end of his speech, he touched momentarily on the question of slavery, appealing to both North and South for calm. "Have not recent events," he queried, "made it obvious . . . that the least deviation from this spirit of forbearance is injurious to every interest, that of humanity included?" As if to underscore the gravity of this question, he firmly stated his determination to disapprove any congressional attempt to abolish slavery in the District of Columbia or to interfere with the peculiar institution in the Southern states. These were bold words, but words alone would not still the controversy.

In closing, it was only natural that he pay tribute to his predecessor. For if this was an inaugural, it was also a farewell. The crowd massed before the Capitol had come to salute the old as well as the new. Many spectators sensed they were seeing Jackson for the last time. Realizing this, Van Buren expressed a determination to preserve the legacy of leadership. "United as I have been in his counsels, a daily witness of his exclusive and unsurpassed devotion to his country's welfare, agreeing with him in sentiments which his countrymen have warmly supported, and permitted to partake largely of his confidence, I may hope that somewhat of the same cheering approbation will be found to attend my path." Then Van Buren added a personal tribute. "For him I but express with my own the wishes of all, that he may yet long live to enjoy the brilliant evening of his well-spent life."[4]

Throughout the entire speech, the crowd stood in respectful silence, greeting Van Buren's oratory with courtesy but without emotion. The quiet lingered as he turned and took the oath of office. Then the presidential party started to descend the steps of the portico. When Jackson reached the carriage, the spectators could contain themselves no longer and unleashed a thunderous ovation that reverberated back down Pennsylvania Avenue. "For once," recalled Senator Thomas Hart Benton, "the rising was eclipsed by the setting sun."[5]

[4] James D. Richardson, ed., A Compilation of the Messages and Papers of the Presidents, 1789–1897, 10 vols. (Washington, D.C., 1900), 3: 313–20; hereafter cited as Richardson, Messages and Papers.
[5] Benton, Thirty Years View, 1: 735.

Chapter 1

The Heir

MARTIN VAN BUREN first stepped onto the national political stage in December 1821, when he .entered the United States Senate. He wasted little time in adapting to his new surroundings; within a month after arriving in the capital, Van Buren sent home a penetrating analysis of political realities in Washington. "The disjointed state of parties," he complained, "the distractions which are produced by the approaching contest for president, and the general conviction in the minds of honest but prudent men, that a radical reform in the political feelings of this place has become necessary, render this the proper moment to commence the work of a general resuscitation of the old democratic party."[1]

Considering Van Buren's background and political experience, this reaction is understandable. He was born December 5, 1782, in the small Hudson River community of Kinderhook, New York. After attending the village academy, Van Buren began work in a local law office; here he mastered the legal trade, developing a mind "usefully disciplined for the examination and discussion of facts."[2] Even while absorbed in the routine of his apprenticeship, the young, aspiring advocate took a pronounced interest in New York politics. He later recalled one vivid experience in 1799, when the town resounded to the raucous sounds of a Federalist victory celebration. Having neither the inclination nor the stamina· for the marathon festivities, Van Buren slipped away to his room, the sounds of "Hail Columbia" ringing in his ears. No sooner had sleep drowned out the jarring noise than he awoke to the vigorous knock of his employer, Francis Sylvester, who entered the room and spent the better part of an hour trying to convert his protégé to the Federalist cause. Van Buren steadfastly refused, claiming that his "course had been settled after much reflection and could not be changed."[3]

6

After completing his studies in 1803, Van Buren gained admission to the bar and began private practice. In the courtrooms of Columbia County he acquired many of the skills on which his political reputation would eventually rest. Van Buren was not a stunning orator; he had neither the physique nor the voice for bombastic delivery. Short, thin, looking more the dandy than the demagogue, he relied on a subtle approach, based on a thorough mastery of detail. "Give him time to collect the requisite information," the frenetic but astute John Randolph later observed, "and no man can produce an abler argument." Van Buren soon became proficient at analyzing complex problems and presenting his conclusions in a clear, concise fashion. Humor often played a part in his presentations. Characteristically, Van Buren relied on deft witticism rather than coarse vulgarity. Never spectacular, he gained renown as a smooth, efficient lawyer.[4]

In 1808 the Republican party captured New York's patronage machinery, and Van Buren received his first political post. As the new surrogate of Columbia County, he assumed responsibility for settling estates, a task that brought him into contact with new and influential clients. The intricacies of wills and testaments did not deflect his political activities in the least. Little record of these early years remains, but Van Buren, like many other lawyers, must have traveled extensively on the circuit, using his leisure time to talk about politics. Taverns, townhalls, courthouse corridors, these were the likely places for partisan conversation. In 1808, shortly after his marriage to Hannah Hoes, Van Buren first dabbled in national affairs by organizing a series of meetings to counteract Federalist opposition to the Embargo.[5] The private speech, the public rally, the occasional resolution—all were crucial elements in grassroots politics. Van Buren became familiar with each.

From the hustings of Columbia County it was but a short step to the legislative assembly in Albany. In 1812 Van Buren won election

[1] Van Buren to Charles E. Dudley, January 10, 1822, in Catharina V. R. Bonney, A *Legacy of Historical Gleanings*, 2 vols. (Albany, N.Y., 1875), 1: 382; hereafter cited as Bonney, *Legacy*.
[2] Martin Van Buren, "The Autobiography of Martin Van Buren," ed. John C. Fitzpatrick, American Historical Association, *Annual Report for the Year 1918*, 2 vols. (Washington, D.C., 1920), 2: 10–11; hereafter cited as Van Buren, *Autobiography*. The most accurate biography of Van Buren is Edward M. Shepard, *Martin Van Buren* (Boston, 1888).
[3] Van Buren, *Autobiography*, pp. 13–14.
[4] Randolph to Andrew Jackson, March 18, 1832, in Jackson, *Correspondence*, 4: 422; Shepard, *Van Buren*, pp. 20–21.
[5] Denis Tilden Lynch, *An Epoch and a Man: Martin Van Buren and His Times* (New York, 1929), p. 78.

as a state senator and took his seat just in time to participate in the special session, called for the purpose of selecting presidential electors. He faced a difficult decision. A vote for New York's Republican nominee, De Witt Clinton, would be a vote against President Madison's conduct of the war; Van Buren had no quarrel with administration policies. Yet he was reluctant to break with his own state party and finally decided to sustain Clinton. Although he could justify his action on the basis of party regularity—a principle he would come to hold most dear—Van Buren long labored under the imputation of being opposed to the great struggle against England.

The alliance with the Clintonians proved temporary. During the presidential balloting, Van Buren grew suspicious of Clinton's blatant solicitation of Federalist votes. A year later these misgivings led to an open break that would have a significant impact on New York politics.[6] For the moment, Van Buren put aside personal feuding and devoted his energies to the Republican preparedness campaign. He soon won renown as a skilled legislator and in 1815 accepted the post of attorney general. During the next four years he would preside over New York's legal affairs at a time when the Empire State, like the rest of the nation, tried desperately to adjust to the postwar world.[7]

Victory celebrations engulfed Albany and other cities the length of the land, as America reveled in the joys of a new nationalism. Although exhilarating, this wave of enthusiasm was but part of the strong tide of wartime fervor. As such it soon receded, revealing once more the antagonisms that had always made Union such a fragile vessel. New York felt the full impact of the forces laying bare this lack of unity. After 1815 the state entered an era of unprecedented social and economic expansion. Migrants from New England moved across its upper reaches in ever-increasing numbers. Barely a trickle in the 1790's, this push westward reached flood stage by 1820. Coupled with this dramatic westward surge was an equally significant rise in the urban population.[8]

The War of 1812 had indirectly accelerated this progress by calling attention to the state's inadequate transportation system. During the height of the fighting, military commanders demanded a more effective link between Lake Erie and Lake Champlain, both scenes of crucial operations. This pressure renewed interest in a grand water-

---

[6] Jabez D. Hammond, *The History of Political Parties in the State of New York*, 2 vols. (Albany, N.Y., 1842), 1: 297–99, 315, 320–22, 342–44; Van Buren, *Autobiography*, pp. 36–46.

[7] Shepard, *Van Buren*, pp. 61–63.

[8] George Rogers Taylor, *The Transportation Revolution* (New York, 1951), pp. 3–9.

way to stretch from Albany to Buffalo. Once a wild dream, this project became a reality in 1817, when the state legislature authorized construction of the first section of the Erie Canal. It is difficult for the modern mind, accustomed to globe-circling transportation and instant communications, to appreciate the public fascination with this undertaking. America greeted its progress with the type of enthusiasm reserved for a startling scientific discovery. The canal promised to provide the answer to myriad economic and geographical problems. It would facilitate westward migration, link the farmer with the marketplace, and promote internal and international trade. No longer need the state remain a composite of isolated communities. The canal would unify New York by creating a miraculous avenue through the wilderness. Thus people dreamed as the construction began.[9]

American political life soon responded to the rapid economic and social expansion symbolized by the Erie Canal. The old habitual pattern of elite politics now began to fade, giving way to an aggressive, less comfortable substitute. The sudden spurt in the number of eligible voters prompted political managers to adopt new techniques. Gone were the days when the candidate could stand confidently before his neighbors on election day, relying on family prestige or social status to carry him to victory. The voters seemed more alive, more interested in the activities of the state and less willing to leave everything to the good judgment of the candidate. Politics was fast becoming a full-time occupation, with success going to those who organized.[10]

Martin Van Buren typified this trend toward professionalization. Since adolescence he had taken politics seriously and was willing to devote both time and energy to the perfection of a sound political organization. By 1820 he had become the acknowledged leader of a Republican clique known as the Bucktails. An association with Tammany Hall and a colorful deer's tail worn in the hat distinguished this ambitious faction from its competitors.

A deep, abiding animosity to De Witt Clinton and all things Clintonian bound the Bucktails together. Van Buren's hostility to-

[9] For a convenient study of the Erie Canal and a guide to other literature on the subject see Ronald Shaw, *Erie Water West* (Lexington, Ky., 1966).

[10] The best brief study of elite politics is Charles Sydnor, *Gentlemen Freeholders: Political Practices in Washington's Virginia* (Chapel Hill, N.C., 1952). On the decline of this pattern see David Hackett Fischer, *The Revolution in American Conservatism* (New York, 1965) and Charles G. Sellers, Jr., "Banking and Politics in Jackson's Tennessee, 1817–1827," *Mississippi Valley Historical Review* 41 (1954): 61–84.

ward the popular governor bordered on fanaticism. Rarely in his later career would he speak with such intensity about a political adversary. In his eyes, Clinton stood convicted of a multitude of sins, not the least of which was a cavalier disregard for allegiance and loyalty. He charged Clinton with collecting "around him a set of desperadoes, who, instigated by the hope of official plunder, will never be content to limit their depredation to the boundaries of the State." Van Buren reserved his utmost scorn for the Clinton organization. "Where are those political blacklegs who have alternately belonged to, deceived & betrayed all parties," he demanded, answering that one might "find them pillars in the Clintonian edifice."[11]

To will Clinton's demise was one thing; to accomplish it was another. In 1819 Van Buren received a temporary setback when the Clintonians removed him as attorney general, a blow all the more bitter because it closely followed his wife's death. This proscription further infuriated the Bucktails, who now hurled themselves into the campaign of 1820 in a manner "violent and abusive beyond example."[12] Clinton eked out a narrow victory but lost all control of the state legislature. The Bucktails trooped into Albany to claim their reward. As a result of triumph, they took control of the council of appointment, key to some 16,000 patronage positions throughout the state. They promptly celebrated their victory by removing Clintonians from office in unprecedented numbers. Rarely had the New York spoils system operated with such devastating efficiency.[13]

Having barely completed this heady conquest, the Bucktails pressed for a constitutional convention to revise the very system they had just exploited to such good advantage. Van Buren and his followers realized they could not resist public clamor for an up-to-date constitution. Furthermore, Clinton was the sworn enemy of innovation; a push for a convention would damage his reputation. By broadening the suffrage, creating new courts, and abolishing the twin councils of appointment and revision, the Albany convocation of 1821 established the Bucktails as champions of a new democracy. Patronage no longer remained the private preserve of a small group of men in the state house. Any party aspiring to dominate the appoint-

[11] Van Buren to Rufus King, January 19, 1820, January 14, 1821, in Charles R. King, ed., *The Life and Correspondence of Rufus King*, 6 vols. (New York, 1894–1900), 6: 253, 376; hereafter cited as King, *Correspondence*.
[12] W. W. Van Ness to Solomon Van Rensselaer, January 5, 1820, in Bonney, *Legacy*, pp. 340–41; Rufus King to Robert Troup, February 29, 1820, in King, *Correspondence*, 6: 284–86.
[13] Alvin Kass, *Politics in New York State, 1800–1830* (Syracuse, N.Y., 1965), p. 14.

ments would have to control the legislature, win the governor's chair, and develop a grassroots organization capable of dictating the election of county officials. Thus while the Bucktails succeeded in embarrassing Clinton, they made their own task more difficult.[14]

Van Buren eventually overcame these obstacles by creating a wide-ranging political network, often regarded as the prototype of the modern state machine. Based in Albany, this "Regency," as it would soon be known, reached into every corner of the state to spread the Republican gospel.[15] By 1823 the Bucktails captured the legislature and the governorship, thereby making themselves masters of the state's law-making process and controlling a lion's share of influential patronage. To retain this ascendancy, the Bucktails imposed a code of strict party discipline evident in both their use of the legislative caucus and their partisan selections of state employees.

Domination of the central legislative and appointive apparatus alone did not ensure Regency success. Van Buren's lieutenants still had to forge effective links with the countryside. Control of the legislative patronage simplified this task; the Albany directorate could appoint outright a number of local judges, clerks, and chancery officials. Candidates for those positions found that a faithful allegiance to the Republican cause was now a prerequisite of preferment. Even for the elective offices of sheriff and justice of the peace, Regency endorsement proved highly advantageous. To assist the public in making wise decisions and to counter opposition calumnies, the Bucktails set up committees of correspondence. This vast network was no mere election-eve phenomenon. Throughout the year, Van Buren and his followers worked to keep open the channels between Albany and the counties. In making appointments and drafting legislation, they paid particular attention to the interests of each locality. This efficiency returned handsome political dividends.

In such an era of limited communication, the press provided one of the main methods of disseminating information. Early in his political career, Van Buren recognized the need for a strong, energetic newspaper to serve the Bucktail cause. As he once remarked,

[14] Henry Shaw to Henry Clay, February 11, 1823, in James F. Hopkins, ed., *The Papers of Henry Clay*, 3 vols. (Lexington, Ky., 1959–), 3: 372–77; hereafter cited as Clay, *Papers*; Kass, *Politics in New York*, p. 15; Robert V. Remini, *Martin Van Buren and the Making of the Democratic Party* (New York, 1959), p. 7.
[15] The term Regency did not become a part of New York's political vocabulary until 1823 but is used here for the sake of convenience. On the structure of this organization see Robert V. Remini, "The Albany Regency," *New York History* 39 (1958): 341–55.

"Without a paper thus edited at Albany we may hang our harps on the willows. With it, the party can survive a thousand such convulsions."[16] Under the capable editorship of Edwin Croswell, the Albany *Argus* soon became the clarion of the Regency. Croswell made no effort to analyze the news objectively. Such impartiality was alien to his profession. The Regency sustained him with a steady flow of state printing contracts, and in return they expected faithful exposition of party policy. Usually Croswell kept his part of the bargain.

Two facets of this Regency experience are of particular importance to an understanding of Van Buren's subsequent career. The Bucktails grounded all their organizational efforts on a doctrine of party loyalty. Long battles with the forces of De Witt Clinton convinced Van Buren of the transcendent importance of maintaining strength through unity. He was always trying to recruit new converts, but only on his own terms. One wavering Federalist learned in 1820 that the Bucktails would be happy to see him and his "friends in the Republican ranks . . . but the idea of making any stipulations to secure the support of Federalists is wholly indefensible."[17] For the remainder of his active political life, Van Buren continued to extol the virtues of party discipline. Unlike so many contemporaries, he did not long for some Nirvana free from the sounds of partisan strife.[18] Political parties were vital; they could lead to "many evils, but not so many as are prevented by the maintenance of their organization and vigilance." Such was the harsh lesson of the New York political environment.[19]

In combating Clintonianism, Van Buren also gained important legislative training. He and the Bucktails had to formulate a set of economic policies geared to the state's rapid expansion. They had to convince the public that the Erie Canal would be safe in their hands and that New York would continue to prosper. By mastering the intricacies of canal construction and finance, the Bucktails took the measure of one of the nation's most ambitious internal improve-

---

[16] Van Buren to Jesse Hoyt, January 31, 1823, in William Lyon Mackenzie, *The Lives and Opinions of Benj'n Franklin Butler and Jesse Hoyt* (Boston, 1845), p. 190.
[17] Van Buren to George Tibbitts, October [?], 1820, Martin Van Buren Papers, Library of Congress.
[18] See, for example, Richmond *Enquirer*, November 7, 1820.
[19] Van Buren, *Autobiography*, p. 125. For a provocative new appraisal of party development in New York that explores Bucktail adherence to regularity, organization, and discipline, see Michael Wallace, "Changing Concepts of Party in the United States: New York, 1815–1828," *American Historical Review* 74 (1968): 453–91.

ments.[20] As a result of this experience, Van Buren gained a deep and lasting impression of the capabilities and importance of state government.[21] This awareness eventually pushed him into a national alliance pledged to safeguard state sovereignty by checking the power of the federal government.

Van Buren's total preoccupation with state affairs came to an abrupt halt in December 1821, when he set out to assume his seat in the Senate. Victorious earlier in the year over Nathan Sanford, Van Buren eagerly anticipated entry into the national political arena. He had no intention, however, of relinquishing his position as leader of the Bucktails. "The transfer from the State to the Federal Service," he later explained, "has generally been considered as a discharge from responsibility for the management of the affairs of the former, but neither friends nor foes would permit such a result in my case."[22] Had he been more candid, Van Buren might have added that his tenure in the Senate and eventually his national reputation depended upon maintenance of power in New York.

When he reached the nation's capital, Van Buren entered an unfamiliar, almost alien environment. He had spent the majority of his career in the bustling city of Albany; as a terminal for the new Erie Canal, this thriving community witnessed New York's dramatic western surge. By contrast, Washington was isolated, cut off from the nation it ruled, a far cry from the imperial metropolis envisioned by its founders. The capital could boast of little save its magnificent distances, vast expanses of undeveloped land, dotted occasionally by islands of architectural grandeur. A city of transients, it came alive for sessions of Congress but languished during the sultry summer months. It was a Southern city; half its federal employees came from Virginia and Maryland. One quarter of the population was black. Slave traders transacted business within sight of Capitol Hill, serving as a grim reminder of national problems yet unsolved.[23]

The political atmosphere was no less alien. The calm of Southern gentility could not cloak the decay of the once triumphant Republican party. Early in the century, Jefferson's organization had thrived

[20] Shaw, *Erie Water West*, p. 112.
[21] Van Buren to Mr. Coleman, April 4, 1828, in James A. Hamilton, *The Reminiscences of James A. Hamilton* (New York, 1869), p. 77; hereafter cited as Hamilton, *Reminiscences*; Van Buren to the Legislature of the State of New York, January 6, 1829, in Albany *Argus*, January 7, 1829.
[22] Van Buren, *Autobiography*, p. 113.
[23] Constance McLaughlin Green, *Washington: Village and Capital, 1800–1878* (Princeton, N.J., 1962), pp. 3–118; James Sterling Young, *The Washington Community, 1800–1828* (New York, 1966).

in the face of a determined Federalist opposition. Yet the champion of state rights contributed to his own undoing; as Federalism declined, so also did the impulse for Republican unity.[24] Although Jefferson's party continued to dominate the political scene after the War of 1812, its leaders found themselves in a precarious situation. Republican strength lay in Congress, and the caucus was its most effective tool. The tie with the legislature was a lifeline the president could not cut; party organization in Congress enabled him to exercise leadership. As long as he had to rely upon the caucus for support and renomination, he could scarcely embark on an independent course that might destroy his only base of power. His cabinet offered little aid, since advisers who aspired to the White House—and the council traditionally included such aspirants—naturally catered to those holding the keys to the succession. The president's strength and that of his party depended upon maintenance of a loyal, disciplined congressional following.[25]

President James Monroe remained oblivious to the need for a well-drilled legislative corps. Rather than stifle dissenting voices, he attempted to overcome the opposition with kindness, inviting its leaders to join in support of his administration. Attractive in theory, such an attempt to eradicate party distinctions was doomed to fail; for as Rufus King shrewdly observed: "notwithstanding we are all federalists and all Reps., that means in the sense of the motto of the Prince of Wales, we may all support, but only a part be rewarded." Monroe's policy of "amalgamation" only exacerbated tensions. By 1820 King recorded the ironic fact that although "Mr. Monroe is reelected unanimously . . . the measures of Govt. are without friends in Congress."[26] The inauguration of Monroe's second term signaled not an end to party strife but the beginning of a vicious struggle for the succession.

Little wonder that Van Buren reacted with dismay. He was accustomed to a different type of politics where quarter was neither asked nor given. Instead of discipline, he encountered laxity. In the place of organization, he found factional chaos. He had abandoned a vigorous, growing city that served as nerve center for an expansive state economy, to enter an isolated community rent by internal dissension.

[24] Rufus King to Christopher Gore, March 13, 1817, in King, Correspondence, 6: 66–67; William N. Chambers, Political Parties in a New Nation (New York, 1963), pp. 191–208.
[25] Young, Washington Community, pp. 232–42.
[26] King to [?], March [?], 1818, King to J. A. King, January 19, 1821, in King, Correspondence, 6: 123, 378.

Van Buren had barely settled in his lodgings when a patronage quarrel placed him in conflict with this strange new system.

In December 1821, the Monroe administration decided to appoint New York Congressman Solomon Van Rensselaer as postmaster at Albany. Neither the president nor the postmaster general discussed the appointment with Van Buren. During their recent removal of Clintonian officeholders, the Bucktails had stripped Van Rensselaer of his position as adjutant general of the militia; Van Buren did not want the aging Federalist marching back to Albany in glory. He tried to build a backfire in New York, hoping to change Monroe's mind. While the president did hold several cabinet meetings on the appointment, he decided that the postmaster general had every constitutional right to name Van Rensselaer to the vacancy.[27]

Angered by this rebuff, Van Buren decided to stage a massive local protest. He called on the Regency to sponsor resolutions in the state legislature, criticizing Van Rensselaer's selection. He also urged creation of a committee to correspond with "republican members of other legislatures" in the hope of generating a nationwide demand for the removal of the postmaster general. In dictating these instructions, Van Buren carefully specified that all criticism be aimed at the postal department and not at the president.[28]

This strategy was too ambitious and too subtle. The Regency dutifully drafted the required resolutions and these appeared in newspapers across the country. Yet the concerted grassroots demonstration never materialized. Legislatures outside New York remained silent, convinced perhaps, as were some of Van Buren's own supporters, that there was little difference between an assault on an executive department and on the chief executive himself. Van Buren soon realized this and gave up his attempt.[29]

It would be easy to dismiss the Van Rensselaer episode as a tempest in a teapot. The administration simply made a patronage decision without consulting all parties concerned. Caught off guard,

[27] Solomon Van Rensselaer to Stephen Van Rensselaer, December 26, 1821, Van Buren to Benjamin Knower et al., January 5, 1822, in Bonney, *Legacy*, 1: 369–70, 374–76; Van Buren to Monroe, January 5, 7, 1822, Van Buren Papers; John Quincy Adams, *Memoirs of John Quincy Adams, Comprising Portions of His Diary from 1795–1848*, ed. Charles Francis Adams, 12 vols. (Philadelphia, 1874–1877), 5: 479–82, 484; hereafter cited as Adams, *Diary*. For a more detailed discussion of this controversy see Remini, *Van Buren and the Democratic Party*, pp. 18–26.
[28] Van Buren to Charles E. Dudley, January 10, 1822, in Bonney, *Legacy*, 1: 382–84.
[29] Michael Ulshoeffer to Van Buren, January 27, 1822, Van Buren Papers.

Van Buren overreacted, desperately trying to avoid a stinging defeat at the outset of his senatorial career. He did not dislike Van Rensselaer; he simply disliked being ignored. He therefore protested the administration decision with great vigor. So it must have seemed to many of Van Buren's contemporaries.

The clash over the Albany postmastership was more than a struggle to refurbish battered reputations. It was a conflict between two dissimilar political systems. For the most part, the president handled the problem as though it existed in a vacuum. He carefully scrutinized the postmaster general's actions, ensuring that they conformed to proper administrative procedure. Once satisfied of this, Monroe turned to the broader question of executive interference. He and his cabinet debated the constitutional issues involved and finally decided that the president should not intervene in a matter of departmental patronage. Although realizing that his decision would spark protests, Monroe took comfort in knowing that he was following longstanding precedents. In short, he used abstract constitutional standards to evaluate a touchy political question.

Van Buren did not appreciate this judicious, impartial approach. He failed to understand how the administration could remain so oblivious to political realities in New York. The Bucktails had recently triumphed over Clinton, thereby establishing themselves as sole agents of the Republican party in the Empire State. During the election in 1820, they wholeheartedly endorsed the policies of the Monroe administration. Now in a seemingly arbitrary fashion, the president was undermining their victory, making a mockery of their claims about the virtue of Republican loyalty. As one disgruntled Bucktail sarcastically put it: "How encouraging to Republicans to adhere to their party."[30] Faced with this unexpected treatment, Van Buren had two choices. He could conform to the president's strange patronage procedure or he could fight the system. Given his previous experience in politics, there was never very much doubt about Van Buren's ultimate decision.

In calling for a "general resuscitation of the old democratic party," Van Buren took the first step down the long road of political opposition, a road that would eventually lead him into a new party and finally to the White House. It is therefore imperative to analyze the ideas that would guide his progress over the next decade and a half.

[30] Ulshoeffer to Van Buren, January 13, 1822, Van Buren Papers. See also Van Buren and Daniel D. Tompkins to Return J. Meigs, January 7, 1822, in Bonney, *Legacy*, 1: 390–92.

At no time during his climb to prominence did Van Buren pause long enough to record his political philosophy. He spoke infrequently in Congress, wrote few pamphlets, and confined most of his analytical observations to private correspondence. Only in the leisure of his retiring years would he attempt a systematic reconstruction of a personal creed.[31] Van Buren was not a creative thinker; he drew his beliefs from the wellspring of Jeffersonian theory. His chief accomplishment as a political theorist was to adapt well-established, abstract tenets to the harsh realities of the 1820's—to give Jefferson's teachings a new sense of relevance and urgency.

Central to Van Buren's political views was an abiding faith in the virtues of party regularity.[32] Formerly he had lashed out against Clinton's lack of consistency; now he assailed Monroe on the same grounds. Having once spoken solely in terms of Bucktails and Clintonians, he now began to talk of Federalists and Republicans. For Van Buren, partisan polarization had long been a fact of life. He continually tried to impress on his contemporaries that the price of success was eternal vigilance.

In addition to calling for more effective discipline, Van Buren increasingly urged reaffirmation of the principles espoused by Thomas Jefferson—especially the twin theories of state rights and limited government. Considering Van Buren's pragmatic nature, these professions seem hopelessly out of character. How could the "magician," as he was known to contemporaries, truly adhere to abstract principles? How could a "subtle and intriguing" man be sincere in his ideological professions?[33] Contradictory though it may seem, Van Buren's pragmatism led directly to his Jeffersonian orthodoxy.

Martin Van Buren was never destined to win fame as a dashing, dynamic statesman. He was too reserved, too cautious, too imperturbable. These qualities, so instrumental in his mastery of New York politics, made him vulnerable to the charge of "noncommittalism." "Even his best friends," remarked a close acquaintance, "were apprehensive that he was over cautious and lacked the moral or political courage . . . in order to meet those exigences which might require

[31] Martin Van Buren, *An Inquiry into the Origin and Course of Political Parties in the United States* (New York, 1867). For a brief description of some of Van Buren's political views see Max M. Mintz, "The Political Ideas of Martin Van Buren," *New York History* 30 (1949): 422–48.

[32] Van Buren to J. A. King, February 4, 1822, in King, *Correspondence*, 6: 458; Remini, *Van Buren and the Democratic Party*, pp. 60–63.

[33] For an acid contemporary sketch of Van Buren see Henry R. Warfield to Henry Clay, May 30, 1822, in Clay, *Papers*, 3: 211.

bold and decisive action."[34] Van Buren could not help but be aware that his public reputation was one of intrigue and indecision.[35] Accordingly, he worked that much harder to establish a record of ideological consistency. Popular leaders such as Calhoun, Webster, and Jackson could overcome frequent political indiscretions, for their appeal was more to the heart than the head. Unable to excite such emotions, Van Buren fell back on doctrinal purity as his next line of defense.

Yet Van Buren embraced Jeffersonian dogma for more than personal reasons. As a conscientious, ambitious craftsman he saw in state rights and limited government a practical solution to the political problems of the day. The Van Rensselaer incident indicated the weakness of the Republican party. The president alone could provide leadership, yet he was trapped in a vicious cycle, dependent on Congress and thus at the mercy of endless legislative bickering. He and his administration were isolated, virtual prisoners in a small, strife-torn community. Preoccupied with the incessant struggle with the legislature, the president could not devote time to cultivating relations with the states, even though they provided the vigor and economic enterprise that revolutionized American society in the Era of Good Feelings. Because communications with the central government were so poor, the states took matters in their own hands; the Erie Canal was but one example of such unaided endeavor.[36] This local activism generated a tremendous amount of political energy. Yet under Monroe, the Republican party was unable to harness this newly released power. Van Buren and others saw in Jeffersonian doctrine a way to justify a more effective cooperation between the states and the federal government. If the party would take cognizance of state problems, rely on the judgment of state leaders, base its operations on the energy of state organizations, it could bind the Union together. The price of such unity was a limit on the activity of the federal government, but Van Buren and his colleagues thought it a fair price.

Although he understood the causes of Republican disunity, Van Buren could not provide an immediate remedy. It would take more than five years of intricate maneuvering before he finally realized his dream of revitalizing the party. During this time his political fortunes

---

[34] Hammond, *Political Parties in New York*, 2: 473.

[35] Van Buren, *Autobiography*, p. 196.

[36] In this analysis I have benefited greatly by reading Seymour Mandelbaum, *Boss Tweed's New York* (New York, 1965). Mandelbaum's comments on the political effects of weak urban communications seem equally applicable to the relations between the states and the federal government.

fluctuated wildly, and he gave serious thought to abandoning the chase.

Shortly after the Van Rensselaer controversy subsided, Van Buren made the first of a series of important visits to the South. Although nominally vacations, these junkets prompted political observers to speculate that the master of the Regency was trying to revive the New York–Virginia axis, once the backbone of the Jeffersonian party.[37] Recent events made this resurrection difficult. To Southerners, long confident of a dominant voice in national politics, the Missouri debates of 1820 had come as a severe shock. Stung by the threat of a hostile Northern coalition, the Southern states demanded a return to strict construction of the Constitution, feeling that in this lay protection for the peculiar institution of slavery. Any Northerner desirous of wooing the South out of its growing isolation would have to submit to careful scrutiny. Already convinced of the utility of state rights, Van Buren enjoyed a decided advantage. Over the next decade, he struck up lasting friendships with powerful Southern leaders, especially Thomas Ritchie, leader of the "Richmond Junto." This machine, similar to the Regency, eventually became the focal point for Van Buren's support in the Old Dominion and primary source of his information about Southern politics.[38]

In all probability, Van Buren made up his mind on the presidential question shortly after returning from this Southern trip in the spring of 1822. Of all possible candidates, Georgia's William H. Crawford seemed to offer the best hope for a Republican renaissance. A Virginian by birth, the affable, six-foot-three-inch secretary of the treasury clearly outshone all other aspirants in declared allegiance to state rights and strict construction. His orthodoxy was not entirely above challenge, but he alone was capable of winning the South.[39] He was also immensely popular in Washington, having built up a loyal cadre of officeholders and an enthusiastic congressional following during his eight years in the cabinet.[40]

Yet even though Crawford's candidacy seemed perfectly suited to

[37] Michael Ulshoeffer to Van Buren, April 2, 1822, Van Buren to Gorham A. Worth, March 16, 1822, Van Buren Papers.

[38] Richard H. Brown, "The Missouri Crisis, Slavery, and the Politics of Jacksonianism," South Atlantic Quarterly 65 (1966): 55–72; Joseph H. Harrison, Jr., "Martin Van Buren and His Southern Supporters," Journal of Southern History 22 (1956): 438–59; Charles H. Ambler, Thomas Ritchie (Richmond, Va., 1913), pp. 90–91, 138–39.

[39] Remini, Van Buren and the Democratic Party, p. 36.

[40] Peter B. Porter to Henry Clay, May 26, 1823, in Clay, Papers, 3: 421–22; Rufus King to Christopher Gore, February 9, 1823, King, Correspondence, 6: 499.

the needs of the national party, Van Buren hesitated because of conditions in New York.[41] The state legislature, key to thirty-six electoral votes, did not favor Crawford but divided its allegiance between John Quincy Adams and Henry Clay.

So bleak did the New York political horizon appear in the spring of 1823 that Van Buren thought momentarily of quitting the presidential arena. Late in March, Secretary of the Navy Smith Thompson inquired whether he would be interested in appointment to the Supreme Court. Having considered the vacancy himself, Thompson wanted to decline and recommend Van Buren instead. Attracted by the calm of the judicial bench, the embattled senator assented, asking only that the president proceed with dispatch. Monroe delayed, and Van Buren soon discovered, to his disgust, that Thompson had never bowed out of the running. Stung by this cavalier treatment, Van Buren abandoned the offer, complaining of Monroe's "habitual indecision and intercourse with court parasites."[42]

Van Buren soon wished that he had escaped to the tranquillity of the Supreme Court. The Empire State was in turmoil, and the Regency struggled to put down a major political revolt. Once again the Clintonians had sprung to life, this time as participants in a coalition called the People's party. This new political force protested primarily against the state legislature's power to choose presidential electors. Van Buren doggedly opposed any reform of the electoral system, fearing that it would cripple his efforts to deliver the state to Crawford. Yet Bucktails throughout New York could not resist public pressure. In the fall voting, the party retained control of the legislature, but many members won reelection only by pledging their efforts to promote electoral revision.[43]

Van Buren's national plans fared little better. In August 1823 Crawford suffered a paralyzing stroke that left him a shattered man. For months he could neither see nor talk. Gradually he regained both vision and speech but was never to mend completely. Close friends carefully guarded the stricken giant and tried to keep his condition a secret, hoping that he would recover in time for the campaign.[44] If Van Buren knew of the disaster that summer, he did not alter plans for nominating Crawford.

[41] King to Charles King, February 26, 1823, in King, *Correspondence*, 6: 504.
[42] Van Buren to Smith Thompson, March 30, April 15, 1823, Van Buren Papers; Van Buren to Rufus King, April 14, 1823, in King, *Correspondence*, 6: 516.
[43] Remini, *Van Buren and the Democratic Party*, p. 42.
[44] J. E. D. Shipp, *Giant Days or the Life of W. H. Crawford* (Americus, Ga., 1909), p. 174.

On the evening of February 14, 1824, the Republicans held their presidential nominating caucus. It was a sorry affair. Crawford's opponents boycotted the meeting; as a consequence, only sixty-eight congressmen appeared. To the accompaniment of jeers from the gallery, Van Buren and his followers went through the ritual of selecting the Georgian and then adopting what proved to be a feeble appeal for Republican unity.[45]

While Van Buren supervised these rump proceedings, his Albany lieutenants were in the process of committing a colossal political blunder. On April 14, 1824, they rammed through the New York legislature a resolution removing De Witt Clinton from the Canal Board. The Regency hoped that the vote would drive a wedge between the former governor and the leaders of the People's party. As a legislative maneuver, the resolution worked to perfection, and the Regency believed that it had destroyed both Clinton and the reform impulse.[46] In concocting this bit of parliamentary legerdemain, Van Buren's followers paid scant attention to probable public reaction. Legislators returning home from Albany encountered a barrage of criticism that "secured to Mr. Clinton a full measure of what he had never before possessed—the sympathies of the People."[47] Overwhelmed by the sudden wave of public sympathy, Clinton made peace with the People's party and accepted its nomination for governor. Once again the Bucktails faced the dread prospect of their archenemy stalking the hustings; worse still, they had only themselves to blame.

In the November balloting, Clinton scored a stunning personal victory and engineered a successful sweep of the lower house of the legislature. For Van Buren, this triumph was but a portent of further disasters. When the state legislature met in mid-November to choose electors, all his plans went awry. He was outgeneraled and outsmarted by the Clay and Adams forces. As a result, Crawford received only five of the state's thirty-six electoral votes. Van Buren gamely tried to rationalize the debacle, but even he had to admit that November 1824 left him "as completely broken down a politician as my bitterest enemies could desire."[48]

The following month he left for Washington to try and salvage something from the ashes of defeat. Neither Henry Clay, John

[45] In his manuscript on the rise of the nominating convention, James S. Chase gives a very detailed account of the caucus of 1824.
[46] Shaw, *Erie Water West*, pp. 164–80.
[47] Van Buren, *Autobiography*, p. 143.
[48] Van Buren to William H. Crawford, November 17, 1824, Van Buren Papers; Van Buren, *Autobiography*, p. 149.

Quincy Adams, William Crawford, nor Andrew Jackson had received a majority of the electoral votes, and as a result, the choice devolved on the House of Representatives. In the wild maneuvering that ensued, Van Buren struggled to hold the New York delegation in line and prevent a bolt to the Adams camp. For a time he succeeded, but at the moment of truth, Stephen Van Rensselaer switched sides and sealed the New Englander's victory.

For Martin Van Buren, the election of 1824 was a sobering experience. He had come to Washington three years earlier, brimming with confidence, eager to assume as important a role in national politics as he had previously played in New York. When confronted with an alien political system, he had boldly raised the standard of reform, searching for a way to bring the party back to meaningful principles. Yet in his zeal, Van Buren lost sight of several crucial facts. Although the logical man to carry the Jeffersonian banner, William H. Crawford was far from an ideal candidate. His main strength lay in Congress; he was thus hopelessly wedded to the very system that Van Buren sought to change. A Crawford victory would not have ensured a greater degree of cooperation between the states and the federal government. On the contrary, it would have been a triumph for the congressional caucus and, while perhaps reaffirming long-cherished ideals, would have perpetuated the machinery that had undermined Republican unity. Van Buren needed a presidential candidate responsive to the will of the people as expressed through state leaders, not an aspirant born of the divisiveness in Washington.

Furthermore, Van Buren's extreme preoccupation with Republican reform jeopardized the Regency's hold on New York. Few state legislators shared the enthusiasm for Crawford. They failed to appreciate the benefits of a New York–Virginia alliance. When Van Buren tried to rally support behind the caucus nomination, he succeeded only in giving his enemies a valuable campaign weapon. The bitter defeat of 1824 taught Van Buren never to venture forth on the high seas of national politics without first securing a sheltered state harbor to ride out the inevitable storms.·

On March 4, 1825, the presidency of John Quincy Adams began in an atmosphere of tension and suspicion, revealing how deeply the election had rent Republican ranks. Van Buren stood aloof from the antiadministration intrigue; he issued strict instructions to his lieutenants not to agitate the presidential question but instead to revive sagging Regency fortunes. While Clinton sat in the governor's mansion, basking in the glory of new-found public favor, Van Buren's agents circulated throughout the state making intensive preparations for the fall legislative elections.[49] No longer burdened by the stigma of Clinton's removal or the onus of electoral reform, they made a dramatic recovery in November 1825, regaining control of the lower house.[50] Despite this political resurgence, Van Buren still hesitated to commit himself to any presidential hopeful. "We of the Crawford school must lay on our oars," he told his friend Benjamin F. Butler.[51] Van Buren delayed for over a year. He was determined not to repeat the mistakes of 1824. Clinton occupied the governor's chair and even bereft of legislative support was a dangerous enemy. Van Buren had to be sure that the unpredictable governor did not conclude an alliance with the administration and thereby disrupt Regency domination of the state. It was not until November 1826 that Van Buren was able to neutralize Clinton's national power.[52]

By the time Van Buren shook free of these local encumbrances, the number of attractive candidates had dwindled drastically. William H. Crawford remained isolated on his Georgia estate, nursing presidential dreams but without political backing. Henry Clay's alleged "corrupt bargain" with the president removed the Kentuckian from serious contention. John C. Calhoun had long since stepped out of the running. Van Buren thus had to choose between the cold, austere John Quincy Adams, whose legislative programs were neo-Federalist, or the ambitious frontier hero, Andrew Jackson, a man of great appeal but an unknown political quantity. Given Van Buren's upbringing, there was really no alternative; in December 1826 he began preparations for the Bucktail march into the Jackson camp.

Having made up his mind, Van Buren wasted little time. He spent the Christmas holidays at a Virginia retreat conferring with Vice President John C. Calhoun, also a recent convert to the Jackson cause. Personal ambition and disagreement over principle would eventually drive the two apart, but for the moment they "united heart and hand to promote the election of General Jackson."[53] as a result of this meeting, Van Buren agreed to work for reconstruction

---

[49] Remini, *Van Buren and the Democratic Party*, pp. 85–92.

[50] Hammond, *Political Parties in New York*, 2: 205–206; Van Buren, *Autobiography*, pp. 157–58.

[51] Van Buren to Benjamin F. Butler, December 25, 1825, Van Buren Papers; Willie P. Mangum to Bartlett Yancey, January 15, 1826, in Henry Thomas Shanks, ed., *The Papers of Willie P. Mangum*, 5 vols. (Raleigh, N.C., 1950–1956), 1: 230–35; hereafter cited as Mangum, *Papers*.

[52] It is not altogether clear exactly how Van Buren achieved this goal. For differing interpretations see Remini, *Van Buren and the Democratic Party*, pp. 120–22; Robert V. Remini, *The Election of Andrew Jackson* (New York, 1963), p. 48; Hammond, *Political Parties in New York*, 2: 232–36.

[53] Van Buren, *Autobiography*, p. 514.

of the New York–Virginia axis that had fallen in 1824 amidst the ruins of the Crawford campaign. Over the next few weeks he drafted a long letter to Thomas Ritchie, setting forth the advantages of Jackson's candidacy. He finally dispatched this crucial appeal on January 13, 1827. Van Buren had never written a more important or revealing document; in it he summarized his own political creed and set forth his hopes for the future of the new Jacksonian alliance.

One persistent theme ran through all Van Buren's remarks. Loyal Republicans had to unite behind Jackson to create an effective national party, grounded on Jeffersonian principles. Van Buren called on Ritchie to revive the battle-tested alliance of "planters of the South and plain Republicans of the North." The nation could ill afford further nonpartisan experimentation; statesmen had to realize that there would always be "party distinctions and that the old ones are the best of which the . . . case admits." Should the voters again ignore the lessons of history, Van Buren feared the outcome would be fatal. If parties failed, he forecast prophetically, "geographical divisions founded on local interests or what is worse prejudices between the free and slave holding states will inevitably take their place." He implied the need for a strong cooperative coalition, anchored firmly in the states, able to bring a degree of national unity without jeopardizing the interests of individual members. For this reason he wanted to commit the Jacksonian alliance to the theories of state rights and limited government.

Although quite specific in his praise for the virtues of political parties, Van Buren did not outline any definite legislative agenda. To commit the new organization to ambitious schemes would only invite trouble. Experience convinced him that the path to Union was not through promotion of national projects, such as those outlined by John Quincy Adams in 1825, but through recognition of local initiative and the capabilities of state government. Van Buren did not ask his fellow Republicans to agree on a positive platform but rather to recognize the common enemy of Federalism.

After sketching the party's aims, Van Buren turned to a frank assessment of its candidate. He praised Jackson's qualifications but was also outspoken about his liabilities. "General Jackson has been so little in public life," Van Buren mused, "that it will be not a little difficult to contrast his opinions on great questions with those of Mr. Adams." Yet this need not be a drawback. Jackson could easily assume the role of outraged virtue; cast as the victim of Washington's clandestine councils, he need not appear their master. Van Buren was much more concerned about Jackson's political orthodoxy.

In 1817 the general had written a letter to President Monroe speaking out strongly against political parties and praising the administration's emphasis on conciliation. This letter had subsequently become a matter of public record, and Van Buren feared that it would hurt the cause. He must also have wondered whether this previous indiscretion was symptomatic of a general lack of consistency. It was too late to demand assurances from the Old Hero. Van Buren's only hope was to direct the campaign in such a way as to commit Jackson to the true doctrines of party loyalty and governmental simplicity. Van Buren touched on this dilemma near the close of his letter: "His election as the result of his military service without reference to party, & so far as he alone, is concerned scarcely to principle, would be one thing. His election as the result of a combined and concerted effort of a political party, holding in the main, to certain tenets & opposed to certain prevailing principles, might be another & far different thing."[54]

It is difficult to determine whether Van Buren succeeded in making the election of 1828 a triumph of party rather than personality. Certainly the Democrats, as the new allies called themselves, put together a superb organization. By the eve of the election, Jackson commanded a vast nationwide network of correspondence committees, congressional cliques, and partisan newspapers geared for rapid dissemination of campaign propaganda and efficient recruitment of voters. Jackson did not invent any new techniques; he simply coordinated the efforts of such strong state machines as the Regency, the Richmond Junto, and his own powerful organization in Tennessee.[55]

Throughout the course of the campaign, Van Buren worked tirelessly to secure Jackson's election. In New York he made the Albany *Argus* a leading Democratic paper and carefully linked its editorial policy with those of the Nashville *Republican* and the Richmond *Enquirer*.[56] He also put his own national ambitions aside for the moment and agreed to run for governor. De Witt Clinton had died earlier in the year, and Van Buren felt his candidacy might promote a final healing of New York's open political wounds. By conducting a personal campaign under the Jackson banner, Van Buren was able to lavish attention on local matters. This close supervision helped prevent the Adams forces from making serious inroads. In particular, Van Buren kept the Regency calm during the anti-Masonic outburst

[54] Van Buren to Thomas Ritchie, January 13, 1827, Van Buren Papers.
[55] For a complete analysis of the election of 1828 see Remini, *Election of Jackson.*
[56] For examples of these ties see Albany *Argus* (Extra), March 24, 1828.

25

that swept the state in 1827. He refused to be stampeded and convinced his colleagues to deemphasize the agitation.[57] The storm eventually subsided without doing any permanent damage. Despite this preoccupation with New York developments, Van Buren took time for several trips through the South, trying to convince former Crawfordites to switch allegiance to Jackson. So notorious became these good will missions that John Randolph drolly observed that his was the only Virginia home Van Buren could visit without inciting the opposition.[58]

Yet without the personal appeal of Andrew Jackson, all this organization efficiency might have gone for naught. He was suited, as few men were, to the task of unifying divergent groups and appealing to an aroused electorate. As a popular hero, he had no equals. His dramatic victory at New Orleans still fired the imagination of a troubled nation; the circumstances surrounding his defeat in 1824 added grist to the campaign mill. Individual factions could unite behind the image of a Cincinnatus leaving the plow to take up arms against a corrupt administration.[59] This personal magnetism became evident in November 1828. Jackson swept to victory, polling an impressive 56 percent of the popular vote. Adams carried all New England but little else. In New York, Van Buren won election as governor by 30,000 votes. Jubilant over the outcome, he wrote Jackson hailing "the truly honorable triumph we have obtained." Only time would reveal whether Jackson regarded the victory as a cooperative enterprise.[60]

The election of 1828 brought hope of a new and dynamic breed of national politics. Jackson's election broke the bonds that had sapped executive power and prestige for over two decades. He owed his triumph not to the efforts of congressional kingmakers but to the work of a devoted corps of state leaders. Jackson successfully tapped the vast reservoir of political strength so long untouched by the members of the Virginia dynasty; his victory ushered in a new era that promised a closer and more productive relationship between the states and the federal government.

[57] Albany *Argus*, August 4, 1828; Van Buren to Churchill C. Cambreleng, July 4, October 23, 1827, Van Buren Papers.

[58] Randolph to Van Buren, October 13, 1828, Van Buren Papers; Van Buren to Azariah C. Flagg, April 2, 1827, quoted in Kass, *Politics in New York*, p. 61; William S. Hoffman, *Andrew Jackson and North Carolina Politics* (Chapel Hill, N.C., 1958), pp. 12–13.

[59] On Jackson as symbol see John William Ward, *Andrew Jackson: Symbol for an Age* (New York, 1955).

[60] Van Buren to Jackson, November 16, 1828, Van Buren Papers; Remini, *Election of Jackson*, p. 187; Albany *Argus*, November 21, 1828.

In order to harness this power, Jackson had to wage a negative campaign. Of necessity, he avoided a definite stand on such crucial questions as the tariff and internal improvements. The Democratic organization was strong because it united dissimilar local interests against the common enemy of Federalism. This diversity all but precluded any specific definition of national goals. The Jacksonian alliance would remain successful so long as its leaders in Washington continued to recognize the needs of the states. For Jackson, the election posed a personal dilemma as well. As triumphant leader of a new and vigorous party, he was in a position to bring necessary reforms, but because of his pledges to combat Adams's latitudinarian programs, these changes were expected to be negative. Jackson promised to uphold the sacred principles of state rights and limited government, and yet this philosophy militated against centralized control. Thus the strong-willed Jackson entered office the servant of a creed that made little provision for a dynamic chief executive.

The election of 1828 dispelled few of Van Buren's doubts about Jackson's political orthodoxy and the future course of the Democratic party. During the next six months, the new governor of New York received numerous letters from close associates, forecasting that the Democracy would founder on the rocks of factionalism. Several correspondents advised Van Buren not to accept the inevitable offer of a cabinet post.[61] Although he dismissed these warnings and agreed to become secretary of state, Van Buren remained apprehensive about Old Hickory's intentions. Shortly before his journey to Washington, he alluded to his misgivings. "I hope the General will not find it necessary," Van Buren said, referring to the inaugural, "to avow any opinion upon Constitutional questions at war with the doctrines of the Jefferson School."[62]

---

[61] Van Buren received the following letters telling of confusion in Washington: John Randolph, December 16, 1828, James Hamilton, Jr., January 23, February 19, 1829, Louis R. McLane, February 19, 1829, James A. Hamilton, February 19, 21, 1829, Elias K. Kane, February 19, 1829; Van Buren Papers.
[62] Van Buren to James A. Hamilton, February 21, 1829, in Hamilton, *Reminiscences*, p. 94.

Chapter 2

The Legacy

On a cool spring evening, late in March 1829, Martin Van Buren arrived in Washington to assume the office of secretary of state. Hoping to rest before his first formal meeting with the president, he was disappointed to find his hotel suite crowded with office seekers. After listening to their supplications for more than an hour, Van Buren escaped and walked to the White House. He found the president's office illuminated by a single candle; Jackson was alone save for his close companion, William B. Lewis. Hesitantly entering the darkened room, Van Buren was surprised by the warmth and sincerity of Old Hickory's welcome. The two fell into animated discussion, and for the moment Van Buren forgot all the gloomy predictions of the past few months.[1] On that night began an unusual political relationship between two men of remarkably dissimilar character. They would never become intimates and at times would clash over important affairs of state. Yet their association helped determine the course of Democratic politics for well over a decade.

Contrary to his earlier fears, Van Buren found the Jackson administration suffering not from intrigue but from aimlessness. Watching the new party take power, former President John Quincy Adams complained that "To feed the cormorant appetite for place, and to reward the prostitution of canvassing defamers, are the only principles yet discernible in the conduct of the President."[2] In the midst of this confusion, Van Buren set about restoring some degree of order. He succeeded in salvaging several inappropriate diplomatic appointments, in mollifying a few disgruntled northern Democrats, and in mediating a potential quarrel between the president and the Richmond Junto.[3] Ironically, the new secretary of state had much more difficulty with a crucial problem of New York patronage.

Late in April 1829 Van Buren learned that Jackson intended to appoint Samuel Swartwout as collector of the Port of New York. A schemer, speculator, and adventurer, Swartwout enjoyed an unsavory reputation earned in part by his complicity in the Aaron Burr conspiracy. Some observers claimed that Swartwout was blackmailing Jackson by demanding a major appointment in return for continued silence about the president's connection with the Burr plot.[4] Regardless of the motives, the Swartwout appointment promised to provoke angry outcries from New York Democrats who wanted the collectorship bestowed on a more worthy recipient. Once aware of the impending nomination, Van Buren wrote his friends in New York City, warning that only a concerted local demonstration would stay Jackson's hand. Next he told the president of his "clear and decided opinion, (and a firmer or better grounded conviction I never entertained in my life) that the appointment of Mr. Swartwout . . . would not be in accordance with public sentiment, the interests of the Country or the credit of the administration." Van Buren could not have stated his case more forcefully, but to no avail. Andrew Jackson refused to desert a friend.[5]

Dismayed by this setback, Van Buren spent a long, lonely evening pacing the streets of Washington. The president's decision placed him in an awkward situation. As master of the Albany Regency and architect of the Democratic triumph in New York, he expected to control patronage in his native state. How could he possibly explain the appointment of an avowed political enemy and incompetent administrator to such a powerful and sensitive post? How could the party survive when its leader treated state interests in such an arbitrary fashion? Van Buren thought of resigning, but soon abandoned the idea. Such a move would have thrown New York's Democratic party into disarray, disrupted the Albany-Richmond axis, and ended

[1] Van Buren, Autobiography, p. 232.

[2] Adams, Diary, 8: 113.

[3] Thomas Ritchie to Mordecai M. Noah, March 14, 1829, Ritchie to Van Buren, March 27, 1829, Andrew Stevenson to Van Buren, April 19, 1829, Van Buren to Jackson, March 31, 1829, Van Buren to Ritchie, April 1, 1829, Jackson to Van Buren (n.d.), Van Buren Papers; Van Buren, Autobiography, pp. 244–62.

[4] William Coleman to James A. Hamilton, April 15, 1829, in Hamilton, Reminiscences, pp. 132–33. On Swartwout's subsequent career see Leo Hershkowitz, " 'The Land of Promise': Samuel Swartwout and Land Speculation in Texas, 1830–1838," New York Historical Society Quarterly 48 (1964): 307–25.

[5] Van Buren to Churchill C. Cambreleng and Walter Bowne, April 20, 1829, Van Buren to Jackson, April 23, 1829, Jackson to Van Buren, April 24, 1829 (2 letters), Van Buren Papers; Van Buren, Autobiography, pp. 264–65.

Van Buren's own presidential aspirations. Consequently, he deferred to Jackson's wishes and tried his best to rationalize the appointment. Van Buren's state supporters accepted the inevitable but not with good grace. "I congratulate you that the appointments in New York are at an end," wrote Congressman Churchill C. Cambreleng, "and now mark me, if our collector is not a defaulter in four years, I'll swallow the Treasury if it was all coined in coppers."[6] Cambreleng's prediction proved as trenchant as his sarcasm.

Although motivated by a sense of party loyalty, Van Buren remained in the cabinet for personal reasons. Had he withdrawn, he would have left the field of battle on the eve of a trial of strength with the forces of Vice President John C. Calhoun. In many ways, the relationship between Calhoun and Van Buren reflected the nature of the Democratic party. Common antipathy to John Quincy Adams brought the two together in 1826 but did not remove the differences between them. For most of the campaign, Calhoun suspected Van Buren of opposing his bid for the vice-presidency. The New Yorker in turn heard disturbing rumors that Calhoun was plotting to seize leadership in the party. Exacerbated by the tariff debates of 1828, these tensions threatened the stability of the Democratic coalition.[7]

Much more than personal advancement depended on the outcome of this struggle. Anxious lest the South slip into a permanent political minority, the mercurial Calhoun desperately searched for new congressional allies. He attempted to construct an alliance with the West, promising support for free public lands in return for lower tariff duties.[8] Such a bargain would have altered the structure of the Democratic party and destroyed Van Buren's dreams of a strong North-South compact. Against this background of clandestine ma-

[6] Cambreleng to Van Buren, April 28, 1829, Van Buren to Cambreleng, April 24, 1829, Van Buren Papers; James A. Hamilton, addressee unknown, April 25, 1829, in Hamilton, *Reminiscences*, pp. 123–24.

[7] Alfred Balch to Van Buren, November 27, 1828, Silas Wright to Van Buren, December 9, 1828, Van Buren Papers; Robert V. Remini, *Martin Van Buren and the Making of the Democratic Party* (New York, 1959), pp. 166, 170–85; John A. Garraty, *Silas Wright* (New York, 1949), pp. 50–74.

[8] Calhoun to James Monroe, July 10, 1828, in J. Franklin Jameson, ed., "Correspondence of John C. Calhoun," American Historical Association, *Annual Report for the Year 1899*, 2 vols. (Washington, D.C., 1900), 2: 266–67; hereafter cited as Calhoun, *Correspondence*; William Freehling, *Prelude to Civil War: The Nullification Controversy in South Carolina, 1816–1836* (New York, 1966), pp. 142–43; Thomas Cooper to Van Buren, March 29, 1829, Van Buren Papers. For a different view of Calhoun's actions during the Jackson administration see Charles M. Wiltse, *John C. Calhoun*, 3 vols. (Indianapolis, Ind., 1944–1951), vol. 2.

neuvering, Van Buren and Calhoun fought their dramatic political duel. During the next two years, the battleground shifted from the cabinet to the banquet hall and finally to the floor of the Senate. During all this time, the prize remained the same—the right to succeed Jackson as head of the party.

Van Buren's eventual triumph was more the result of political good fortune than masterly planning. He first confronted Calhoun during the famous Peggy Eaton affair, when the vice president surreptitiously supported the cabinet wives in their social ostracism of the bride of Jackson's secretary of war. Calhoun hoped to provoke an administrative shakeup during which his own supporters could gain access to the president's inner councils. By the time Van Buren reached Washington, the contestants in this petticoat war were already choosing sides, and the new secretary of state saw his advantage. As a widower, he had nothing to fear from feminine reprisals and therefore was free to pay Mrs. Eaton the respect due her station. In private calls and at public dinners, Van Buren practiced the subtle diplomacy that was his trademark. Jackson noted this attention with pleasure and placed more confidence in Van Buren's judgment. The two began a regular series of rides outside the city during which they discussed affairs of state. No doubt the Eaton scandal proved a primary topic of conversation. At first Jackson held Henry Clay responsible for the commotion, then gradually shifted the blame to Calhoun. Whether Van Buren engineered the change is unclear, but he became the beneficiary of the new policy.[9]

Early in December 1829, Jackson fell dangerously ill, and his close friend, William B. Lewis, persuaded him to draw up a political will. In a long letter to an old comrade, John Overton, the president sharply criticized Calhoun and then wrote a glowing tribute to Van Buren. "He, my dear friend, is not only well qualified, but desires to fill the highest office in the gift of the people, who in him, will find a true friend and safe depository of their rights and liberty." Should Jackson die, Lewis was to use the letter as he saw fit.[10] As on several other occasions, the Old Hero rallied, and the praise, penned under fear of death, was filed away for posterity. He was not yet ready to name an heir.

---

[9] For the most complete account of the Eaton affair see John Spencer Bassett, *The Life of Andrew Jackson*, 2 vols. in 1 (New York, 1931), pp. 458–74. For a modern corrective see Robert V. Remini, *Andrew Jackson* (New York, 1966), pp. 111–16.

[10] William B. Lewis, endorsement on Jackson to John Overton, December 31, 1829, in Jackson, *Correspondence*, 4: 108–109.

Ironically, the feud with Calhoun first attracted public attention at a banquet celebrating Democratic unity. For weeks prior to the Jefferson birthday dinner, rumors spread that the Calhounites would use the occasion to advance the idea of nullification, not state rights. When apprised of this, Van Buren reacted with characteristic caution. He had long hoped that the Democrats would avoid debate over constitutional theory—that the rubric of state rights would shelter all. Now Calhoun pressed for definition and acceptance of the principle of minority veto. Van Buren regarded this theory as a bastard offspring of legitimate Jeffersonian axioms but recognized that the subject "required the utmost prudence and circumspection on the part of the President."[11]

Although he stood to gain from a rupture between Calhoun and Jackson, Van Buren seems to have been more the worried bystander than the intriguing manager of the Jefferson birthday dinner. He did not help prepare the challenge that Jackson hurled so defiantly at Calhoun. The morning of the banquet, the president consulted with William B. Lewis and Andrew J. Donelson before deciding on his dramatic toast. "Our Federal Union—it must be preserved." Van Buren later assented to the wording but probably with reluctance, fearing its effects on the South. Contrary to his later claim, his own offering did not follow the "spirit and tenor" of Jackson's thunderbolt. To the distracted celebrants, Van Buren proposed: "Mutual forbearance and reciprocal concessions; thro' their agency the Union was established—the patriotic spirit from which they emanated will forever sustain it."[12]

Van Buren simply did not enjoy enough influence to serve as the mastermind of the dinner. "If he is managing at all," observed one influential administration spokesman, "it is so adroitly that nobody perceives it."[13] Van Buren had won the president's respect, but he was far from being the power behind the throne. Throughout Jackson's two terms, the Western clique of Amos Kendall, William B. Lewis, Andrew J. Donelson, and Francis P. Blair stood closest to the chief executive. Significantly, the one area in which the secretary of

[11] Van Buren, *Autobiography*, pp. 413–14.

[12] Ibid., pp. 414, 416; James Parton, *The Life of Andrew Jackson*, 3 vols. (New York, 1861), 3: 284. For a different interpretation appearing in several later accounts see Richard R. Stenberg, "The Jefferson Birthday Dinner, 1830," *Journal of Southern History* 4 (1938): 334–35.

[13] Amos Kendall to Francis P. Blair, April 25, 1830, quoted in Charles G. Sellers, Jr., *James K. Polk: Jacksonian, 1795–1843* (Princeton, N.J., 1957), p. 148.

state did assume a dominant position concerned the party's adherence to true republican doctrine.

Late in May 1830 Congress passed and sent to the White House a bill authorizing government purchase of stock in a proposed road between Maysville and Lexington, Kentucky. Sponsors of this type of legislation had long been arguing that appropriation of federal revenue for internal improvements would bind the states into an effective Union. Van Buren disagreed. During his career in the 1820's he saw New York seized by a speculative mania touched off by construction of the Erie Canal. He and his Regency associates made every effort to discourage reckless spending and to channel the state's activity into meaningful projects, fearing that if they failed, a mad race for the spoils would disrupt their political organization. During his congressional career, Van Buren exhibited the same reserve. He argued on several occasions that the unchecked appetites of the states would produce discord, not harmony. Twice he urged the Senate to sponsor a constitutional amendment defining the responsibility of the federal government for internal improvements.[14]

Jackson's views were not so neatly delineated. "Internal improvement and the diffusion of knowledge," he remarked obliquely in his inaugural, "so far as they can be promoted by the constitutional acts of the Federal Government, are of high importance."[15] No one was exactly sure what the new president meant by "constitutional." When the Maysville bill cleared the House, Van Buren saw an excellent opportunity to end this uncertainty and reaffirm the administration's dedication to simple government. Not only was the proposed road entirely local, and therefore objectionable on constitutional grounds, it also ran practically to Henry Clay's front door. On one of their early morning rides, Van Buren convinced Jackson to disapprove the measure.

On May 27, 1830, the president dispatched the Maysville veto in which he deliberately stated that the federal government should not assume responsibility for local projects. By this defiant act, he served notice that he would not allow his administration to be disrupted by continuous legislative logrolling. Instead he reasserted the pledge implicit in his campaign—to combat latitudinarian constructions of

[14] Van Buren, Message to the New York State Legislature, January 6, 1829, in Albany *Argus*, January 7, 1829; *Annals of Congress*, 18th Cong., 1st sess., 1823–1824, p. 135, 19th Cong., 1st sess., 1825–1826, 2: 20–21. On the Regency's economic policies see Garraty, *Silas Wright*, pp. 44–49.

[15] Richardson, *Messages and Papers*, 2: 437.

the Constitution by keeping the national government "within its proper sphere" and allowing "the states to manage their own concerns in their own way."[16] By persuading Jackson to sound the Jeffersonian tocsin, Van Buren helped ease the fears of many Southern Democrats who had grown restive since the inauguration.[17]

The Maysville message marked the emergence of Van Buren as one of the president's confidants. For the next six years Jackson would seek his advice on internal improvements.[18] Calhoun viewed this close cooperation as a direct challenge and determined to oust his New York rival from power. In February 1831 he initiated a newspaper campaign charging Van Buren with promoting dissension in order to win the succession. As proof of this perfidy, Calhoun printed a complete account of the Eaton affair and of his own quarrel with Jackson over the Seminole War. The vice president assumed that Jackson would stand aside while an outraged citizenry drove Van Buren from the cabinet in disgrace. This proved to be a mistake. The Old Hero did not view Calhoun's actions as a public service and was incensed at the publication of court secrets. Instead of sacrificing Van Buren for the sake of party harmony, Jackson branded Calhoun as the instigator of all discord. In all this excitement, Van Buren alone remained relatively aloof. "I have no doubt," he said during the early stages of the controversy, "but an attempt will be made to hold me responsible for it."[19] Van Buren's circumspection undoubtedly helped convince the president that Calhoun's slanders lacked foundation.

Van Buren weathered the initial storm, but he knew that more tempests would follow. So long as John Eaton remained in the cabinet, he would serve as a source of embarrassment and an easy

[16] Ibid., 2: 489; Van Buren, *Autobiography*, pp. 312–38; Jackson to Van Buren, June 26, 1830, Van Buren Papers.

[17] Thomas Ritchie to Archibald Ritchie, June 8, 1830, in Charles H. Ambler, ed., "Unpublished Letters of Thomas Ritchie," *John P. Branch Historical Papers of Randolph Macon College* (1911), 3: 208; hereafter cited as Branch Historical Papers; Van Buren to Jackson, July 25, 1830, in Jackson, *Correspondence*, 4: 166–67. See also James Hamilton, Jr., to Van Buren, June 8, 1830, Ritchie to Van Buren, June [?], 1830, Van Buren Papers.

[18] Jackson to Van Buren, October 18, November [?], 1830, Van Buren, notes on internal improvements, December 6, 1830, Jackson endorsement on William H. Crawford to Van Buren, January 3, 1831, Van Buren to Andrew J. Donelson, August 26, 1832, Van Buren to Jackson, November 5, 1834, Van Buren Papers.

[19] Parton, *Jackson*, 3: 327; Jackson to Van Buren, July 31, 1840, Van Buren Papers; John Overton to Jackson, February 3, 1831, in Jackson, *Correspondence*, 4: 236–38; James A. Hamilton to General Van Sholten, May 28, 1831, in Hamilton, *Reminiscences*, pp. 221–22.

target for opposition ridicule. Yet Jackson spurned all demands for Eaton's removal.[20] Knowing that party harmony hung in the balance, Van Buren resolved to break the deadlock himself. He persuaded the president to accept his resignation, preparing the way for Eaton's withdrawal and a thorough reorganization of the cabinet. During the spring and summer of 1831, Jackson formed a new council of state, decidedly hostile to Calhoun's interests. Van Buren accepted appointment as minister to England and in August sailed for London as the acknowledged champion of Democratic unity.[21]

Van Buren's departure shows that he was not master of the Democratic party. Jackson alone ruled the alliance, as indicated by his willingness to send Van Buren abroad for an extended stay. Neither man anticipated that the Senate would soon cut the visit short. Resignation may have increased Van Buren's presidential stock, but it also removed him from the center of power. Politics required rapid decisions; he would now be isolated by more than three thousand miles of ocean. At least one of the new minister's friends thought this seclusion would be a definite political asset, since it would remove Van Buren from public view at a time when the administration was heading toward uncharted waters. Calling the resignation the "stroke of a master," New York's James A. Hamilton argued that Van Buren could now avoid "all the difficulties and perhaps disasters which events . . . may bring about."[22] Specifically Hamilton referred to the imminent collision between the administration and the Second Bank of the United States.

Both personal and political considerations prompted the president to enter the lists against the "Monster of Chestnut Street." As the result of a youthful financial imbroglio and his experience during the Panic of 1819, Jackson came to the White House deeply distrustful of banks and paper money. Over the course of the next few years, he gathered around him several Western advisers who shared this bias. Yet the bank war was to be more than an individual crusade. Jackson

[20] Samuel Bradford to Jackson, February 28, 1832, quoted in Bassett, *Jackson*, p. 521; William S. Archer to Van Buren, March 12, 27, 1831, Van Buren Papers; Charles H. Ambler, *Thomas Ritchie* (Richmond, Va., 1913), pp. 138–39.

[21] Van Buren, *Autobiography*, pp. 402–408; Jackson to Hugh Lawson White, April 9, 1831, in Jackson, *Correspondence*, 4: 258–60; Benjamin F. Butler to Van Buren, April 22–23, 1831, Thomas Ritchie to Van Buren, April 20–21, 30, 1831, Peter V. Daniel to Van Buren, April 22, 1831, Richard E. Parker to Van Buren, April 23, 1831, Van Buren Papers.

[22] James A. Hamilton to Van Buren, May 1, 1831, Van Buren Papers. See also Albany *Argus*, August 12, December 2, 1831; Richmond *Enquirer*, January 10, 1832.

appealed to an aroused electorate, many of whom were unable to adjust to the rapid economic expansion of the era. In their confusion, they could not turn to the economists for guidance, since economics as a separate, respectable discipline did not exist. Nor could they seek the impartial advice of the business community, for as the British minister, Henry Fox, observed, "finance and adverse systems of banking have been chosen by political antagonists as their battleground."[23] While the general causes of economic instability thus remained unexplained, the bank was real, a symbol of corporate wealth and monopolistic intrigue. It seemed to represent everything wrong with the American economy. Thus when Nicholas Biddle foolishly pitted its strength against Jackson's personal prestige, the enraged president found an audience ready and willing to support his cause.[24]

Van Buren held more moderate and less emotional economic views. He did not distrust banks, but he did object to "over-banking." In his brief tenure as governor of New York, Van Buren introduced legislation creating the famed safety fund system that established guidelines for chartering banks and protecting the individual creditor against financial failures. This emphasis on state regulation did not lead him to oppose a national bank. No doubt Van Buren viewed Biddle's excesses with alarm; still, he must have been aware that an assault on so strong a political corporation would injure the party, especially in the crucial state of Pennsylvania.[25] Since the Supreme Court had already decreed the bank to be constitutional, Van Buren saw no need to challenge this decision. In his devotion to strict construction, he accepted the Constitution as he found it, not as he wished it would be.

Van Buren displayed a similar reticence for the duration of the bank war. In December 1829, he arranged to have his friend James A. Hamilton peruse Jackson's annual message in the hope of preventing an assault on the bank. Hamilton managed to compress the crude invective but could not convince Jackson to "omit everything as to

[23] Fox to Lord Palmerston, May 21, 1837, Public Records Office, London, Foreign Office: 5, Vol. 314, Pt. IV, Photostats in the Library of Congress; hereafter cited as PRO:FO: 5, etc. For a brief introduction to the bank war see Robert V. Remini, *Andrew Jackson and the Bank War* (New York, 1967).

[24] On the symbolic significance of the bank see Marvin Meyers, *The Jacksonian Persuasion, Politics and Belief* (Stanford, Calif., 1957), pp. 10–14.

[25] Garraty, *Silas Wright*, pp. 44–45; Albany *Argus*, April 8, 1828, January 7, May 5, June 2, 1829, January 11, 1830. For a major reassessment of the Regency's role in the bank war see Frank Otto Gatell, "Sober Second Thoughts on Van Buren, the Albany Regency, and the Wall Street Conspiracy," *Journal of American History* 53 (1966): 19–41.

the bank."[26] During the next eighteen months, Van Buren stood on the fringes of power while Jackson's Western colleagues amassed evidence of Biddle's political sins.[27] When he left for England, the retiring secretary of state seemed grateful for the chance to escape from Washington. "I am so tired of the slang about intrigue, and management," he moaned, "that there is scarcely anything I would not do." The only way to achieve peace was to "go for the usual period of four years out of the country."[28]

This quiet interlude came to an abrupt halt six months later, and Van Buren found himself thrust again into the political spotlight. On January 25, 1832, Vice President John C. Calhoun broke a Senate deadlock by casting the deciding vote against Van Buren's nomination. "It will kill him, sir, kill him dead," the exultant South Carolinian exclaimed. "He will never kick sir, never kick." Age had not improved Calhoun's political judgment; as Senator Thomas Hart Benton observed, "You have broken a minister, and elected a Vice-President."[29]

Without doubt, the Senate's rejection won Van Buren the public sympathy that he had always lacked. Democratic politicians, who six months before denied that he would be the next vice president, now reversed themselves. "All prior objections & hostile feelings are now merged in the recent outrage upon him, the President and the Country," said one influential Virginia spokesman.[30] Convinced by his correspondents that his candidacy would promote the interests of the party, Van Buren agreed to have his name brought forward for the vice-presidential nomination. Late in May 1832 the Democrats held their first national nominating convention in Baltimore and on the

[26] Hamilton, *Reminiscences*, p. 150; Richardson, *Messages and Papers*, 2: 462.

[27] Felix Grundy to Jackson, May 22, 1829, Francis P. Blair to Jackson, August 17, 1830, Worden Pope to Jackson, August 6, 1831, in Jackson, *Correspondence*, 4: 37, 174, 326–27; Kendall to Francis P. Blair, November 23, 1829, quoted in Gatell, "Sober Second Thoughts," p. 39n.

[28] Richmond *Enquirer*, February 4, 1832; Van Buren to James A. Hamilton, December 14, 1831, in Hamilton, *Reminiscences*, pp. 234–35; Adams, *Diary*, 8: 338.

[29] Thomas Hart Benton, *Thirty Years View*, 2 vols. (New York, 1854–1856), 1: 215, 219; Isaac Hill to Van Buren, January 29–February 12, 1832, Van Buren Papers.

[30] Andrew Stevenson to Thomas Ritchie (copy), February 4, 1832, Van Buren Papers. See also Francis P. Blair to Van Buren, January 28, 1832, Van Buren to William L. Marcy, March 14, 1832, Levi Woodbury to Van Buren, April 10, 1832, Van Buren Papers; Churchill C. Cambreleng to James A. Hamilton, February 9, 1832, William B. Lewis to Hamilton (n.d.), Hamilton, *Reminiscences*, pp. 240–41, 243; John Eaton to Jackson, March 13, 1832, in Jackson, *Correspondence*, 4: 418.

initial ballot selected the New Yorker to serve as Jackson's running mate. Although pleased by this popular outpouring, Van Buren was in no hurry to return from England. For one thing, he did not wish to appear the overeager suitor rushing to his intended with open arms. This was not his style. By delaying his homecoming, he also neatly sidestepped the growing conflict over the bank.

Van Buren arrived back in the United States shortly before Congress adjourned but took no part in preparing Jackson's veto of the bank recharter. This task fell chiefly to Amos Kendall, a wizened Kentucky newspaper editor noted for hostility to banks.[31] When Van Buren reached Washington, the message was all but complete, and he was forced to adopt a policy not totally to his liking. Contrary to Van Buren's earlier expectations, the bank veto proved a potent political weapon, calculated to please Democrats of all persuasions. Those attracted to Jackson because of his martial image could once again thrill to the sight of the Old Hero astride the executive ramparts thrusting aside congressional assaults. Those who in 1828 recoiled from the "corrupt bargain" could now vent their frustration on an even more convenient scapegoat. Finally, the ardent believers in state rights saw in the closing paragraphs of the message a reaffirmation of Jeffersonian principles. Van Buren greeted this enthusiasm with unfeigned pleasure. "The veto is popular beyond my most sanguine expectations," he wrote during the summer of 1832.[32]

The sheer volume of this antibank chorus all but drowned out several minor but discordant notes. During the course of his campaigning in New York, Van Buren received an urgent request from a committee of North Carolina politicians asking for his views on the tariff. This appeal reflected a renewed concern for the safety of Southern institutions. Both the founding of William Lloyd Garrison's *Liberator* and the Nat Turner rebellion struck fear in the hearts of slaveholders. The Albany *Argus* pledged its support for the Southern cause, but this was not enough. Van Buren dutifully repeated his belief that while Congress had the right to erect tariff barriers, it should not do so in a manner injurious to a minority of Americans. Near the end of his reply, Van Buren touched briefly on the theory of

[31] Albany *Argus*, July 9, 1832; Jackson to Van Buren, July 7, 1832, in Jackson, *Correspondence*, 4: 461–62; Lynn Marshall, "The Authorship of Jackson's Bank Veto Message," *Mississippi Valley Historical Review* 50 (1963): 466–77.

[32] Van Buren to Andrew J. Donelson, August 26, 1832, Van Buren Papers. See also Van Buren to James A. Hamilton, August 5, 1832, in Hamilton, *Reminiscences*, p. 247; Jackson to Amos Kendall, July 23, 1832, in Jackson, *Correspondence*, 4: 465; Albany *Argus*, September 25, October 1, 1832; Ambler, *Thomas Ritchie*, p. 149; Remini, *Jackson and the Bank War*, pp. 88–108.

nullification, arguing that it was "destitute of constitutional author-ity."[33]

Swept up in the enthusiasm of the campaign, Democrats ignored these warning signals; November 1832 was a time for rejoicing, not for worry. Andrew Jackson easily defeated his rival, Henry Clay, and Van Buren won election as vice president without difficulty. At the height of the celebration, Amos Kendall wrote to Van Buren suggest-ing that in view of the president's certain triumph, the party might well consider a new strategy. Would it not be wise, he asked, to hold out the olive branch to the remnants of the Clay corps? "By prompt attention to these men," the Democrats could "secure a majority of the Senate at the coming session." Such an entente would enable men "of all parties in the Northern, middle and Western states" to form a united front against nullification.

Van Buren quickly dispatched a rejoinder. Obviously he was shocked by Kendall's disregard for both party discipline and ideolog-ical consistency. Such a policy as Kendall outlined would have been fashionable during the Monroe administration, but it hardly suited a party created to combat the "amalgamationist heresy." Whether or not Kendall spoke for Jackson, it was not encouraging to have so trusted an adviser expound such views. Creation of a Northern coalition would deal a deathblow to the New York–Virginia axis and might well provoke the sectional confrontation that Van Buren wanted to avoid. Kendall seemed much more concerned with the importance of the West than of the South.

Chastened but not cowed by Van Buren's reply, Kendall explained that of course he had never intended to bring about a complete unification of the Democrats and National Republicans. "In relation to the Nationals *as a party* and in relation to their leaders *as men* and politicians," Van Buren was right. "We must not court them nor meet their advances. The effect of either, as you well remark, would be to strengthen the nullifiers of the South." Still, Kendall felt that some "moral force" had to "be arrayed on the side of the administra-tion" to check "the incipient treason of the South." Kendall closed with the assurance that he was inflexibly committed to "genuine republican principles." Then he added a clumsy threat. "At this

[33] Van Buren to Joseph H. Bryan et al., October 4, 1832, Van Buren Papers. This letter was subsequently printed as a pamphlet and is reproduced in Samuel R. Gammon, *The Presidential Campaign of 1832* (Baltimore, Md., 1922), pp. 163–67. See also Richmond *Enquirer*, April 27, October 19, 1832; Thomas Ritchie to Van Buren, June 25, 1832, Van Buren Papers; Albany *Argus*, May 19, 28, June 4, October 7, 1832.

moment I look upon you as the rallying point of the republican party; but events of a few years may make it necessary . . . that its favor shall be bestowed upon another."[34] Here the correspondence broke off. Kendall's suggestions were disconcerting. They raised serious doubts about Jackson's political orthodoxy and the administration's professed intention of dealing with the threat of nullification in a calm, deliberate manner.

Less than a month after the election, the president found himself confronted by the worst sectional crisis in the nation's history. Since the tumultuous Jefferson birthday dinner, South Carolina had been edging closer and closer to defiance of the tariff laws that in their eyes symbolized Northern tyranny. Although viewing the mounting tension with alarm, Van Buren hoped for a reasonable solution. He maintained correspondence with several important South Carolinians and urged Jackson to proceed with caution.[35] For a time in the late fall of 1832, the president seemed to be heeding this advice. "As to nullification in the south," he said in reference to his forthcoming annual message, "I mean to pass it barely in review." Jackson kept his word. In reporting to Congress on the state of the Union, he called for tariff reduction and made only a passing reference to the question of nullification.[36]

While preparing this conciliatory message, Jackson learned that South Carolina's state convention had overwhelmingly approved an ordinance declaring the tariff laws of 1828 and 1832 null and void. The president was furious. He immediately began preparing a new document designed to strike directly at the nullifiers. For the task he selected his secretary of state, Edward Livingston, a man of ultranationalistic views, about whom Jackson had earlier written: "he is a polished scholar, an able writer, and a most excellent man, but he knows nothing of mankind."[37]

On December 10, 1832, Andrew Jackson issued the famous nullification proclamation that has earned him fame as a staunch defender

[34] Amos Kendall to Van Buren, November 2, 10, 1832, Van Buren Papers. Van Buren's reply of November 7 is not extant but is referred to in the second of Kendall's letters.

[35] James Hamilton, Jr., to Van Buren, April 20, May 27, June 8, September 20, 1830, Robert Y. Hayne to Van Buren, October 23, 1830, Van Buren Papers; Van Buren to Jackson, September 21, 1831, in Jackson, Correspondence, 4: 351–52.

[36] Jackson to Van Buren, November 18, 1832, in Jackson, Correspondence, 4: 489–90; Richardson, Messages and Papers, 2: 591–606.

[37] Jackson to Van Buren, December 17, 1831, Jackson to Joel R. Poinsett, December 2, 1832, Jackson to Anthony Butler, December 4, 1832, in Jackson, Correspondence, 4: 385, 493–94, 495–96; Parton, Jackson, 3: 465–66; William B. Hatcher, Edward Livingston (Baton Rouge, La., 1940), pp. 382–86.

of the Union. This momentous state paper was boldly patriotic in tone, but some of its principles shocked administration supporters. Not content to discuss nullification as a threat to the nation, Jackson felt impelled to tell how the nation came into being. In this constitutional discourse, he clearly departed from the hallowed ground of state rights. In phrases more reminiscent of Hamilton than Jefferson he declared, "The Constitution of the United States, then, forms a *government* not a league." "It is a Government in which all the people are represented, which operates directly on the people individually, not upon the States." When asked if he might eliminate such objectionable passages, Jackson answered, "Those are my views and I will not change them nor strike them out."[38]

These dramatic developments took Van Buren by surprise. At the time of the annual message, he was in Albany, looking forward to a few months' rest before his inauguration as vice president. The nullification proclamation rudely interrupted this vacation and placed him in a very difficult position. As an official spokesman of the administration, he could scarcely disavow the president's declarations. Yet neither could he ignore those loyal Democrats who bitterly complained of Jackson's doctrinal heresies. To many it seemed that the president had indulged in a constitutional discourse when a simple appeal to patriotism would have sufficed. "Had the proclamation been empty and inflated as a balloon," commented Churchill C. Cambreleng, it would have "carried . . . through the Union with applause."[39]

During the next few weeks, Van Buren tried to prevent the administration from making further inflammatory statements. At the same time, he pressed for tariff reform to alleviate the major cause of Southern complaint. Early in January 1833 Van Buren's young protégé, Silas Wright, arrived in Washington to take his newly acquired seat in the Senate. Having left Albany but a short time before, Wright was in an excellent position to lay Van Buren's views before Congress. To anxious queries from Southerners, Wright replied that Van Buren was "decidedly in favor of a reduction of the revenue to the wants of the government" and for "preserving the Union at any personal or local sacrifice." In turn Wright told the Regency that

---

[38] Richardson, *Messages and Papers*, 2: 648; Parton, *Jackson*, 3: 466–67.

[39] Cambreleng to Van Buren, December 18, 29, 1832, Van Buren Papers; Richmond *Enquirer*, December 13, 1832, March 9, 1837; Willie P. Mangum to Charity Mangum, December 15–16, 1832, John L. Bailey to Mangum, December 25, 1832, in Mangum, *Papers*, 1: 589–91; Sellers, *Polk*, p. 157; Francis Fry Wayland, *Andrew Stevenson* (Philadelphia, 1949), p. 92.

Southern leaders felt only an immediate reduction in duties would ease tensions.[40]

When Van Buren recommended this conciliatory approach to the president, he encountered sharp resistance. "No, my friend," Jackson wrote in rebuttal, "the crisis must be now met with firmness, our citizens protected, and the modern doctrine of nullification and secession put down forever." As to the prospect for tariff reform, the president wondered "whether some of the eastern states may not secede or nullify, if the tariff is reduced. I have to look at both ends of the union to preserve it," he concluded testily. This curt rejoinder indicates that Jackson did not, as many historians argue, array the full might of his administration behind a compromise tariff. In fact by February 1833 Democratic legislative forces were in such disorder that they could not even elect Jackson's personal friend Francis P. Blair as a congressional printer.[41]

From the moment he issued his proclamation, Jackson seemed to forswear a legislative solution and to treat the nullification crisis as a private war between the executive branch and the state of South Carolina. When he did go to Congress on January 16, 1833, it was not to appeal for a reduction in duties but to request authority to use the militia should the need arise. In this famous "force bill message," Jackson yielded nothing to his critics but restated many of the objectionable arguments from his proclamation.[42] Then in an effort to buttress his position, the president called upon the party for support. In particular he wanted the Empire State to take the lead. When the Regency showed little sign of action, Jackson wrote angrily to Van Buren, asking, "Why is your Legislature silent at this eventful crisis?" "I cannot but sincerely regret, that the great state of Newyork has not come forth in her majesty and strength at this eventful moment."[43]

[40] Silas Wright to Azariah Flagg, January 14, 20, 1833, Flagg to Wright, January 21, 1833, Flagg-Wright Papers, New York Public Library; Albany *Argus,* December 15, 19, 20, 22, 1832.

[41] Van Buren to Jackson, December 27, 1832, Jackson to Van Buren, January 13, 1833, in Jackson, *Correspondence,* 4: 506–508, 5: 2–4; Thomas Hart Benton to Van Buren, February 16, 1833, Van Buren to Silas Wright, February 20, 1833, Van Buren Papers. For a different view see Freehling, *Prelude to Civil War,* p. 288; Major Wilson, "Andrew Jackson: The Great Compromiser," *Tennessee Historical Quarterly* 26 (1967): 64–78.

[42] Richardson, *Messages and Papers,* 2: 610–32.

[43] Jackson to Van Buren, January 25, 1833, in Jackson, *Correspondence,* 5: 12–13; Louis R. McLane to Van Buren, January 23, 1833, Van Buren Papers; James A. Hamilton to Jackson, January [?], 1833, in Hamilton, *Reminiscences,* pp. 249–50.

Van Buren hesitated because he feared that in its rush to put down nullification, the party might desert its principles. Late in January 1833 the state legislature finally responded to the president's appeal. The lawmakers adopted a carefully worded report that approved administration policy but also reiterated a belief in the viability of state rights. The report closed with a call for tariff reform.[44] After carefully shepherding this local reply, Van Buren again turned his attention to events in Washington. In late February he asked the president if the administration could drop the military provisions of the force bill. "If you can see your way perfectly clear in advising our friends in the house to waive for the present session the militia force part of the bill it would I have no doubt instantaneously revive the kindest feelings in the South."[45] This recommendation came too late. Jackson had already lost the initiative to Henry Clay, whose compromise tariff bill promised to provide the legislative relief required for a settlement. Stung by this reversal, Jackson insisted even more strenuously on passage of the force bill. "Lay *all* delicacy on this subject aside," he commanded one senatorial lieutenant, "and compell every mans name to appear upon the journals that the nullifiers may *all* be distinguished from those who are in support of the laws, and the union."[46] Jackson won his vote of confidence, but Henry Clay earned the distinction of resolving the dispute. From the ashes of the nullification crisis would rise the nucleus of a strong, new congressional opposition.

By his headstrong actions, the president also injured the Southern wing of the party. He boldly accepted South Carolina's challenge, but in so doing abandoned many cherished Democratic principles. The proclamation of December 10, 1832, deviated from his professed adherence to state rights and placed his supporters in the unprecedented position of having to choose between their allegiance to the leader of the Democracy or to the states that put him in power.[47] Jackson did not make the choice easy.

[44] Albany *Argus*, February 1, 1833. Adverse reaction to the report is reflected in Albany *Argus*, February 15, 1833. On the response in the South see Nathaniel Macon to Van Buren, March 2, 1833, Van Buren Papers.

[45] Van Buren to Jackson, February 20, 1833, in Jackson, *Correspondence*, 5: 19–21; Thomas Hart Benton to Van Buren, February 16, 1833, Van Buren Papers.

[46] Jackson to Felix Grundy, February 13, 1833, quoted in Joseph H. Parks, *Felix Grundy* (Baton Rouge, La., 1940), p. 197.

[47] Ambler, *Thomas Ritchie*, p. 155; Alvin L. Duckett, *John Forsyth* (Athens, Ga., 1962), pp. 162–63; Mangum, *Papers*, 2: 55n; Arthur C. Cole, *The Whig Party in the South* (Washington, D.C., 1913), pp. 17–23.

At no time during their long, eventful relationship did Jackson and Van Buren differ so markedly as during the nullification crisis. Consistently the New Yorker met the president's impassioned outbursts with pleas for moderation. "You will say that I am on my old track—caution—caution," he remarked in one revealing letter, "but my Dr Sir, I have always thought, that considering our respective temperaments, there was no way in which I could better render you that service which I owe you." Van Buren was fully aware of the dangers of disunion; he simply believed that the party could meet the challenge without resorting to destructive theoretical bickering. Democratic political theory had always been purposely vague; but in the heat of battle, Jackson demanded definition and branded all disagreement as disloyal.[48] The president's bold and decided opinions enlisted public sympathies but also raised new questions about his ideological sincerity. Had Van Buren come to Washington, he might have presented his case more effectively. Instead, he chose to remain in Albany. He thus viewed the conflict from the state level, while Jackson tried to think in terms of the entire Union. Doubtless their divergent responses stemmed in part from this difference in perspective.

The aftermath of the nullification crisis dispelled none of these disagreements. At the time of his inauguration as vice president, Van Buren heard distressing rumors about a possible coalition between Jackson and Massachusetts Senator Daniel Webster. During the past few months, Webster had emerged as a staunch defender of Jackson's proclamation and an active backer of the force bill. This transformation seemed to lend substance to Amos Kendall's ominous suggestions of a new political coalition. In the summer of 1833 Jackson made an extended visit through New England that heightened speculation about a major political realignment; this prospective merger between Jackson and Webster threatened both the structure of the Democratic party and the presidential ambitions of Van Buren.

The climax to this clandestine movement occurred shortly before the opening of Congress in December 1833. Summoned to the White House for an early morning meeting, Van Buren found Jackson in company with Tennessee's Senator Felix Grundy, another strong supporter of the force bill. Grundy stated that the party could increase its congressional power by concluding a bargain with Web-

---

[48] Van Buren to Jackson, December 27, 1832, Jackson to John Coffee, March 16, 1833, in Jackson, *Correspondence*, 4: 506–508, 5: 30–31.

ster. Such an entente would guarantee selection of favorable committees at a time when the Democrats faced renewed opposition. At this point Van Buren interrupted to lodge a strong protest against an arrangement that would subject the administration to a charge of proselytizing. Webster had long been a friend of the bank; since the battle with Nicholas Biddle was about to enter a new stage, Van Buren felt that the president could ill afford to blur party lines. Throughout this entire exchange, Jackson said nothing. After Van Buren finished, the Old General quietly told Grundy to forget the entire plan. "Between neither of these gentlemen and myself," Van Buren later recalled, "was the subject ever revived."[49]

Jackson's acquiescence indicated that he and Van Buren had reached a new understanding, putting an end to the disagreement of previous years. Van Buren helped achieve this rapprochement by agreeing to the removal of deposits from the Second Bank of the United States. When Jackson first proposed this withdrawal early in 1833, Van Buren hesitated, feeling that such precipitate action would only create more turmoil in a party already disrupted by charges of executive tyranny. Congress had overwhelmingly expressed its confidence in the safety of the deposits, and there seemed little reason to flout the will of the legislature. Van Buren soon discovered that Jackson was adamant and that further opposition would be pointless. He therefore relented.[50] As Van Buren feared, a congressional battle ensued, producing strong outcries against highhanded administration policies and further weakening the party in Virginia.[51]

Van Buren's willingness to support a policy that he knew to be politically unwise reveals the depths of his desire to be president. Jackson's second term was nearing its midpoint and the vice president could not remain the moderate, cautious adviser. He had to step forward and prove himself worthy of the mantle of leadership. No

[49] For a comprehensive treatment of the prospective alliance see Norman D. Brown, "Webster-Jackson Movement for a Constitution and Union Party in 1833," *Mid-America* 46 (1964): 147–71. See also Albany *Argus*, July 12, 1833; Van Buren, *Autobiography*, pp. 677–79.
[50] Hamilton, *Reminiscences*, p. 258; Amos Kendall, *Autobiography of Amos Kendall*, ed. William Stickney (Boston, 1872), pp. 376, 383; hereafter cited as Kendall, *Autobiography*; Kendall to Van Buren, June 9, 1833, Van Buren to Jackson, July 29, 1833, Francis P. Blair to Van Buren, August 17, 1833, Van Buren Papers; Van Buren to Jackson, August 19, September 4, 11, 1833, Jackson to Van Buren, August 16, September 8, 1833, in Jackson, *Correspondence*, 5: 158–60, 179–84.
[51] Francis P. Blair to George Bancroft, June 24, 1845, in Jackson, *Correspondence*, 5: 238n; Kendall, *Autobiography*, pp. 402–403; Ambler, *Thomas Ritchie*, pp. 157–58; Cole, *Whig Party*, pp. 27–34.

doubt the threat of a Webster-Jackson coalition hastened this decision. By coming out strongly against the bank, Van Buren accentuated the one issue on which the prospective allies could not agree. He obviously preferred a crusade against Nicholas Biddle to continued attacks on Southern extremists.

After the furor over the removal of deposits died down, Van Buren began planning for the Democratic nominating convention scheduled to meet in Baltimore in May 1835. Before the delegates assembled, the vice president hoped to reestablish meaningful communications with Virginia, where the nullification crisis threatened the hegemony of the Richmond Junto. Under the leadership of John Tyler, a new political faction emerged in the Old Dominion, opposed to the executive excesses of the Jackson regime. In 1834 this coalition handed the Junto its first major defeat. The heated political campaign touched off a lively debate that soon raised the specter of a Northern conspiracy. Once again, Van Buren found it necessary to repeat his devotion to Jeffersonian principles. "Never was a poor devil subjected to such cross examination as I have been by the Old Dominion," he lamented. Despite these grumblings, he reaffirmed his belief that the Constitution did not sanction interference with slavery in the South.[52]

These words of reassurance did not prevent a major Southern protest at the Baltimore convention in May 1835. As expected, Van Buren won nomination on the first ballot. Confident that their candidate could win the South, Democratic managers sought a running mate who could carry the Jackson banner in the West. They finally selected Kentucky's Senator Richard M. Johnson, a hero of the War of 1812 and reputed slayer of the Indian warrior Tecumseh. Johnson's proponents felt that the martial image would complement Van Buren's urbane demeanor. This strategy offended Virginia's disgruntled Democrats, who brought forward Van Buren's friend William C. Rives, former minister to France and a strong congressional defender of the president. In the hectic balloting that followed Johnson won 178 to 87, and representatives from the Old Dominion left Baltimore doubting Democratic sincerity.[53] Van Buren wrote directly to Rives and tried to restore party harmony, but

[52] Van Buren to Mrs. William C. Rives, April 1, 1835, Rives Papers, Library of Congress; Thomas Ritchie to Silas Wright, March 2, 1835, Elias K. Kane to Ritchie, March 10 [?], 1835, Silas Wright to Ritchie, March 10, 1835, Van Buren Papers. Drafts of the letters by Kane and Wright are in Van Buren's hand.
[53] Albany Argus, May 25, 27, 1835; Leland W. Meyer, The Life and Times of Colonel Richard M. Johnson of Kentucky (New York, 1932), pp. 393–425.

the effort availed little. A firm friendship was foundering on the rocks of political necessity.[54]

In accepting the call of his party, Van Buren invoked two themes that he would raise again and again during the campaign. "I consider myself the honored instrument, selected by the friends of the present administration to carry on its principles and policies." To the chairman of the convention, Van Buren expressed an equal determination to work for cooperation between the states and to uphold true republican doctrines.[55] These familiar, predictable responses reveal a candidate confident that the party organization he helped create would again prove victorious. Only the clouds on the Southern horizon caused Van Buren any concern.

The Democratic nominee had reason to be optimistic, for his opponents had yet to display any significant signs of solidarity. United solely by their opposition to executive despotism, the Whigs, as these new political allies styled themselves, enjoyed more strength in the Congress than in the countryside. They calculated that by running a number of sectional candidates they could capitalize on regional animosities and prevent Van Buren from winning a majority of the electoral votes. Such a decentralized strategy had merit; a Whig nominee in one section could speak directly to local issues without needing to explain the statements of other Whig candidates. The plan also had defects. Unable to agree on one suitable national candidate, the Whigs might also prove incapable of coordinating their local efforts. Of the announced Whig aspirants, Tennessee's Hugh Lawson White presented the most immediate threat to Van Buren's chances. A former Democrat and once a close friend of the president, he could pose as the true savior of republican principles and thus draw support from Southern malcontents.

During the summer and fall of 1835, abolitionist agitation made Van Buren even more uneasy about the Southern wing of the party. In a move to publicize its preachings, the American Anti-Slavery Society flooded the mails with tracts and pamphlets telling of degrading conditions among the black population. A great deal of this promotional literature reached the South, where distraught postmasters disposed of it as best they could. In Charleston, on July 30, 1835,

[54] Van Buren to Rives, May 26, 1835, Rives to Van Buren, June 2, 1835, Van Buren Papers. On the previous friendship between the two men, see their extensive correspondence in both the Van Buren Papers and the Rives Papers.
[55] Van Buren to the Committee of Notification of the Baltimore Convention, in *Niles Register*, 48: 257–58; Van Buren to Andrew Stevenson, May [?], 1835, Van Buren Papers.

an angry mob publicly burned incendiary material and hung leading abolitionists in effigy. This catharsis did not allay suspicions of a Northern conspiracy, for as John Quincy Adams noted, "Rouse in the heart of the slave-holder the terror of his slave, and it will be a motive with him paramount to all others never to vote for any man not a slave-holder like himself."[56]

When Van Buren learned of the excitement, he redoubled his efforts to promote calm. The Albany *Argus* spoke out sharply against abolitionist extremism, and the Regency sponsored a meeting at which prominent New York Democrats expressed their sympathy for the South. Van Buren also persuaded Governor William L. Marcy to denounce antislavery agitation in his annual report to the state legislature.[57] Such forthright statements helped disprove the charges that Van Buren covertly sanctioned the postal campaign, but they did not still the demand for explanations. Finally in March 1836 the Democratic candidate issued a public avowal of his views on abolition. While recognizing that Congress had the right to abolish slavery in the District of Columbia, Van Buren declared that he would "go into the White House the inflexible and uncompromising opponent" of any such legislation.[58] To Van Buren's dismay, this candid exposition did not ease all fears. No matter how often he pledged his support, many Southerners would continue to regard him an outsider.

Having done his best to dampen the fires of sectional discord, Van Buren proceeded with the more routine aspects of the campaign. He had at his disposal the same network that had proved so effective in two previous national elections. In New York, the Regency was enjoying its finest hour; even the activities of a new equal rights party in New York City did not disrupt Van Buren's hold on the state. At the other end of the axis, Virginia's Democrats had regained power. Although unhappy about Johnson's place on the ticket, the Rich-

[56] Adams, *Diary*, 9: 251; Bertram Wyatt-Brown, "The Abolitionists' Postal Campaign of 1835," *Journal of Negro History* 50 (1965): 227-38; Freehling, *Prelude to Civil War*, pp. 340-43.

[57] The following letters in the Van Buren Papers tell of Southern fears: Richard E. Parker, August 21, December 25, 1835, William Schley, August 22, 1835, Romulus Saunders, August 25, 1835, Peter V. Daniel, September 25, 1835, Dabney Carr, December 21-22, 1835, William C. Rives, January 29, 1836, Gideon J. Pillow, March 2, 1836. On Van Buren's response see Van Buren to William Schley, September 10, 1835, Van Buren to William L. Marcy, November [?], 1835, Van Buren Papers. See also Albany *Argus*, July 31, August 3, 13, 21, 24, September 4, 5, 7, 16, December 16, 28, 1835.

[58] Van Buren to Junius Amis, et al., March 4, 1836, Peter V. Daniel to Van Buren, June 7, 1836, Van Buren Papers.

mond Junto worked actively in Van Buren's behalf. To coordinate
the efforts of these two powerful state machines, Van Buren kept in
close communication with Francis P. Blair to ensure that the editorial policy of the Washington *Globe* reflected Democratic strategy.
Only the revolt against Jackson in Tennessee deprived the party of
one of its essential state organizations.[59]

In his conduct of the campaign, Van Buren employed no fancy
innovations. He stated his position on the major issues of the day and
defended himself from the inevitable calumnies that creep into every
presidential election. Because of his personality, he did not try to
make his a triumph of individual over party. As the masthead of the
Albany *Argus* proclaimed: "Union, Harmony, Self-Denial—everything for the cause, nothing for men." Below that appeared this
slogan: "The support of state governments in all their rights, as the
most competent administration of our domestic concerns, and the
surest bulwark against anti-republican tendencies."[60] Both quotations
expressed the heart of Van Buren's political creed.

The fall election crowned this appeal with success. Van Buren
received 170 electoral votes to his opponents' 124. The margin was
comfortable, but not overwhelming. To a large extent, Van Buren
won because the Whigs could not agree. He was, in the words of one
contemporary political observer, the only "National candidate."[61] In
Virginia and North Carolina, for instance, many antiadministration
voters despaired of casting their ballots for Hugh Lawson White
because they knew he could not win and because they feared he was
only a stalking horse for William Henry Harrison. A similar rivalry
between Harrison and Daniel Webster disrupted Whig forces in
Pennsylvania allowing Van Buren to unite a badly splintered party
and eke out a narrow victory. Although able to defeat the pluralistic
Whig strategy, Van Buren could not rest on his laurels. The loss of

[59] Jabez D. Hammond, *The History of Political Parties in the State of New York*, 2 vols. (Albany, N.Y., 1842), 2: 428–65; Garraty, *Silas Wright*, p. 130; Albany *Argus*, April 25, August 8, 10, 13, 1836; Ambler, *Thomas Ritchie*, pp. 175–86; William C. Rives to Van Buren, August 29, 1836, Thomas Ritchie to Van Buren, June 9, 1836, Francis P. Blair to Van Buren, July 14, August 28, October 8, 1836, Van Buren Papers; Van Buren to Francis P. Blair, August 22, 25, September 15, October 15, 1836, Blair and Woodbury Family Papers, Library of Congress.
[60] For a sample of campaign material see Van Buren to Sherrod Williams, August 8, 1836, Van Buren Papers; Albany *Argus*, August 5, October 27, 31, November 3, 1836; Washington *Globe*, July 30, August 26, 27, September 23, 27, October 1, 31, 1836; Richmond *Enquirer*, August 16, 23, September 27, 30, October 21, 1836.
[61] Jabez D. Hammond to Edwin Croswell, July 19, 1835, Van Buren Papers.

such Democratic strongholds as Georgia and Tennessee indicated that the road ahead might prove rough.[62]

At the time Martin Van Buren prepared to take office, the Democratic party showed signs of severe strain. Ironically, these tensions resulted from the actions of a man who brought the alliance into being. During his eight years in the White House, Andrew Jackson fulfilled much of the promise of 1828. In his battles with Nicholas Biddle, in his defiance of congressional assaults, in his dramatic confrontation with the nullifiers of South Carolina, the president set a tone sharply in contrast to the atmosphere of previous administrations. While Jackson displayed unprecedented energy, he did not materially enhance the powers of his office. He did use the veto more frequently than all his predecessors combined, but the veto was a defensive move, as were most of the triumphs of Jackson's long career. The negation of an act of Congress may have signified determination, but it also indicated an inability to manage legislative proceedings. Furthermore, in asserting the independence of the executive branch, Jackson helped create a staunch opposition that rallied to the cry of presidential despotism.

In the final analysis, Jackson was only as strong as his party. He had no independent electorate pledged to defend him against all critics. Poor communication facilities forced him to transmit his appeal through the states. Yet during the nullification crisis and the bank war, the president proceeded as though the Democrats were a national party instead of an amalgamation of state organizations. In his determination to destroy the hated doctrine of nullification, he dismissed the idea of state rights as if it were an abstract proposition instead of a realistic political blueprint for the America of the 1830's. Jackson's independent actions created consternation within the party and led to serious defections, especially in the South. Despite all this, Jackson survived, primarily because his opponents were so ill organized.

For Martin Van Buren, the election of 1836 ended a long, uncertain campaign for the nation's highest office. His success in securing Jackson's blessing was a triumph of temperament not strategy. At no time did he challenge the president for popular support. This, as Calhoun rudely discovered, was to risk defeat and political exile. Although Van Buren took issue with many of Jackson's decisions, he

---

[62] Ambler, *Thomas Ritchie*, p. 179; William S. Hoffman, *Andrew Jackson and North Carolina Politics* (Chapel Hill, N.C., 1958), pp. 102–12. Sister Mary Raimonde Bartus, "The Presidential Election of 1836" (Ph.D. diss., Fordham University, 1967), came to my attention too late for use in this study.

did so in a quiet, unobtrusive manner. He preferred to remain in the background, not as manager, but as a counselor whose advice often seemed timid but rarely provocative. Because he never became a rival, Van Buren proved an acceptable heir.

Van Buren seemed uniquely qualified to restore Democratic solidarity. Extended immersion in New York politics gave him an acute appreciation for state problems. By carefully disassociating himself from Jackson's doctrinal heresies, Van Buren emerged from the nullification crisis with his Jeffersonian principles intact. He hoped to capitalize on his continuing friendship with key Southern spokesmen to prevent further Whig inroads. So, too, he planned to utilize his long legislative experience to good advantage. If he could repair damaged relations with Congress, he might well deprive the new Whig party of its central base of operations.

Despite obvious qualifications, Van Buren entered office with one severe handicap. He did not enjoy widespread popularity. While able to master the intricacies of grassroots politics and coordinate the activities of far-flung organizations, he never enlisted the heartfelt enthusiasm of his countrymen. No matter how often he reiterated his basic political beliefs, or reaffirmed his devotion to the Jeffersonian creed, Van Buren remained the "magician." Americans might begrudgingly recognize the necessity of political expertise, but they would not worship its practitioners. The true test of the Democratic party would come when the hero stepped aside and the party professional took his place.

Chapter 3

In Search
of Calm

ALTHOUGH pleased with the outcome of the election, Van Buren wasted little time in celebration.[1] He had always greeted success with the same dignity with which he accepted defeat. Ahead lay months of hard work and planning, during which he would try to place his own imprint on the Democratic party without destroying the vital link with his predecessor. High on his list of priorities was the need to restore good relations with the South, in the hope of checking the growth of Whig power.

In view of these imperatives, selection of a cabinet took on paramount significance. The council of state was crucial for two reasons. It served to satisfy regional demands for national recognition and it offered a barometer of the political atmosphere in the administration. The proliferation of modern bureaucratic agencies and the demand for technical expertise have removed the twentieth-century cabinet from the center of political attention. By contrast, the Jacksonian council stood alone in the Democratic spotlight. History had shown it to be a breeding ground for intrigue.

As a participant in the cabinet struggles of Jackson's first term, Van Buren recognized the perils of controversy. The upheavals occasioned by the Eaton affair and the removal of deposits shook the party to its foundations. As new head of the alliance, Van Buren wanted to avoid such turmoil. By retaining the cabinet intact, he would establish valuable continuity and disarm his opponents, many of whom were hoping for a collapse of the new regime. Such a policy would also discourage a mad race for the spoils. "You have no conception what conflicting interests will immediately present themselves the moment a place is open," he told his son shortly after the election.[2] Yet total acceptance was almost as hazardous as complete change. No matter how much Van Buren owed his predecessor, he did not want to cultivate the image of subservience. Fortunately, Jackson had left one post vacant. In October 1836 Lewis Cass resigned to become minister to France. Rather than name a successor, the president instructed his attorney general, Benjamin F. Butler, to assume the duties of the war department with the express understanding that Van Buren would fill the position the following year.[3]

In looking for a new secretary of war, Van Buren was determined to appease Southerners who had long complained that they shared too little in the councils of the nation.[4] In 1836 Georgia's John Forsyth was the only cabinet member from the South. Acutely aware of this fact, Van Buren's Virginia friends urged the appointment of another Southerner, arguing that such a move would demonstrate the new president's determination to safeguard the interests of the slave states. "The mass of the Southern people would feel more confidence in the good disposition of the administration," wrote the Junto's Richard E. Parker, "by seeing in the cabinet men born amongst them entertaining, if you will, the same prejudices."[5]

Van Buren needed little urging. On the evening of February 1, 1837, he held a long meeting with Virginia's disgruntled senator, William C. Rives, and tried once again to overcome the animosity created by the vice-presidential battle in 1835. When asked to accept the cabinet vacancy, Rives demurred, hinting that the position of secretary of state might be more acceptable. Van Buren undoubtedly appreciated Rives's diplomatic experience and his high standing with Virginia's Democrats, but he could only meet this request by removing the incumbent, John Forsyth. This would inflame tensions in Georgia, a crucial Southern state already lost to the opposition. Rather than offend Rives, Van Buren suggested that he accept the vacancy with the hope of advancing to a more suitable post at a later date. Rives declined and, in so doing, signaled the start of an open break that would have a significant impact on the success of the new administration.[6]

From Virginia, Van Buren turned to South Carolina, writing to

[1] Silas Wright to Azariah Flagg, December 16, 1836, Flagg-Wright Papers.
[2] Van Buren to John Van Buren, December 30, 1836, Van Buren Papers.
[3] On March 3, 1837, Jackson officially nominated Butler as secretary of war and told the Senate of the previous arrangement whereby Butler had assumed Cass's duties. U.S. Senate, *Journal of the Executive Proceedings of the Senate, 1789–1948*, 90 vols. (Washington, D.C., 1828–1948), 4: 628; hereafter cited as *Senate Executive Journal*.
[4] Van Buren to George M. Dallas, February 16, 1837, Van Buren Papers.
[5] Richard E. Parker to Van Buren, February 7, 1837, Van Buren Papers.
[6] Transcript of a memorandum dated February 1, 1837, Letterbook (1835–1839), Rives Papers.

Joel R. Poinsett and urging him to become secretary of war. Remembering the trend of his conversation with Rives, Van Buren made it clear to Poinsett that neither the position of secretary of state nor that of secretary of the treasury was open. On February 9, 1837, Poinsett, despite his concern about the Washington climate, accepted the proposal.[7]

Poinsett was a man of fifty-eight whose frail constitution had not prevented an active career. A native of Charleston, South Carolina, Poinsett received his early education in England, where he developed an interest in natural science and a mastery of four languages. This training qualified him for service in the diplomatic corps, and in 1801, he began a series of extensive travels that would continue for the next two decades. During this period he visited Russia and served as a commercial agent in Latin America. In 1825 Poinsett accepted an appointment as minister to Mexico and set off on what proved to be a stormy diplomatic mission. He became deeply involved in Mexican politics and his democratic prejudices compromised whatever efforts he might have made to advance the cause of peace during the Mexican revolution of 1828. The following year President Jackson reluctantly recalled his partisan minister.

Poinsett's subsequent career in South Carolina politics was as turbulent as his stay in Mexico. After his return to the United States in 1830, he became an active opponent of nullification and served as leader of the Unionist party in his native state. He frequently wrote to Jackson of the need for federal assistance to stem the potential insurrection. Poinsett earned Jackson's respect, although the president tended to treat his ally's militance with a good deal of caution. In selecting Poinsett, Van Buren offended the nullifiers, but their opposition was no longer of political consequence. More important, he chose a man identified with both the South and the Union.[8]

Although successful in recruiting new Southern support, Van Buren barely managed to avoid an embarrassing situation in his own state. On February 15, 1837, New York's Benjamin F. Butler announced his intention to resign as attorney general. For some time, Van Buren had been aware of Butler's feelings and had written to the Regency urging them to put pressure on the attorney general to remain in his post.[9]

[7] Van Buren to Poinsett, February 4, 1837, Poinsett Papers in the Gilpin Collection, The Historical Society of Pennsylvania; Poinsett to Van Buren, February 9, 1837, Van Buren Papers.
[8] On Poinsett see J. Fred Rippy, *Joel Roberts Poinsett* (Durham, N.C., 1935).
[9] Butler to Van Buren, February 15, 1837, Van Buren to John Van Buren,

Van Buren had both personal and political reasons for wanting to keep his former law partner in the cabinet. Butler was a skilled jurist who had served in the New York legislature and as a member of the Regency. He once refused an opportunity to become a United States senator, preferring the quiet of a law practice to the whirl of national politics. The calm was short-lived. In 1833 Van Buren wrote to offer Butler the post of attorney general in Jackson's cabinet. In a revealing passage the vice president argued: "Although you are not the slave of mad ambition, you are, as you ought to be, tenacious of your professional standing. That cannot be *increased* at home, and can only be made *national*, by becoming identified with national concerns."[10] More effective than the appeal to Butler's ambition was the observation that Jackson had no objection to his attorney general's continuing a private law practice. Butler accepted and served for the remainder of Jackson's term. Again in 1837 Van Buren's arguments proved persuasive and Butler agreed to withdraw his resignation.[11]

The president-elect narrowly averted two additional cabinet explosions. On December 23, 1836, Mahlon Dickerson came to Van Buren's lodgings to discuss his role in the new administration. The secretary of the navy was still recovering from a severe attack of influenza suffered earlier in the fall. Appreciating this, Van Buren tried to persuade his visitor to accept appointment as chargé d'affaires to Belgium, but Dickerson declined, considering the post of secondary importance. The two men were unable to reach an agreement, and Dickerson left the meeting "altogether in doubt" about Van Buren's intentions. For the next month there were persistent rumors that Dickerson would retire.[12]

The sixty-six-year-old Dickerson had a long career in local and

December 30, 1836, Van Buren Papers; Van Buren to John A. Dix, January 28, 1837, Dix Papers, Columbia University Library; John L. Graham to Van Buren, February 4, 1837, Benjamin F. Butler Papers, Princeton University Library.

[10] Van Buren to Butler, November 8, 1833, in William A. Butler, *A Retrospect of Forty Years* (New York, 1911), pp. 39–43.

[11] On Butler's career to 1833 see Rev. William D. Driscoll, "Benjamin F. Butler: Lawyer and Regency Politician" (Ph.D. diss., Fordham University, 1965).

[12] Mahlon Dickerson, MS Diary, October 15–31, December 23, 1836, New Jersey Historical Society; James Graham to William A. Graham, January 29, 1837, in J. G. de Roulhac Hamilton, ed., *The Papers of William A. Graham, 1825–1856*, 4 vols. (Raleigh, N.C., 1957–1961), 1: 482; hereafter cited as Graham, *Papers*. On Dickerson's previous experience see Josiah C. Pumpelly, "Mahlon Dickerson," New Jersey Historical Society *Proceedings* 11 (1891): 143. Robert Beckwith, "Mahlon Dickerson of New Jersey, 1770–1853" (Ph.D. diss., Columbia University, 1967), came to my attention too late for use in this study.

national politics. Rising through the ranks of the New Jersey legislature, he served his state first as governor and then senator. In 1834, after seventeen years in Washington, he agreed to join Jackson's cabinet. Dickerson had no experience in naval affairs; his age and delicate health were definite liabilities. Furthermore, his fiscal views ran counter to those of the majority of Jackson's advisers. Van Buren would have been happier had Dickerson accepted a position in the diplomatic corps, but the president-elect was not prepared, at such a crucial time, to have a member of the council resign in anger. It was much safer to wait for a more propitious moment for Dickerson's replacement.[13]

With Butler and Dickerson continuing to serve in the cabinet, Van Buren considered his problems solved and approached his term with confidence. One evening in the midst of a postinaugural party, the new president, in an expansive mood, expounded on his oft-repeated belief that a harmonious cabinet was one in which no member harbored presidential ambitions. Standing within earshot were two of Van Buren's counselors, Secretary of the Treasury Levi Woodbury and Secretary of State John Forsyth. Woodbury let the remark pass, but Forsyth took immediate offense at what he considered a deliberate innuendo.

The next few days were filled with confusion. Forsyth went to see Van Buren and suggested the possibility of going abroad in a diplomatic capacity. Taken aback, the president mused over several openings but made no attempt to dissuade the Georgian or force him to reconsider. Forsyth then petulantly asked who would become secretary of state, and Van Buren mentioned Butler. Now convinced of a presidential plot to drive him from the cabinet, Forsyth refused a foreign mission, submitted his resignation, and prepared a letter to his Georgia constituents justifying his actions. He delivered this angry missive to the office of the Washington *Globe*, where it was dutifully set in type.

Van Buren was totally unprepared for this outburst. He promptly prevented the publication of Forsyth's letter and then tried to improve the deteriorating situation. He wrote to his distraught adviser, explaining that he had not meant to imply that Forsyth was a candidate and had only meant to include in this category men actively campaigning for the presidency. Forsyth then agreed to

[13] Pumpelly, "Dickerson," 133–43; Dickerson, MS Diary, June 18, 21, 1836. On the dissatisfaction with Dickerson see Prosper M. Wetmore to William L. Marcy, March 19, 1837, Simon Gratz Autograph Collection, The Historical Society of Pennsylvania.

remain in the cabinet; the crisis was over. There is little reason to believe that Van Buren sought Forsyth's removal, especially since a few weeks before he had told Rives and Poinsett that the secretary of state would remain.[14]

This was not the first, nor would it be the last time that Forsyth acted with haste and indiscretion. As minister to Spain in 1819, he had seen fit to deliver a pompous lecture to Spanish diplomats on the duties of their king. The address drew prompt criticism from the Spanish foreign office. Forsyth's later career was more promising. A resident of Georgia, he served in both the House and the Senate. In 1832 Forsyth headed a strong movement against nullification and was in part responsible for Georgia's refusal to follow in the footsteps of South Carolina. His support of Jackson's policies made him a logical choice for the job of secretary of state in 1834. To this post Forsyth brought a modicum of diplomatic experience, a tremendous talent for debate, and a strong devotion to the Democratic party. He had mellowed somewhat by his fifty-seventh year, but age did not completely eliminate the impulsiveness of youth. No matter what Forsyth's shortcomings as a diplomat, Van Buren could not afford to alienate such a strong Southern ally.[15]

Although Van Buren avoided a public airing of these problems, there were numerous rumors to liven the inauguration atmosphere. A popular topic of speculation was the possibility that Jackson's nephew Andrew J. Donelson would be a member of the new administration. Shortly after the election of 1836, Van Buren had asked Donelson to accept a cabinet post, presumably as secretary of war. Donelson did not enjoy a national reputation, and some thought his appointment would draw criticism from the West. On the advice of Jackson and other political associates, Van Buren withdrew the offer.[16]

Doubt concerning Van Buren's intentions only added to the frustration of those not assured of sharing in the spoils. One observer,

14 William B. Lewis to Andrew Stevenson, March 13, 1837, Andrew Stevenson Papers, Library of Congress; William B. Hodgson to William C. Rives, May 23, 1837, Rives Papers; Van Buren to Forsyth, March 9, 1837, Van Buren Papers; Albany Argus, January 12, 1837. For a somewhat different account based in part on less contemporary sources see Alvin Laroy Duckett, John Forsyth (Athens, Ga., 1962), p. 182.
15 Eugene I. McCormac, "John Forsyth," in Samuel Flagg Bemis et al., eds., American Secretaries of State and Their Diplomacy, 14 vols. (New York, 1927–1965), 4: 302–303; Duckett, Forsyth, p. 55.
16 Thomas Ritchie to Thomas Green, January 26, 1837, in Branch Historical Papers, 4: 381–82; William S. Derrick to Nicholas P. Trist, February 15, 1837, Trist Papers, Library of Congress; Van Buren, Autobiography, pp. 345–47.

visiting Washington in the winter of 1837, direly predicted that "the formation of the new cabinet will cause another rupture, there are not enough loaves and fishes to feed all the hungry swarm of Expectants who are looking for office."[17] Senator James Buchanan, upset by Van Buren's secrecy, pressed for representation for Pennsylvania. Van Buren appreciated the importance of the Keystone State; he also knew that honoring it with a cabinet selection might further agitate a precarious political situation. In offering the Russian mission to Buchanan's colleague George M. Dallas, Van Buren made it clear that a cabinet post was out of the question. The Dallas appointment temporarily placated Buchanan, but other elements of the Democratic party in Pennsylvania continued to demand recognition. Van Buren persisted in his course and tried to make the best of a difficult situation, but he obviously could not please all factions.[18]

Rumors, resignations, pressures, and negotiations—they touched all the members of the cabinet except Levi Woodbury and Amos Kendall. Both men strongly supported Andrew Jackson, and there seemed little doubt that they would continue to serve Van Buren.

Small, frail Amos Kendall was a giant in the Jackson administration. A vitriolic Kentucky newspaper editor, he deserted Henry Clay's camp in 1826 and found Jackson's Democracy more responsive to local interests. Kendall brought to Washington a wealth of political experience. Raised in Massachusetts, he emigrated to Kentucky in 1814 and took a job as tutor for Henry Clay's children. This association soon made him known to the political elites; Kendall obtained a postmastership and turned to journalism. He learned that newspapers, to be successful, must be partisan and appeal to the prejudices of patrons and subscribers. In 1816 Kendall took over the *Argus of Western America* and strengthened his position by winning election as state printer. For the next decade he sharpened the tools that would make him an indispensable political practitioner.[19]

---

[17] James Graham to William A. Graham, January 29, 1837, in Graham, *Papers*, 1: 482.

[18] Buchanan to William N. Irvine, December 23, 1836, Irvine Family Papers, The Historical Society of Pennsylvania; Buchanan to William Norris, January 11, 1837, Buchanan Misc. Papers, Library of Congress; Buchanan to Van Buren, February 19, 28, 1837, Simon Cameron and Ovid Johnson to Van Buren, February 24, 1837, Van Buren to Dallas, February 16, 1837, Van Buren Papers; Philadelphia *Sentinel*, March 16, 1837, quoted in *National Intelligencer*, March 18, 1837; Philip Shriver Klein, *President James Buchanan* (University Park, Pa., 1962), p. 113.

[19] Lynn Marshall, "The Early Career of Amos Kendall" (Ph.D. diss., University of California, Berkeley, 1962); Richard P. Longaker, "Was Jackson's Kitchen Cabinet a Cabinet?" *Mississippi Valley Historical Review* 44 (1957): 94–108;

Under Jackson, the forty-year-old Kendall began his career in the inconspicuous position of fourth auditor of the treasury. His journalistic skill and his flair for strong, effective rhetoric gained him access to the president's closest circle of advisers. As a Westerner, Kendall shared Jackson's animosity to banks and was a leading participant in the attack on Biddle's financial empire. In 1834 he officially joined the cabinet as postmaster general, soon exerting an influence over his department that struck the ubiquitous John Quincy Adams as "perfectly despotic."[20] Kendall brought needed reforms to the postal service and also won Southern political support by helping limit the spread of abolitionist literature in 1835.[21] Van Buren had quarreled with Kendall in the past, but he did not want to lose so talented a politician.

Levi Woodbury was the lone cabinet member from New England. Born in New Hampshire in 1789, he attended Dartmouth, studied law, and in 1817 became an associate justice of the New Hampshire court. After six years on the bench, he turned to more active political pursuits, winning election first as governor, and then as senator; in 1831 he became secretary of the navy. While in Jackson's cabinet Woodbury sided with Blair and Kendall in approving the removal of deposits from the Bank of the United States. In 1834, after the Senate rejected Roger B. Taney as secretary of the treasury, Jackson transferred Woodbury to the vacant post.[22]

By the middle of March 1837, the excitement of the inauguration had passed. The president had completed his cabinet arrangements and had survived several near crises. His council of state was not the most impressive in the nation's history, but it was competent. All the members had college education, and four of the six men were lawyers. Both Forsyth and Poinsett had previous diplomatic experience. Three of Van Buren's advisers had served in Congress and all had an exposure to local politics. Amos Kendall alone was conspicuous by his

---

Lynn Marshall, "The Authorship of Jackson's Bank Veto Message," *Mississippi Valley Historical Review* 50 (1963): 98–99; Harriet Martineau, *Retrospect of Western Travel*, 2 vols. (New York, 1838), 1: 155–56.

[20] Adams to Edward Everett, November 14, 1837, John Quincy Adams MS Letterbook (1837), Adams Family Papers, Massachusetts Historical Society.

[21] Bertram Wyatt-Brown, "The Abolitionists' Postal Campaign of 1835," *Journal of Negro History* 50 (1965): 227–38; Frank Otto Gatell, "Postmaster Huger and the Incendiary Publications," *South Carolina Historical Magazine* 44 (1963): 193–201. On Kendall's later career see Kendall, *Autobiography*.

[22] On Woodbury's early career see Vincent J. Capowski, "The Making of a Jacksonian Democrat: Levi Woodbury, 1789–1831" (Ph.D. diss., Fordham University, 1966).

lack of significant congressional, legal, or diplomatic training, yet he was by far the most talented politician. If there was a weakness in Van Buren's council, it was that of ill health. Dickerson, Poinsett, and Kendall would each suffer some disabling ailment during the next four years.

The new president was pleased with his handiwork. He had achieved his goal of increasing representation for the South while retaining continuity with his predecessor. Furthermore, he believed that his councilors worked "together harmoniously and gloriously."[23] Considering the political consequences of Jackson's cabinet upheavals, such unity was essential. To maintain this spirit of cooperation, Van Buren held weekly cabinet meetings, following a precedent established by Jackson in 1831. The pattern of these deliberations indicates that the cabinet was no mere perfunctory body. Before delivering any important message to Congress, Van Buren met with his department heads, both to listen to their suggestions and to brief them on his own recommendations. During time of domestic or international turmoil, the president called his counselors into emergency session; on occasion these crisis deliberations took place daily.[24]

Van Buren's role during a cabinet meeting is conjectural. Apparently he posed questions, but remained aloof during proceedings, recording impressions and reserving judgment. Such reticence was characteristic; the president had long been averse to giving his opinions in a committee session because such a course was "contrary to parliamentary usage, according to which the Chairman is regarded as a mediator, and, to some extent, an umpire between the conflicting opinions of the Committee."[25] He did not shy away from difficult decisions; he simply chose to make them in private, thereby reducing the risks of open controversy.[26]

In seeking advice, the president did not depend on the cabinet alone. Throughout his career, Van Buren had solicited opinions from important state leaders, and he continued this practice while in the White House. A large percentage of his correspondence concerned

[23] Van Buren to Jackson, April 24, 1837, Van Buren Papers. See also John M. Niles to Gideon Welles, September 3, 1837, Welles Papers, Library of Congress.

[24] Dickerson, MS Diary, gives the only account of cabinet meetings. These generalizations are based on a study of his report of eighty-one council sessions between March 4, 1837, and his resignation in the summer of 1838. For Jackson's use of the cabinet see James C. Curtis, "Andrew Jackson and His Cabinet: Some New Evidence," *Tennessee Historical Quarterly* 27 (1968): 157–64.

[25] Van Buren, *Autobiography*, p. 106.

[26] See, for instance, Van Buren, endorsement on a questionnaire on the specie circular, March 24, 1837, Van Buren Papers; Dickerson, MS Diary, April 5, 1837.

affairs in New York and Virginia; it is clear that he regarded these two states as the foundation of the Democratic alliance. John A. Dix, Azariah Flagg, and William L. Marcy, all Regency members, commented on a range of topics affecting the Empire State. Thomas Ritchie and his brother-in-law, Richard E. Parker, sent a constant flow of information on affairs in Virginia, while Andrew J. Donelson wrote occasionally on Tennessee politics and on his uncle's condition. The majority of news from the Hermitage filtered through Francis P. Blair, who remained in Washington to edit the *Globe*. Silas Wright and Churchill C. Cambreleng supervised Congress and counseled Van Buren on legislative problems. The president could also consult his sons, two of whom held posts in the General Land Office.[27]

Van Buren enjoyed a close rapport with most of his department heads; several took on added duties well outside their designated administrative spheres. The new secretary of war continued an active interest in finances and foreign affairs.[28] Postmaster General Amos Kendall was equally concerned with the nation's economy; during the Panic he proved quite willing to experiment with his department. Once the banks suspended specie payments, Kendall discontinued depositing funds in these institutions and kept money in the hands of postal employees. On a small scale he displayed the feasibility of dispensing with banks as fiscal agents for the government, thus demonstrating the merits of the sub-Treasury scheme.[29] Attorney General Benjamin F. Butler was Van Buren's intimate confidant and was most influential in devising legislation for the special session.[30]

That cabinet members ranged far afield is not surprising. The council of state was primarily a political, not an administrative, entity. In selecting advisers the president sought to reward local interest, not to obtain technical proficiency. If the nominee was a skilled administrator, so much the better. If not, the chief executive

[27] *Senate Executive Journal*, 5: 18, 216. Such nepotism was by no means unusual; see Sidney H. Aronson, *Status and Kinship in the Higher Civil Service* (Cambridge, Mass., 1964).

[28] Robert Greenhow to Poinsett, August 14, 1837, Poinsett Papers in the Gilpin Collection; Van Buren to Poinsett, May 8, 1838, Poinsett to Van Buren, May 9, 1838, Poinsett Papers, The Historical Society of Pennsylvania; Poinsett, Notes on banking and currency reforms, September 4, 1837, Van Buren Papers; Nicholas Biddle to E. C. Biddle, October 31, 1838, in Reginald C. McGrane, ed., *The Correspondence of Nicholas Biddle* (Boston, 1919), p. 307; hereafter cited as Biddle, *Correspondence*.

[29] Jackson to Kendall, May 26, June 23, 1837, Jackson-Kendall Papers, Library of Congress; John M. Niles to Gideon Welles, December 6, 1837, Welles Papers.

[30] Jackson to Kendall, March 23, 1838, Jackson-Kendall Papers; William Gouge to Van Buren, July 17, 1840, Van Buren Papers.

had the additional responsibility of overseeing departmental routine. In most instances Van Buren allowed his subordinates wide latitude in their endeavors. To lighten the overwhelming burden of patronage, he established the precedent of permitting department heads to appoint clerks and other minor functionaries. The president could thus devote more time to filling the increasing number of posts requiring Senate confirmation.[31] Van Buren did not ignore the lower civil service and was quick to reprimand any indiscriminate appointments that created political controversy.[32] Although lenient, the president was not lax. When Dickerson bungled naval affairs, Van Buren stepped in.[33] During financial and foreign crises, he also superintended the work of both his secretary of the treasury and secretary of state.

To a great extent, Van Buren succeeded in maintaining cabinet harmony throughout his administration. He endured the normal turnover of advisers. Dickerson departed in 1838 after a quarrel concerning the Navy Department; New York's James Kirke Paulding took his place. Benjamin F. Butler finally retired in the spring of that year, and Tennessee's Felix Grundy became the new attorney general, only to resign eighteen months later to return to the Senate. As Grundy's successor, Van Buren named Pennsylvania's Henry D. Gilpin, thus at long last rewarding the Keystone State with a cabinet post. The final change in the council came a scant six months before the election, when Amos Kendall decided to devote his full energies to editing the *Extra Globe*. Connecticut's John M. Niles filled out Kendall's term as postmaster general. Except for a sharp newspaper debate over Dickerson's withdrawal, none of these changes created any significant political turmoil.[34]

The calm at the outset of the new administration was in sharp contrast to the frantic confusion of the old. Jackson's mercurial personality and his uncertain health had affected social life as well as politics. On occasion, the executive mansion teemed with visitors indulging in saturnalian festivities reminiscent of the inaugural in

---

[31] Leonard D. White, *The Jacksonians: A Study in Administrative History, 1829–1861* (New York, 1954), p. 73.

[32] James K. Paulding to Van Buren, October 11, 1838, in Ralph M. Aderman, ed., *The Letters of James Kirke Paulding* (Madison, Wis., 1962), pp. 237–38; hereafter cited as Paulding, *Letters*.

[33] Dickerson, MS Diary, January 23, February 5, 1838.

[34] For a complete discussion of developments in the cabinet between 1837 and 1840 see James C. Curtis, "The Heritage Imperiled: Martin Van Buren and the Presidency, 1837–1841" (Ph.D. diss., Northwestern University, 1967), pp. 54–71.

1829. At other times, the old general sat alone in his drafty room, rocking by the side of a blazing fire, looking haggard and worn. Under Van Buren the pace of entertainment was more leisurely and the atmosphere more formal. Gone were the days when any visitor might burst into the president's office unannounced. Uniformed guards now carefully screened all guests. So, too, the large raucous receptions gave way to small intimate dinner parties at which Van Buren jovially presided, taking obvious pleasure in the splendor of his board and the talents of his imported chef. The president did not eliminate the normal holiday levees, but he did prevent "the mob-ocracy from intruding themselves."[35] Clearly, Van Buren did not cultivate the role of champion of the common man.

The president's search for administrative harmony and his empha-sis on formality and punctilio reflect his approach to the problems of the Democratic party. He did not propose to unite the faithful behind a vast legislative program; such an idea was alien to his day. He hoped to cooperate with Congress and to end the legislative bickering that had marred Jackson's second term.[36] Beyond that, Van Buren simply sought to preserve the status quo. Convinced that the party needed a hiatus from quarreling and dissension, he was content to watch over the Democratic alliance as a paternal peacemaker, mediating political feuds in the same diplomatic manner with which he managed social affairs. Unforeseen events soon shattered these dreams forever.

[35] Jessie Benton Fremont, *Souvenirs of My Time* (Boston, 1887), pp. 88–99; John Fairfield to Anna Fairfield, January 24, 1836, Fairfield Papers, Library of Congress; Frederick Marryat, *A Diary in America with Remarks on Its Institu-tions*, ed. Jules Zanger (new ed.; Bloomington, Ind., 1960), p. 190.

[36] In some areas Van Buren did succeed in improving relations with the legislative branch. For instance, he had a much easier time with appointments than did his predecessor. Perusal of the *Senate Executive Journal* indicates that the upper chamber rejected only thirty-two of Van Buren's nominations and none of these involved a major post. This was in marked contrast to the quarrels of the Jackson administration of which Van Buren himself was a victim.

Chapter 4

Panic
and Response

BEFORE Van Buren could concentrate on eliminating Democratic dissension, he had to resolve several difficult financial problems left over from the Jackson administration. The most crucial of these concerned the specie circular, an executive order issued by Jackson shortly before the election in an attempt to curb reckless speculation. Since 1831 the nation's economy had expanded at a frenzied rate. Although part of a general international upswing, this growth related directly to the country's westward surge. Cotton paced the advance; as its price rose, so did the desire for land. Boom times hit the South and West. Eager merchants took advantage of improved transportation facilities to rush needed manufactures and foodstuffs into the area. Wherever money went, banks were sure to follow, and soon the nation's monetary structure strained to keep abreast of the times. By 1836 a great deal of this economic energy found its way into unsound ventures; land sales skyrocketed; so, too, did the indiscriminate chartering of new banks.[1]

Against this background Jackson fought his titanic war with the Second Bank of the United States. Despite his energy and dedication, Old Hickory seemed to have little idea of how to check the rampaging economy or fill the void created by the demise of Biddle's monster. From beginning to end, the president regarded the struggle as a political duel, undertaken for political reasons and fought in the political arena. Jackson did not ignore the financial consequences of his actions; he simply could not stand back and objectively survey the forces at work in the nation's economy. Few men could. For the duration of the bank war, Jackson remained on the defensive, constantly reacting to some anticipated move by Biddle. This posture prevented the president from developing any coordinated plans for fiscal reform.

Some historians have argued that during the bank war, the Democrats followed a consistent course aimed at controlling the economy.[2] This theory has its drawbacks because it presumes that the Jacksonians preached, and consciously pursued, a policy of federal intervention. From a post–New Deal vantage point this appears logical, but unfortunately there is little proof to support such a supposition. Those who cite evidence of paternalistic governmental concern usually focus on the activities of local agencies.[3] In fact, the very intensity of state campaigns for internal improvements made national action politically hazardous. Democrats found that only a negative theory of federal government was compatible with local activism, and upon assuming power in 1829 they were determined to avoid enacting legislation that might arouse sectional animosities.

Of all Jackson's advisers, Martin Van Buren was the most concerned with political implications of economic policy. He did not join eagerly in the antibank onslaught but remained aloof, fearful that constant agitation would disrupt the party. When in 1833 he reluctantly lent his voice to the rising chorus, he did so because he believed corporate monopoly offered a more convenient scapegoat than Southern particularism. Despite his decision to support the removal of deposits, Van Buren did not advocate an endless multiplication of banking facilities. The same caution that prompted his recommendation of the safety fund in 1829 continued to influence his judgment four years later.[4]

The Democrats soon realized that by removing deposits from the Second Bank of the United States and placing them in state institu-

[1] For a much more detailed description see Douglass C. North, *The Economic Growth of the United States 1790 to 1860* (Englewood Cliffs, N.J., 1961); George Rogers Taylor, *The Transportation Revolution* (New York, 1951).

[2] The most recent, comprehensive statement of this theme is John M. McFaul, "The Politics of Jacksonian Finance" (Ph.D. diss., University of California, Berkeley, 1964). See also several articles by Richard Timberlake, Jr.: "The Independent Treasury and Monetary Policy before the Civil War," *Southern Economic Journal* 27 (1960): 92–103; "The Specie Circular and the Distribution of the Surplus," *Journal of Political Economy* 68 (1960): 109–17; "The Specie Standard and Central Banking in the United States before 1860," *Journal of Economic History* 21 (1961): 318–41. In addition see Harry N. Schieber, "The Pet Banks in Jacksonian Politics and Finance, 1833–1841," *Journal of Economic History* 23 (1963): 196–214. These works seem bent on refuting Bray Hammond, *Banks and Politics in America from the Revolution to the Civil War* (Princeton, N.J., 1957), which pictures the Jacksonians as acquisitive, unenlightened entrepreneurs.

[3] Taylor, *Transportation Revolution*, p. 352. See his bibliographical essay for a guide to works developing this theme.

[4] Frank Otto Gatell, "Spoils of the Bank War: Political Bias in the Selection of Pet Banks," *American Historical Review* 70 (1964): 35–58.

tions, they reaped temporary political rewards but sowed the seeds of economic chaos. They now had to control the rapidly expanding fiscal structure without violating Jeffersonian principles of simple government and state rights. One wing of the party, under nominal leadership of Missouri's Thomas Hart Benton, favored a return to hard money. Such a policy raised many political problems; deflationary measures would tend to undermine the state banks, so recently enlisted as allies. Furthermore, since Congress would not cooperate in such a plan, the only recourse would be to executive fiat, opening the administration to charges of tyranny.

Although equally opposed to an unchecked expansion of credit, Van Buren advocated more moderate remedies than did Benton. Regarding banks as a necessary evil to be tolerated, not attacked, Van Buren favored control by state machinery such as provided by New York's safety fund system.[5] He thus stood midway between those who actively promoted further speculation and those who, out of fear, rushed to embrace hard money doctrines. His ambivalence was the product both of his New York experience and of a concern for the political consequences of establishing a specie standard by executive order.

The deposit system remained in effect from 1833 to 1837. If the Jacksonians had planned to use it to reform the economy, they soon found they were dealing with unwieldy machinery. Congress would not act to provide safeguards, and so the secretary of the treasury was left to his own devices. He could influence state banking practices by establishing restrictions on specie reserves, but this was a clumsy means of control and was effective only so long as banks reacted favorably to administration exhortations.[6]

In June 1836 Congress seriously weakened even this influence by passing an act requiring the distribution of surplus revenue to the states and the selection of additional depositories. No longer could the president work solely with friendly banks; he would lose both political and economic leverage.[7] Jackson hesitated to sign this bill because it was clearly inflationary in intent. By providing additional

---

[5] Fritz Redlich, *The Molding of American Banking: Men and Ideas* (New York, 1947), pp. 88–94; McFaul, "Politics of Jacksonian Finance," pp. 212–14.
[6] McFaul, "Politics of Jacksonian Finance," p. 88.
[7] Gatell, "Spoils of the Bank War," p. 36. In this connection see Amos Kendall's statement of the government's desire to keep from increasing the number of deposit banks: Kendall to the Postmaster of Lagrange, Tenn., March 21, 1837, Letters from the Postmaster General to Postmasters, Postal Department Records, National Archives; hereafter cited as Letters from Postmaster General.

funds to state banks, it would encourage further speculation and strain an already overheated economy. Yet the nation was not in a self-denying mood, and the president frankly did not know what to do with the burgeoning Treasury surplus. The sworn enemy of federally sponsored internal improvements, he believed he had little choice but to unburden the national government by giving the money to the states. Besides, it was an election year and distribution promised to be a popular issue. After obtaining assurances that the states would regard the money as a "loan" and not a "gift," Jackson relented. So alarming were the prospects of an increase in speculation that he issued the specie circular to neutralize the effects of the deposit act. This order specifically required that all public land be paid for in gold and silver. The new directive did not go far enough to satisfy Benton and raised an outcry from Jackson's congressional opponents, who once more protested executive interference in the economy.

Although it curtailed speculation, the specie circular placed a heavy burden on the nation's financial institutions. Banks in the West and Southwest increased their specie reserves in order to anticipate the effects of the Treasury order. This necessitated a transfer of specie from East to West and a stockpiling of revenue at a time when Eastern banks were under pressure to honor their commitments abroad and to comply with the requirements of the deposit act. In the summer and fall of 1836 the Bank of England raised its discount rate, thereby tightening credit. All this occurred in a year when Americans were already suffering an unfavorable balance of trade and had gone in debt to English merchants. These developments combined to create acute economic instability.[8]

On the eve of his inauguration, Van Buren drew fire both from those who wanted relief from the credit restrictions associated with the specie circular and from those who favored even more drastic deflationary measures. On March 1, 1837, by an overwhelming majority, Congress passed a bill altering, but not repealing, the specie circular. Although Jackson prevented the measure from becoming law, the legislature had expressed its displeasure with his stringent policies. This response transcended party lines; Van Buren found many of his state supporters eager proponents of revision. While Congress indicated its dissatisfaction with the specie circular, Benton

[8] North, *Economic Growth*, pp. 198–200; Taylor, *Transportation Revolution*, pp. 338–43; Reginald C. McGrane, *The Panic of 1837* (Chicago, 1924), pp. 43–69.

urged the president-elect to take immediate actions to halt the spiraling economy.[9] As soon as the excitement of the inauguration passed, Van Buren turned to this inherited dilemma.

What to do with the specie circular? The new president considered this question countless times during the next month. His mail, once brimming with congratulations, now brought daily complaints, warning of dire economic consequences should the order remain in effect.[10] Continuous reports of impending financial failures made it imperative that Van Buren act, if only to reassert current policy. Adding to this predicament was a growing restlessness in Congress and in the Democratic press. Several key senators warned that by ignoring the legislature's demand for a new policy, Van Buren risked open revolt. Both the Albany *Argus* and the Richmond *Enquirer* assured their readers that the new president would alter the Treasury directive.[11]

As he had done so often in the past, Van Buren turned to his native state for advice before making any firm decisions. Silas Wright was preparing to return to his home in Canton, New York, and the president persuaded him to make a brief detour to determine the opinions of the state's commercial community.[12] While Wright was so employed, Van Buren asked the Treasury Department to evaluate the probable consequences of a repeal of the specie circular. Woodbury's clerk and sometime adviser, William Gouge, prepared a lengthy statement in response to Van Buren's request. Gouge argued that abrogation of the order might provide temporary relief in New York and New Orleans but would eventually increase the amount of

[9] U.S. Congress, *The Congressional Globe*, 24th Cong., 2d sess., 1837, 4: 272–73. Jackson received the bill on March 2, 1837, and the following day notified Congress that he would not affix his signature. He objected to the loose construction of the measure which he felt would be open to conflicting interpretation: Richardson, *Messages and Papers*, 3: 282–83; Silas Wright to Azariah C. Flagg, February 26, 1837, Flagg-Wright Papers; Jackson to Nicholas P. Trist, March 2, 1837, Trist Papers; Thomas Hart Benton, *Thirty Years View*, 2 vols. (New York, 1854–1856) 2: 10–11. ·

[10] See, for example, letters from the following individuals in the Van Buren Papers: Henry Toland, March 9, 1837, Gorham Worth, March 12, 1837, James Lee, March 14, 1837, Campbell P. White, March 14, 1837, Cornelius Van Wyck Lawrence, March 18, 1837, Robert I. Ward, March 22, 1837, Myndert Van Schaick, March 28–29, 1837.

[11] Nathaniel P. Tallmadge to Van Buren, March 15, 1837, Van Buren Papers; Nathaniel Niles to William C. Rives, April 15, 1837, Tallmadge to Rives, April 16, May 1, 1837, William C. Rives to Thomas Ritchie, May 4, 1837, Rives Papers. Albany *Argus*, March 11, 16, 1837; Edwin Croswell to Benjamin F. Butler, March 13, 1837, Butler Papers; Richmond *Enquirer*, April 21, 1837.

[12] Wright to Van Buren, March 21, 1837, Van Buren Papers.

paper in circulation and endanger the government's ability to meet scheduled payments of surplus revenue. In urging retention of the circular, Gouge stated, "The fault of the measure is, (regarded in an economic point of view) not that it is too powerful, but that it is not powerful enough." Lest these economic reasons be insufficient, he added that repeal would disappoint those "sturdy Democrats" who looked on Van Buren as pledged to uphold Jackson's policies.[13] The president next consulted his cabinet, conducting preliminary discussions on the specie circular on March 22, 1837. Despite Gouge's strong urgings, Van Buren worried about the party and was giving serious consideration either to suspending or to modifying the Treasury order; the next day he asked his advisers to submit written opinions of these alternatives.[14]

While the cabinet mulled over this question, Van Buren wrote to the Hermitage to prepare Jackson for a major shift in policy. His letter is a masterpiece of ambiguity, telling of the "bundles of letters, & memorials from our friends in favor of rescinding the Treasury order, but in almost every case breathing a kind & liberal spirit toward yourself, admitting that much good has been accomplished by it, but insisting that it ought to be discontinued now." In the next breath, Van Buren discredited these "friendly" sources, stating flatly that "Every man who has become embarrassed by his own improvident speculations relieves himself from self reproaches by laying his misfortunes at the door of the Treasury order."[15] The juxtaposition of these two statements tends to confound the modern reader, but Jackson knew that his successor was exploring the possibility of change. On March 30, 1837, the former president replied that he placed little faith in the protestations of gamblers and speculators and that a "common share of prudence would await the memorials of the people—*the real laboring classes,* for the suspension of the Treasury Order." Three days later, Jackson's nephew Andrew J. Donelson

[13] William Gouge [?], Memorandum, March 19, 1837, Van Buren Papers. This document is in Gouge's handwriting although the calendar of Van Buren's papers, ed. Elizabeth H. West (Washington, D.C., 1910) attributes it to Woodbury. The ideas are clearly Gouge's as Woodbury later expressed doubts about the utility of the specie circular.

[14] Dickerson, MS Diary, March 22, 23, 1837; Van Buren, Memorandum, March 24, 1837, Van Buren Papers. On Van Buren's inclination to rescind, see Nathaniel Niles to William C. Rives, June 13, 1837, Rives Papers.

[15] Van Buren to Jackson, March [?], 1837, Van Buren Papers. McFaul suggests that this letter may never have been sent. Admittedly, it is fragmentary, but only the last page is missing, and it is here that Van Buren usually dated his letters. Furthermore, Jackson's letter to the president on March 30, 1837, makes reference to several key phrases and ideas that appear in Van Buren's letter.

wrote a less impassioned note, expressing the hope that Van Buren might find a middle way to uphold the spirit of Jackson's policies while extending more credit to purchasers of public lands.[16]

Initial cabinet response was mixed. Most members felt uneasy about the circular but could not agree on a remedy. Dickerson advocated total repeal, Kendall toyed with the idea of a temporary suspension, and Levi Woodbury all but disassociated himself from any responsibility for the measure. Poinsett, Forsyth, and Butler remained silent. Preferring to reach a decision alone and fearing the effects of fruitless discussion, Van Buren decided not to insist on the written opinions of his advisers.[17]

The president found himself in a difficult position. Time seemed to be running out. Although he favored modification, news of repeated failures made him doubt whether any executive action could avert a crisis. Silas Wright reported that members of New York's financial community now thought it "nonsense to talk any longer of Treasury orders . . . or of any action of the sectional or state governments as either having occasioned the mischief, or as being able to furnish the remedy." He maintained that frenzied speculation created the crisis and only a further restriction of credit would help. Churchill C. Cambreleng argued much the same line, blaming a ruthless opposition, bent on restoring a national bank, for manufacturing cries for repeal. "Drowning men clutch at straws," said the Regency's Azariah C. Flagg, "and hence many are attaching consequence to the repeal of the specie order as a measure of relief. The specie order did not cause the disease & its repeal cannot cure it."[18]

Persuaded by the opinions of these trusted state leaders, Van Buren decided to stand by the specie circular. He made no official pronouncements, but by mid-April 1837, the Washington *Globe* launched into a lengthy defense of Jackson's policies. Blair carried the fight to the opposition, arguing that repeal would only facilitate

[16] Jackson to Van Buren, March 30, 1837, Van Buren Papers. There is a draft of this letter, somewhat milder in tone, in the Jackson Papers, Library of Congress; Donelson to Van Buren, April 2, 1837, Donelson Papers, Library of Congress.

[17] William B. Lewis to William C. Rives, March 29, 1837, Dickerson to Rives, May 2, 1837, Nathaniel Niles to Rives, April 9, 22, May 4, 1837, Rives Papers; Woodbury to Henry Toland, March 27, 1837, Woodbury to John P. King, April 29, 1837, Woodbury Papers, Library of Congress; Dickerson, MS Diary, April 5, 1837; Van Buren, Endorsement on third copy of "questions to cabinet on repeal of the specie circular," March 24, 1837, Van Buren Papers.

[18] Wright to Van Buren, March 21, 1837, Cambreleng to Van Buren, April 8, 1837, Flagg to Van Buren, April 10, 1837, Van Buren Papers.

Nicholas Biddle's scheme of draining specie from the West for export to England. Overtrading and speculation were the real causes of distress, but Jackson's foresight would lessen the impact of the eventual crash. Privately, Van Buren now remarked that the specie order was "the only measure that could save the country."[19] Opposition critics, he believed, were trying desperately "to make the distress of the country subservient to party politics."[20]

Such a change of heart reflects Van Buren's basic political orientation. Despite the strong economic arguments of Gouge, the president explored a possible suspension or modification of the specie circular and even prepared Jackson for such an eventuality. Only after his New York advisers made their political report did Van Buren reverse course. Most observers never even guessed that the president seriously considered departing from the policy of his predecessor.[21] Had the pace of financial decline been less rapid, there is every reason to believe that Van Buren would have decided on a compromise solution such as that suggested by Donelson.

By the end of April 1837 danger signals appeared everywhere and the government braced itself for the coming tempest. Woodbury had warned the banks not to overextend and hoped they would survive. He took consolation in the knowledge that the specie circular would preserve some revenue that might otherwise have been lost.[22] The merchants of New York City thought the government should act to relieve corporate distress and dispatched a delegation to Washington to plead with the president. Van Buren agreed to a meeting, insisting that all communications be in writing. In the past, Jackson's informal statements had often provoked controversy and Van Buren wanted no misunderstanding.[23] On May 3, 1837, the president received his guests and listened patiently to their statement. After a review of the causes of the crisis, the merchants asked for a repeal of the specie circular, convocation of Congress, and an eight-month moratorium on payment of custom-house bonds. In reply, Van Buren was courteous and firm; he challenged their views on the origins of distress and

[19] Washington *Globe*, April 14, 15, 17, 19, 1837; Nathaniel Niles to William C. Rives, April 22, 1837, Rives Papers.
[20] Van Buren to Jackson, April 24, 1837, Van Buren Papers.
[21] For Jackson's suspicions see Jackson to Francis P. Blair, April 24, 1837, Jackson Papers.
[22] Levi Woodbury to Campbell P. White, April 3, 1837, Woodbury to C. Macalister, April 22, 1837, Woodbury Papers; Albany *Argus*, April 10, 1837.
[23] Peter V. Daniel to Van Buren, April 29, 1837, Jesse Hoyt to Van Buren, April 30, 1837, Van Buren Papers.

stated his intention to retain the Treasury order. There would be no immediate call of Congress, but the president did promise to consider some indulgence for payment of custom-house dues.[24] The meeting adjourned, and the disconsolate merchants returned to New York.

During the next few days there were several desperate attempts to avert a crisis. Joel R. Poinsett dashed off a note to Nicholas Biddle, asking if there were not some way to control the country's exchanges without resorting to a national bank. If the secretary of war hoped to present a compromise plan to the president, he was sorely disappointed. Biddle enthusiastically replied that "the simplest & easiest form of relief would be to make the present Bank of the U.S. the depositors of the public revenue."[25] In essence, he urged the administration to forge anew the link so dramatically broken by Jackson in 1833. Van Buren would never have agreed to depart so radically from Democratic tradition. During the first week in May 1837, the president and his advisers were swept along by forces beyond their comprehension or control. They tried earnestly to arrive at some solution to the impending crisis but in retrospect they seem helpless and pitiable. Never had the party advocated a centralized control of the economy; the rapid deterioration of financial confidence did not create a climate for experimentation.

On May 10, 1837, the long-awaited storm broke with devastating fury. New York's banks, unable to meet the continuing demands for specie, closed their doors. In a matter of days financial houses throughout the country followed suit. Chaos reigned. Trade in the normally bustling ports of New York and New Orleans ground to a halt. Debtors across the country faced the grim prospect of meeting their obligations with depreciated currency. In the South and Southwest planters saw their crops rot in the fields and the price of slaves plummet to a new low. Laborers in urban areas faced mounting unemployment as America's infant industrial complex felt the full impact of the Panic. To the general public it was as though a major war had erupted, threatening to rend the entire fabric of society. The

[24] Isaac S. Hone et al. to Van Buren, May 3, 1837, Van Buren to Isaac S. Hone et al., May 3, 4, 1837, in *National Intelligencer*, May 13, 1837; Levi Woodbury to Samuel Swartwout, May 8, 1837, Letters from the Secretary of the Treasury to the Collectors of Customs, Small Ports, Treasury Department Records, National Archives; hereafter cited as Letters to Collectors.

[25] Poinsett to Biddle, May 6, 1837, Biddle to Poinsett (2 letters), May 8, 1837, in Biddle, *Correspondence*, pp. 273–75. For a different interpretation of this correspondence see Thomas P. Govan, *Nicholas Biddle* (Chicago, 1959), pp. 310–11. On Biddle's plans for a new national bank see Henry D. Gilpin to Van Buren, May 21, 1837, Van Buren Papers.

British minister, Henry Fox, read the accounts of distress in disbelief and then sent his government a moving dispatch on the crisis. "It would be difficult to describe, or to render intelligible in Europe, the stunning effect which this sudden overthrow of the commercial credit and honor of the nation has caused, in a Country like America where mercantile business fills the greater part of every man's time, and forms the general politics of society. The conquest of the land by a foreign power could hardly have produced a more general sense of humiliation and grief."[26]

In the midst of this confusion, the president struggled to get his bearings. He called the cabinet into immediate session, and these emergency meetings continued for nearly a week. Primarily concerned about the safety of public revenue, Van Buren directed Woodbury to issue a circular stating that no defaulting bank could remain a depository of government monies. The secretary of the treasury added assurances that all removals would be gradual. The administration could not press the banks too far, as a massive call for government deposits would only touch off a wave of complete bankruptcies, making recovery of these funds impossible. Privately, the secretary of the treasury tried to persuade one bank in each state to resume specie payments in the hope of setting an example for others to follow. In addition to protecting government revenue, Van Buren acted to relieve debtors by authorizing delays in payment of duty bonds. Realizing the inadequacy of such stopgaps, the president issued a call for Congress to meet in special session in September.[27] Under the pressure of financial crisis, he adopted measures spurned barely a week before.

From the cabinet, the debate shifted to the press, and for the next few weeks administration supporters and opposition critics traded venom and invective. Long the Democratic editorial spokesman, Francis P. Blair rushed to the defense of current policy. Then,

[26] Fox to Lord Palmerston, May 21, 1837, PRO:FO: 5, Vol. 314, Pt. IV. For a brief summary of the impact of the Panic see McGrane, *Panic of 1837*, pp. 91-144.

[27] Dickerson, MS Diary, May 10-18, 1837; Woodbury, Circular to Banks, May 16, 1837, Letters from the Secretary of the Treasury to Banks, Treasury Department Records, National Archives; hereafter cited as Letters to Banks. See also Amos Kendall to John A. Webber, May 25, 1837, Letters from Postmaster General, National Archives; Woodbury to George Newbold, May 12, 1837, C. P. White to Woodbury, May 14, 1837, Woodbury Papers; Levi Woodbury to William Price, May 16, 1837, in *National Intelligencer*, May 23, 1837; Van Buren, Memorandum on cabinet meeting, May [?], 1837, Van Buren Papers; *National Intelligencer*, May 18, 1837.

switching tactics, he launched an offensive against Biddle, state banks, and the financial community. Blair charged that New York merchants, returning empty-handed from their interview with the president, diabolically prompted the suspension of specie payments. Surprised after two weeks of such harangue to find himself classed as an enemy of mercantile interests, Blair narrowed his focus and blamed a select portion of the commercial community for bringing the country to ruin. Once so effective in the crusade against Biddle's bank, the Washington *Globe* now created consternation by its indiscriminate attacks. New York's Senator Nathaniel P. Tallmadge, an emerging spokesman for congressional conservatism, saw in the newspaper campaign an attempt to "excite the worst passions of the people" and feared that the assault would "prostrate our whole credit system."[28]

More disconcerting than Blair's irresponsible behavior were the reactions of the two most important Democratic state newspapers. After the suspension of specie payments, Thomas Ritchie ignored the plight of the federal government and spent most of his time defending Virginia's banks. In a series of provincial editorials he blamed the collapse of credit on forces outside the Old Dominion. Only after several weeks of such handwringing did he admit that perhaps the state banks were in part to blame for the crisis in public confidence. The Panic produced a similar response in Albany. Where Ritchie had been outspoken in his support for state banks, Edwin Croswell preferred a quiet neutrality, refraining from extensive discussion of New York's responsibility for the Panic.[29] The onset of the depression thus deprived Van Buren of two vital channels of communication. Loyal Democrats had little way of appreciating the problems facing the president.

Against this turbulent background, the administration began to plan for the special session of Congress. Van Buren followed no master design or blueprint for fiscal reform but tried to formulate remedies that Congress would speedily approve. With public funds already in jeopardy, there was little sense in continuing to distribute

[28] Washington *Globe*, May 10–24, 1837; Tallmadge to William C. Rives, May 31, 1837, Rives Papers. Van Buren's contemporaries used the term "Conservative" to refer to those Democrats who actively dissented from administration fiscal policy and proclaimed their devotion to the cause of state banks. I will hereafter adhere to this usage. On the origin of the movement in Virginia see Howard Braverman, "The Economic and Political Background of the Conservative Revolt in Virginia," *Virginia Magazine of History and Biography* 60 (1952): 266–87.
[29] Richmond *Enquirer*, May 16, June 2, 13, 1837; Albany *Argus*, May 6, 18, June 9, 28, 1837.

surplus revenue. In fact, the government was so uncertain of income that Van Buren decided to ask for an issue of Treasury notes to cover expenses. Customs collectors daily faced an angry barrage of abuse from merchants demanding some leniency on the payment of custom-house dues. Having already stretched the law to its limit, the president wanted Congress to assume responsibility for eventual settlement of these cases. Up to this point, Van Buren was reacting to the immediate problems raised by the bank suspensions.

Short-term solutions could not still the controversy, for the Panic raised doubts about the wisdom of all previous Democratic fiscal policy. The state bank deposit system, once considered ideally suited to the decentralized nature of the Democratic party, lay in ruins. The president had long recognized that the party could not afford to "meet Congress with broken Deposit banks."[30] His worst fears were now realized. When the legislature convened in September, congressmen would demand more than an explanation; they would expect the government to recommend some new method of safeguarding its revenue. Worse still, the nation in its disgust might rally to the Whig banner and demand the recharter of a national bank.[31]

Van Buren searched for a way to disarm his enemies while still preserving the financial integrity of the government. As he told William C. Rives, the great question of the special session would be the "nature & character of the future fiscal agency of the Treasury." Among possible alternatives Van Buren listed "a national Bank—a continuance of the present system with improvements & alterations . . . or the adoption of . . . [a plan] by which the Government will be separated from all connection with Banks." Rejecting a recharter as unthinkable, Van Buren left little doubt that he favored the last of the three proposals. He tried to impress Rives with the importance of presenting Congress with a single solution upon which all Democrats could unite.[32]

Van Buren had in mind a separation of bank and state similar to that first proposed by Virginia Congressman William F. Gordon in

[30] Van Buren to William C. Rives, April 8, 1837, Rives Papers.
[31] On fear of a new national bank as a factor in Democratic policy see Levi Woodbury to Jackson, May 10, 1837, Silas Wright to Van Buren, May 28, 1837, Woodbury Papers; Franklin Pierce to John McNeil, May 18, 1837, Pierce Papers, New Hampshire Historical Society; Jackson to Amos Kendall, May 26, 1837, Jackson-Kendall Papers; James K. Polk to Van Buren, May 29, 1837, Van Buren Papers; William R. King to James Buchanan, June 2, 1837, Buchanan Papers, The Historical Society of Pennsylvania.
[32] Van Buren to Rives, May 25, 1837, Van Buren Papers.

1834.[33] At that time, Jackson was still committed to state depositories, but William Gouge kept the plan alive and circulated his views among influential members of the party.[34] These ideas might well have been destined for oblivion had not the Panic destroyed the administration's faith in the existing deposit system. Soon after the suspension, the president of the Bank of Virginia, John Brockenbrough, wrote to Van Buren suggesting that the government sever its connection with state banks, as they were hard to control and primarily concerned with their own profits. "Instead of employing any corporation to transact its business," Brockenbrough contended that the Treasury could "employ its own agents to collect and disburse the public funds." He did not advocate either a destruction of all banks or a reliance on an exclusively metallic currency; the federal government should worry only about its own funds and leave reforms to the states. On May 24, 1837, the Washington *Globe* endorsed similar ideas and Van Buren sent copies of Brockenbrough's letter to key advisers for comment.[35]

In essence, Brockenbrough sought to relieve the government from financial embarrassment. By adopting his plan, the administration would cease to rely upon deposit banks, thereby avoiding association with institutions instrumental in bringing on the Panic. In short, the banks would be *"left to their fate."*[36] The Treasury would control its own revenues but would exercise only incidental influence over the economy as a whole; hopefully, the states would then act to correct

---

[33] McFaul, "Politics of Jacksonian Finance," pp. 129–31, maintains that the plan for an independent Treasury was not "hastily conceived" but "had been under discussion within the administration for a long time and had gained increased support since the 'experiment' of reforming the currency through selected state banks was unsuccessful." He is undoubtedly correct in his interpretation of the origins of the measure, but deemphasizes the impact of the Panic of 1837. That the scheme for a divorce of bank and state had antecedents in Jackson's administration should not imply that it was therefore part of a logical chain of reform. Few Democrats in 1835–1836 envisioned the collapse of the state bank system. This crisis alone made Gordon's plan both attractive and feasible.

[34] Thomas Ritchie to Richard Parker, May [?], 1837, quoted in Parker to Benjamin Butler, May 27, 1837, Van Buren Papers; Gouge to Levi Woodbury, June 29, 1837, Woodbury Papers; Gouge to Gideon Welles, July 18, 1837, Welles Papers.

[35] Brockenbrough to William C. Rives, May 20, 1837, contained in Brockenbrough to Van Buren, May 22, 1837, Silas Wright to Van Buren, June 4, 1837, James Buchanan to Van Buren, June 6, 1837, Van Buren to John M. Niles, June 10, 1837, mentioned in Niles to Van Buren, July 1, 1837, Van Buren Papers. See also a copy of Brockenbrough's letter in the Buchanan Papers, The Historical Society of Pennsylvania; Washington *Globe*, May 24, 1837.

[36] William B. Hodgson to William C. Rives, June 3, 1837, Rives Papers.

abuses within their jurisdiction. Jackson had a somewhat similar idea in mind in 1836, when he toyed with the possibility of asking Congress to charter a bank for the District of Columbia that could serve as an example to the states.[37] Brockenbrough's scheme would necessitate only minimal legislation. Since the suspension of specie payments, the president had been required by law to store, collect, and disburse funds through Treasury agents and post office employees.[38] Congress merely needed to make the arrangement more permanent. Continuation of this system admirably suited the traditional policy of reducing the surplus and keeping federal receipts to a bare minimum.[39] For these reasons, Van Buren brought Brockenbrough's ideas to the attention of the party.

The president's suggestions did not find favor with all Democrats. The most vocal critic, William C. Rives, left little doubt that he would oppose any attempt to sever the ties between the Treasury and the state banks. New York's Nathaniel P. Tallmadge joined his Virginia friend in planning strategy for the special session and laying groundwork for a new Washington newspaper to represent this Conservative viewpoint. Tallmadge objected to the contemplated divorce of bank and state because, by increasing presidential patronage, it would expand the political power of the federal government.[40] Rives was even more explicit, and on June 3, 1837, presented his opinions to the president. The Virginia senator felt that in spite of the Panic, the state bank system was still adequate and worthy of reform. "Is it right," he asked, "to *isolate* the government from the general interests & wants of the community?" Unlike Tallmadge, Rives argued that the executive should have more power and that discontinuing state banks as depositories would only diminish the means for controlling the economy. "One of the strongest considerations in my mind, in favour of continuing to employ the fiscal agency of the State

---

[37] Jackson to Amos Kendall, November 24, 1836, printed in the Cincinnati *Commercial*, February 4, 1879. Jackson asked Kendall about the "propriety of chartering a bank in the District of Columbia . . . such as will be a model for the States." See also Francis P. Blair to Jackson, June 25, 1837, Jackson Papers.

[38] Out of an original eighty-eight deposit banks, all but six ceased to be depositories for government funds after the suspension of specie payments. U.S. Congress, *House Documents* (No. 2 appendix, K.L.), 25th Cong., 1st sess., 1837, pp. 55–56. See also Amos Kendall to Jackson, June 6, 1837, Jackson Papers; Kendall to Postmasters in New York, May 9, 1837, Letters from Postmaster General, National Archives.

[39] James Buchanan to Van Buren, June 5, 1837, Van Buren Papers; Jackson to Amos Kendall, June 23, 1837, in Cincinnati *Commercial*, February 4, 1879.

[40] Tallmadge to Rives, May 1, 21, 31, 1837, Rives Papers; Thomas Allen to Tallmadge, June 20, 1837, Tallmadge Papers, Wisconsin State Historical Society.

Banks is that thro' that connection, the government may exert a powerful & salutary influence on the condition of the general currency."[41]

The president was not surprised by the protestations of his critics, but he did not anticipate the reservations of his friends. In a candid letter, Silas Wright frankly appraised the merits and drawbacks of Brockenbrough's proposal. He approved of the government's having closer control over its own funds rather than again entrusting them to the care of state banks, but was apprehensive about the political consequences of such a scheme. For one thing, he argued, the administration had no way to convince the public of the feasibility of an independent Treasury. The opposition would brand it as "one of the most fearful attempts to extend executive patronage and power" that the nation had yet witnessed. Chances of congressional approval were slim and a defeat would be disastrous. While the country generally favored separation along the lines suggested by Brockenbrough, Wright thought bank forces would mount a vicious assault in Congress and prevent enactment of the president's plan. Without congressional sanction, the mechanism could not work, and so Wright appealed to Van Buren not to rule out the alternative of reforming the state banks.[42]

James Buchanan echoed many of Wright's apprehensions but was equally at a loss to make positive recommendations. Although he admitted the simplicity of Brockenbrough's scheme, the Pennsylvania senator thought it failed to meet the needs of the average citizen and therefore might prove less attractive than a recharter of a national bank. The government needed some institutional tie to the states. Further discouragement came from Virginia, where Thomas Ritchie militated against "any sudden jar in the social system."[43]

Van Buren respected Wright and Buchanan as experienced politicians but was obviously annoyed at their response. On the back of

[41] Rives to Van Buren, June 3, 1837, Van Buren Papers. See identical sentiments in Reuben Whitney to Rives, July 20, August 12, 1837, Rives Papers.

[42] Wright to Van Buren, June 4, 1837, Van Buren Papers. For a somewhat different interpretation of this letter see John A. Garraty, *Silas Wright* (New York, 1949), pp. 144–45. For Wright's previous views on the necessity of state banks, despite their flaws, see Wright to Azariah Flagg, February 26, 1837, Flagg-Wright Papers. Garraty (p. 126) interprets the letter to Flagg as indicating Wright's espousal of an independent Treasury. This is clearly inconsistent with Wright's hesitations in June 1837, and a careful reading will not support Garraty's contention.

[43] Buchanan to Van Buren, June 5, 1837, Van Buren Papers; Buchanan to Mrs. Francis P. Blair, June 7–8, 1837, Buchanan Papers, The Historical Society of Pennsylvania; Richmond *Enquirer*, June 13, 1837.

Wright's letter he scrawled, "discouraging, evidently written in a moody state of mind."[44] The president should have anticipated such a reaction, for his proposal constituted a break with Democratic tradition. No matter how simple it might prove in practice, a divorce of the federal government from the banks would require legislative effort and might provoke a realignment of political allegiances. The plan aided only the central government and appeared to threaten state institutions. Ostensibly consistent with Jeffersonian principles of governmental simplicity, Brockenbrough's proposal actually challenged sectional interests and violated the usual practice of skirting issues incapable of translation into local terms. Both Wright and Buchanan sensed this, and while they doubted the reliability of state banks, each felt the cure might be more dangerous than the disease.

Van Buren's intolerance to opinions that reflected his own former political preachments is an indication that he was under extreme pressure. He undoubtedly realized that his plan would create a certain amount of local unrest, but he felt he had little choice. None of his advisers had suggested a reasonable remedy. Congress had repeatedly refused to reform the state banking structure, and there was little hope of a coordinated local effort to this end. It was not because of any intense dislike for state banks that Van Buren embraced Brockenbrough's plan; it seemed the only means of countering opposition pressure for a national bank and of shifting attention away from the defects of previous Democratic policy. By disassociating himself from the states, the president could employ an antibank rhetoric in his drive for adoption of a divorce bill. As Connecticut's John M. Niles put it, "our opponents charge the difficulties . . . to the government; we charge them to the Banks. This is the issue between us."[45]

Not all Van Buren's advisers were so discouraging as Wright and Buchanan. During the early weeks in June, Butler and Gouge worked closely with the president, drafting legislation for the special session.[46] On June 12, 1837, Van Buren sent several of these proposals to Wright for comment and evidently calmed some of his friend's fears, for ten days later the Senate leader responded: "I am most happy to

[44] Van Buren, endorsement on the letter of Silas Wright to Van Buren, June 4, 1837, Van Buren Papers. The endorsement was evidently written some time later but still indicates Van Buren's displeasure with Wright's opinions.

[45] Niles to Van Buren, July 1, 1837, Van Buren Papers.

[46] Butler to Jackson, June 10, 1837, Jackson Papers; Nathaniel Niles to William C. Rives, June 8, 1837, William B. Hodgson to Rives, June 20, 1837, Rives Papers; Gouge to Van Buren, July 17, 1840, Van Buren Papers.

infer from your last that your mind is made up so far and that, while you place the alternatives before Congress, you will give strong preference in favor of separation." While Wright commended Van Buren's decision, he still was hesitant to have Congress grapple with such an explosive issue.[47]

Van Buren now moved to insure party acceptance of plans for the special session. He did not want to publicize specific proposals, lest a sudden bank resumption render legislation unnecessary. Although he did not rule out future association with the state banks, the president nevertheless proceeded on the assumption that they would do nothing to redeem themselves before September.

As the first step in his preparations, Van Buren sent a circular to his political associates, asking for their advice, and indicating his own preferences. Essentially an outline of legislation for the special session, this document contained seven questions, three of which concerned relations with the mercantile community. The president recommended that Congress sanction the existing policy of delayed payment of custom-house bonds, that it grant a definite postponement of suits against defaulting banks, and that it give the banks in the District of Columbia sixty to ninety days to resume specie payments. Such proposals indicated Van Buren's willingness to execute the laws with as much leniency as possible. The president also thought it desirable to postpone the fourth installment of surplus revenue, due the states on October 1, 1837. To cover future expenses, Van Buren wanted Congress to authorize an issue of interest-bearing Treasury notes. Primarily concerned about the future of government deposits, he inquired, "What substitute, for the present at least, shall be adopted, instead of the discontinued Banks?" Answering his own question, he proposed that the government keep its funds in the Treasury, the mint, and the offices of collectors and postmasters.[48]

After sending his private questionnaire, Van Buren initiated a campaign of public education. On June 20, 1837, Silas Wright began a series of seven articles discussing the causes of the Panic and suggesting possible remedies. Significantly, these treatises appeared not in the Albany Argus but in the St. Lawrence Republican, a Democratic paper of secondary rank. The Regency's disenchantment with administration policy was beginning to have its effect. In the

[47] Wright to Van Buren, June 22, 1837, Van Buren Papers; Wright to William L. Marcy, June 22, 1837, Gratz Collection.
[48] Van Buren, memorandum, June 21 [?], 1837, Van Buren Papers. The handwriting is that of Gouge, but Van Buren obviously directed the preparation of this document.

course of his journalistic meanderings, Wright listed possible cures for the diseased body politic. Making a definite distinction between the duties of the state and national governments, he urged a separation of the Treasury from the banks. A reduction of federal influence would allow the states to reform their own affairs. The administration in Washington should do no more than set an example for local leaders to follow.[49]

While Wright labored in New York, William Gouge supervised publication of a pamphlet entitled "An Inquiry into the Expediency of Dispensing with Bank Agency and Bank Paper in the Fiscal Concerns of the United States." So that his tract would not appear as a *"feeler* put forth by the Administration," Gouge made arrangements to publish it in Philadelphia rather than Washington.[50] He outlined a system much more intricate than that envisioned by John Brockenbrough. On essential principles the two agreed; the government would collect, store, and disburse its own funds. But where Brockenbrough advocated the use of existing machinery, Gouge proposed creation of at least thirty-six new sub-Treasuries. In commenting on Gouge's plan, the Washington *Globe* took note of this complexity and assured its readers that reform need not be so involved.[51]

As mouthpiece for the president and primary organ of the Democratic party, the Washington *Globe* followed a circuitous path during the summer of 1837. After the bank suspension, Francis P. Blair struck out against all elements of the opposition, gradually becoming more selective in his approach. In order to explain the Panic and justify government plans for the special session, he attacked state banks. Finding this an explosive issue, he soon shifted tactics, blaming Nicholas Biddle and the Whig press for forcing the bank failures. Unfortunately, this logic did not deter the opposition, and Blair spent much of the summer trying to defend the administration from charges of being hostile to all banks.[52] As a final solution, he appealed to the party faithful to unite on a plan for separating the government from the banks. "The states only are competent," he concluded, "to bring their own institutions under proper subjection."[53]

---

[49] These articles appear in somewhat condensed form in Ransom H. Gillet, *The Life and Times of Silas Wright*, 2 vols. (Albany, N.Y., 1874), 1: 527–65.

[50] Washington *Globe*, July 7, 12, 1837; Gouge to Levi Woodbury, June 29, 1837, Woodbury Papers; Gouge to Gideon Welles, July 18, 1837, Welles Papers.

[51] Washington *Globe*, July 13, 1837.

[52] Ibid., June 22, 23, July 1, 2, 22, 28, 31, August 15, 16, 1837.

[53] Ibid., June 28, July 21, 1837.

Blair's inconsistencies plagued the president and made his preparations for the special session all the more difficult. Eastern elements in the party resented the *Globe's* strong language and obvious sectional bias. "The Globe is not what it should be," lamented Hartford's influential postmaster Gideon Welles. "It is deficient in tact, it wants suavity, it neglects its friends and betrays great ignorance of, or great indifference toward the states, except Kentucky, Tennessee, New Hampshire and a slight smattering of affairs in New York and Virginia."[54] Welles urged Van Buren to bypass Blair and found a new press in Washington. Although the president paid little heed to this specific request, he had given some thought to establishing a second administration journal. Van Buren had shown enthusiasm for the *United States Magazine and Democratic Review*, a projected monthly publication devoted to politics and the arts. One of the editors, John L. O'Sullivan, later claimed that the "project rested on the presumed basis of the executive printing—an 'understanding' which the President in person took certain preliminary . . . steps to carry into effect."[55] In April 1837 Levi Woodbury started mailing out a prospectus of the new magazine, asking loyal Democrats to subscribe. Originally scheduled to appear in July 1837, the first issue did not come out until October.[56]

In the interim, political developments forced the president to withdraw support from the new journal. By August 1, 1837, Nathaniel P. Tallmadge and William C. Rives, both emerging Democratic critics, had completed arrangements for publishing *The Madisonian* under the editorship of Thomas Allen. At first this paper posed as a friend of the administration, claiming to support the president on all issues except that of separating bank from state.[57] Van Buren saw through the ruse immediately; in an interview with Allen, the presi-

[54] Welles to Van Buren, June 9, July 24, 1837, Van Buren Papers. See also Nathaniel Niles to William C. Rives, June 8, 1837, Rives Papers; Welles to Francis P. Blair, July 22, 1837, Welles Papers; William L. Marcy to Prosper M. Wetmore, August 18, 1837, Marcy Papers.

[55] O'Sullivan to Benjamin F. Butler, December 16, 1839, Butler Papers. See also Thomas Cooper to Joel R. Poinsett, May 24, 1838, Poinsett Papers; Butler to Thomas Olcott, June 21, 1838, Olcott Papers, Columbia University; Hugh A. Garland to Francis P. Blair, December 30, 1839, Blair-Lee Papers, Princeton University; Garland to Van Buren, February 4, 1840, O'Sullivan to Van Buren, February 8, 1840, Van Buren Papers.

[56] Woodbury to Postmasters, April 17, 1837, Welles Papers. See the statement on the delay in the *United States Magazine and Democratic Review* 1 (1837): iv.

[57] Thomas Allen to Rives, March 14, August 15, 1837, Tallmadge to Rives, May 21, 31, June 28, 1837, Rives Papers; Allen to Tallmadge, June 20, 1837, Tallmadge Papers; *The Madisonian*, August 16, 1837.

dent stated that "he should be sorry to see another opposition paper started" in Washington.[58] Since the bank suspensions, Van Buren had struggled to unite the party in preparation for the special session. In trying to establish a common area of agreement, he had minimized local problems and ignored the plight of state banks. Just when it seemed that this tactic might succeed, *The Madisonian* began exploring chinks in the Democratic armor. Loudly praising the deposit system, Allen and his staff cataloged the serious consequences of a divorce of bank and state. To make matters worse, the new paper had an air of respectability, because two of Jackson's advisers, William B. Lewis and Reuben Whitney, promised their services to the fledgling enterprise.[59] In view of this serious challenge, Van Buren abandoned any thought of supplanting the *Globe* and quickly let it be known that *The Madisonian* had no presidential blessing.[60]

As if these journalistic difficulties were not enough, Van Buren found several influential party leaders opposed to his special session program. Unexpected criticism came from the Hermitage. Jackson agreed with the need for an independent Treasury but thought the other recommendations too lenient. The government should cancel the fourth installment, not merely postpone it; under no circumstances should there be an issue of Treasury notes. The financial community deserved little sympathy. Jackson urged immediate action against merchants and bankers who failed to meet their obligations. Van Buren took these comments in stride, respectfully replying that the government would protect its own interests but giving little indication that he would alter his specific plans for the special session. He defended the issue of Treasury notes and then closed with the dubious assurance that "upon the genl. subjects referred to in your letter you will find a striking concurrence between your own views & ours."[61]

---

[58] Allen to Rives, August 3, 1837, Rives Papers.

[59] Allen to Rives, August 1, 1837, Reuben Whitney to Rives, July 20, August 12, 1837, Rives Papers; Whitney, circular letter, July 15, 1838, Blair-Lee Papers; John M. McFaul and Frank Otto Gatell, "The Outcast Insider, Reuben Whitney and the Bank War," *Pennsylvania Magazine of History and Biography* 91 (1967): 115–44.

[60] Allen to Rives, August 3, 1837, Rives Papers.

[61] Van Buren to Jackson, July 28, 1837, Van Buren Papers. Jackson's sentiments are in an undated and unsigned memorandum, in Jackson's handwriting, in Vol. 7, 2d series, Jackson Papers. There is little doubt that Jackson was referring to Van Buren's questionnaire, since he mentions specifically all seven points. Van Buren's response would indicate that the president received Jackson's opinions, though perhaps not in the precise form in which they appear in the Jackson memorandum. See also the following in the Van Buren Papers indicating replies

Virginia responded in a different but equally negative manner. Where Jackson thought Van Buren too moderate, Rives feared the president's intentions were too extreme. To make matters worse, Thomas Ritchie was gradually moving away to "a point of suspense" between the administration and the Conservatives. Violating canons of partisan reporting, he opened up his columns to arguments for and against an independent Treasury.[62] Van Buren wrote to convince Ritchie that the administration bore no malice toward state banks. "If the system had not fallen to pieces itself," the president argued, "I certainly would not have sustained the idea of breaking it up."[63] He closed by telling Ritchie that he would present all the alternatives to Congress. Presidential persuasiveness did not make the Richmond *Enquirer* alter its neutral course. By trying to air opposing views, Ritchie only provoked hostility.[64] Van Buren encountered similar problems in New York, where the Albany *Argus* displayed little enthusiasm for the government's separation from the banks.[65]

Such hesitancy frustrated the president. In trying to prepare the party for the coming congressional campaign, he had drawn up several concrete proposals to combat opposition demands for a national bank. Van Buren felt that without such a program, the Democrats would lose the initiative and party unity might well disintegrate. Consequently he solicited the support of his state allies, trying to make them see that the problems of the federal government were, in effect, their problems also. Unprepared for such strong pressure, Democrats reacted vigorously, as if to remind the president that theirs was not a national party but an amalgam of state organizations. Just as Jackson contemptuously dismissed local objections during the nullification crisis, Van Buren now complained that his correspondents were "influenced more by their apprehension of coming in contact with the states than by a calm view of the whole ground."[66] For the defender of state rights, this represented a startling shift in attitude.

---

to the circular: Isaac Hill to Levi Woodbury, July 4, 1837, John A. Dix to Van Buren, July 5, 1837, Azariah Flagg to Benjamin Butler, July 12, 1837, Robert Rantoul to Woodbury, July 20, 1837, Roger B. Taney to Van Buren, July 20, 1837.

[62] John Brockenbrough to Van Buren, August 7, 1837, Van Buren Papers; William B. Hodgson to William C. Rives, July 13, 1837, Rives Papers; Richmond *Enquirer*, July 18, 1837.

[63] Van Buren to Ritchie, August 11, 1837 (2 letters), Van Buren Papers.

[64] David Campbell to William C. Rives, July 1, 1837, Rives Papers; Silas Wright to Azariah Flagg, September 5, 1837, Flagg-Wright Papers.

[65] Albany *Argus*, July 21, 25, August 16, 1837.

[66] Van Buren to Benjamin F. Butler, July 27, 1837, Butler Papers.

Despite this dissent, Van Buren went ahead with preparations for the special session. The next few weeks would provide the most crucial test of his presidency. Forced by unfortunate and unexpected circumstances to call Congress into extra session, he now had to present the legislature with a program of recovery, which, although necessitating minimal legislation, still required prompt approval. Not since 1825 had a president staked his prestige and popularity on a bid for congressional support. Success would heal the breach in the party; defeat might presage the end of Democratic rule.

Chapter 5

The Special
Session

For more than four months the Panic had swept the land, and now all attention focused on Washington. As legislators streamed into the capital, Van Buren put the finishing touches on his message, scheduled for delivery shortly after Congress convened. Despite all his careful preparations, the president was nervous. He realized that the success of his program depended upon quick, decisive action. Yet he was appealing to a headstrong body accustomed to power and resentful of executive dictation.

In the 1830's Congress resembled a debating society whose members sought personal glory and prestige. Alexis de Tocqueville thought this a unique feature of a democratic country. "Parties are so impatient of control," he observed after watching Congress in action, "and are never manageable except in moments of great public danger. Even then the authority of leaders, which under such circumstances may be able to make men act or speak, hardly ever reaches the extent of making them keep silence." Another traveler of the era, Frederick Marryat, noticed the same phenomenon. He was struck not so much by the legislators' freedom, as by their propensity for oratorical forays, each of which had to be "full of eagles, star-spangled banners, sovereign people, claptrap, flattery, and humbug." "It is astonishing," he added, "how little work they get through in a session at Washington."[1]

Such permissiveness often encouraged irrelevant debate and led to personal slanders that occasionally spilled from the legislative chambers onto the field of honor. Not all congressional duels ended as harmlessly or humorously as that between Henry Clay and John Randolph, where the only casualty was Randolph's waistcoat. In February 1838 Maine's Jonathan Cilley and Kentucky's William

Graves stalked each other with rifles; the encounter proved damaging to congressional prestige and fatal to Jonathan Cilley.[2]

To control such an assembly was no easy task. Van Buren was fortunate to have in the Senate a talented and devoted friend, Silas Wright. A native of Massachusetts, Wright studied law in New York before becoming a member of the Regency. Under Van Buren's tutelage, he served as a state legislator, comptroller, and finally succeeded William L. Marcy in the United States Senate. By 1837 Wright headed the Finance Committee; from this post he would supervise the important legislation of the next three years.[3] Less flamboyant than some of his Senate colleagues, Wright always presented his arguments with remarkable clarity. At times he could be brutally frank, and his letters, while rambling and discursive, breathe a refreshing honesty. Wright occasionally overanticipated objections to proposed legislation, but his pessimism proved valuable in arming administration forces for battle. Van Buren also received strong support from Pennsylvania's James Buchanan, chairman of the Foreign Relations Committee, from Missouri's Thomas Hart Benton, and from Connecticut's John Niles.

Not coincidentally, a former New York associate also acted as Van Buren's chief lieutenant in the House. In Churchill C. Cambreleng the president had a skillful ally and efficient manager. Cambreleng spent his youth in New York City, where he enjoyed a successful mercantile career. Entering politics in 1821, he won election to Congress and remained in Washington for the next sixteen years. Business experience proved valuable in a time of rapid economic change, and Cambreleng advanced to the chairmanship of the powerful House Committee on Ways and Means. He tended to be dogmatic on financial matters and lacked the political acumen of Wright. Nevertheless, Van Buren thought Cambreleng "honest as the steelyard and as direct in the pursuit of his purpose as a shot from a culverin," and had no qualms about entrusting him with responsibility for administration measures.[4] Maryland's Benjamin C. Howard, Ohio's Thomas Hamer, and Virginia's John W. Jones assisted

---

[1] Alexis de Tocqueville, *Democracy in America*, trans. Henry Reeve, ed. Phillips Bradley, 2 vols. (New York, 1945), 2: 89; Frederick Marryat, *A Diary in America with Remarks on Its Institutions*, ed. Jules Zanger (new ed.; Bloomington, Ind., 1960), pp. 189–90; Richmond *Enquirer*, March 18, 1837.

[2] For a brief, vivid account of this duel see Charles G. Sellers, Jr., *James K. Polk: Jacksonian, 1795–1843* (Princeton, N.J., 1957), p. 334.

[3] John A. Garraty, *Silas Wright* (New York, 1949).

[4] Van Buren, *Autobiography*, p. 655.

Cambreleng in organizing the Democratic forces in the House.

During the Jacksonian era, the Speaker of the House emerged as the key congressional leader. By appointing faithful Democrats to legislative committees, he could at once strengthen the party and insure a friendly reception for presidential proposals. In an age when sectional tensions threatened to erupt at any moment, the Speaker frequently stood between order and chaos. He was charged with the difficult assignment of preventing antislavery agitation from making a shambles of parliamentary procedure. He thus served as both party disciplinarian and keeper of the peace. In 1835 James K. Polk defeated his Tennessee rival, John Bell, in a hotly contested battle for the position of Speaker. Once elected, Polk adhered to the tradition of partisan committee selections. While presiding over the troublesome sessions of 1836, he and his supporters secured adoption of the gag rule to silence abolitionist agitation; this measure infuriated men like John Quincy Adams but helped restore calm. As overseer of a contentious Congress, Polk could not avoid all possible pitfalls. Fortunately, his erroneous rulings were infrequent.[5]

When the House convened on September 4, 1837, Democratic managers concentrated on reelecting Polk as Speaker. For more than a month Van Buren's aides had circulated appeals urging prompt attendance at the opening session and warning of the dire consequences of a Whig victory in this contest.[6] These preparations paid handsome dividends. The newly arrived legislators had barely settled in their seats when the Democrats called for the vote on the speakership question. On the first ballot, Polk defeated his perennial Whig rival, John Bell, 116 to 103.[7] The party was now ready to act on the president's program. The following day, Congress met in joint session to hear Van Buren's special report on the state of the Union—a message that combined bold recommendations with appeals to the past.

As expected, the president confined himself to economic issues. In

---

[5] Adams to petitioners of the twelfth district of Massachusetts, January 31, 1837, MS Letterbook (1837), Adams Family Papers; Sellers, *James K. Polk*, pp. 304–18.

[6] Jackson to Van Buren, June 6, 1837, Van Buren Papers; Polk to Francis P. Blair, June 20, August 16, 1837, Blair-Lee Papers, Princeton University Library; Polk to Andrew J. Donelson, August 6, 1837, Donelson Papers, Library of Congress; Churchill Cambreleng to Levi Woodbury, July 21, 1837, Woodbury Papers; Donelson to Polk, July 20, 1837, Blair and Rives circular, August 9, 1837, Polk Papers, Library of Congress; Albany *Argus*, August 24, 1837; Washington *Globe*, August 28, 1837.

[7] *Congressional Globe*, 25th Cong., 1st sess., 1837, 5: 3; Adams, *Diary*, 9: 365–67.

setting forth his reasons for convening a special session, Van Buren paid brief tribute to congressional competence. All the passions and the emotions engendered by the Panic, he stated, could not "prevent a community so intelligent as ours from ultimately arriving at correct conclusions." After this characteristic bit of flattery, he began his analysis of the Panic and its consequences. The chief evils, according to Van Buren, were a "redundancy of credit" and a "spirit of reckless speculation"; both had combined to precipitate a crisis that was international in origin.

To remedy these economic ills, the president asked his listeners to consider a new means for collecting and disbursing revenue. He rejected the idea of a national bank, maintaining that a recharter proposal would "disregard the popular will, twice solemnly and unequivocally expressed." Nor were state banks fit depositories. Since all such corporations were prone to take advantage of funds at their disposal, Van Buren suggested the removal of government monies. This would end the practice of having public resources spur private speculation. The Treasury could safely collect, keep, and pay its own funds without the services of any bank. Van Buren asked Congress to enlarge the responsibilities of existing public officials to facilitate this end. He anticipated no excessive annual surplus to complicate this arrangement, nor did he feel that an independent Treasury would enlarge executive patronage.

From the mode of keeping federal funds, Van Buren turned to the type of currency to be received in government transactions. He praised the effects of Jackson's specie circular and indicated a marked preference for hard money. Still, he made no attempt to incorporate a specie clause in his plan for an independent Treasury and did not exclude the possibility of allowing bank notes convertible into gold or silver. The president was reluctant to take a strong stand on this question for fear of endangering the rest of his program. He hoped that Congress and the nation would accept his recommendations as a simple adjustment in the mode of keeping public revenue. By confining legislation to this question alone, Van Buren could capitalize on current discontent without committing himself to a radical hard money policy that might encourage a crusade against all banks. Since the war against Biddle, state banks had formed a powerful and vocal element in the Democratic alliance; although they had now failed, Van Buren did not want to split the party by seeking their destruction.

As if to convince Congress that his proposals did not deviate from Democratic tradition, the president closed with an appeal to the

Jeffersonian creed. "All communities are apt to look to government for too much," he said, referring to the clamor for federal relief. "Even in our own country, where its powers and duties are so strictly limited, we are prone to do so." "But this ought not to be. The framers of our excellent Constitution . . . wisely judged that the less government interferes with private pursuits the better for the general prosperity." "If, therefore," he concluded, "I refrain from suggesting to Congress any specific plan for regulating the exchanges of the country, relieving mercantile embarrassments, or interfering with the ordinary operations of foreign or domestic commerce, it is from a conviction that such measures are not within the constitutional province of the General Government."[8] In his own, subtle way, Van Buren sought to emphasize that his recommendations did not threaten the country's banks, that the general government was simply solving its own financial problems and did not intend to meddle in the economic affairs of the states. These reassurances failed to calm Democratic fears, for the president's program contradicted the very nature of the party. Van Buren's message implied that the interests of the administration differed from those of the states. Many Democrats found this implication disturbing.

Response to Van Buren's message was immediate and predictable, ranging from indiscriminate praise to unthinking condemnation. Francis P. Blair endorsed it as the "boldest and highest stand ever taken by a chief magistrate" and "a second declaration of independence." Future Secretary of the Navy James K. Paulding waxed eloquent in saluting Van Buren's devotion to laissez faire principles. "The great vice of our Government," Paulding observed, "is meddling legislation." Similar encouragement came from the Hermitage, although Jackson fretted about an issue of Treasury notes. By contrast, the opposition pictured the president as pursuing a radical experiment inherently hostile to all banks.[9]

These charges caused Van Buren little concern. He had long since anticipated Whig objections and had recommended the independent Treasury to counter their demands for a new national bank. The president hoped that his message would convey this sense of urgency —that all Democrats would join in meeting the common enemy.

[8] Richardson, *Messages and Papers*, 3: 324–46.

[9] Washington *Globe*, September 5, 1837; Paulding to Van Buren, September 10, 1837, in Paulding, *Letters*, pp. 196–97; Jackson to Van Buren, September 14, 1837, Van Buren Papers; Millard Fillmore to Thurlow Weed, September 9, 1837, in Frank H. Severance, ed., "Millard Fillmore Papers," *Buffalo Historical Society Publications* (Buffalo, N.Y., 1907), 11: 164; hereafter cited as Fillmore, *Papers*.

Within a week after delivering his report, Van Buren began to receive distressing news. Instead of uniting the party, his appeal had touched off an intense nationwide debate that jeopardized Democratic strength in Congress.

By far the most disturbing response to the special session message came from *The Madisonian*, a paper that posed as the true defender of Jeffersonian principles. Thomas Allen and his editorial colleagues attacked the independent Treasury as a threat to "the interests of the states" and urged Democrats to convince the president of the error of his ways.[10] These statements revealed that *The Madisonian* had no intention of adhering to the party line and that Conservative Senators Nathaniel P. Tallmadge and William C. Rives now had a national paper to publicize their cause. To prevent these insurgents from recruiting a local following, Van Buren appealed to state leaders to endorse his proposals. In so doing, he forced them to make a cruel choice—to decide whether their loyalty to the national party outweighed their devotion to state interests. Although Van Buren's policies created confusion throughout the party, they had the greatest impact in New York and Virginia, long considered by the president to be the crucial Democratic strongholds.[11]

The actions of New York's Governor William L. Marcy provide a good example of the dilemma confronting Van Buren's followers. When the New York banks suspended specie payments in May 1837, the governor faced the responsibility of executing a law requiring all defaulting institutions to forfeit their charters. Since the failures were so widespread, Marcy decided against invoking this harsh penalty; instead he convinced the assembly to give the banks a year's leeway. Van Buren accepted Marcy's solution, but obviously worried about its implications.[12] To have the president arguing that state banks had failed while the head of the Regency granted them grace was an embarrassing contradiction, bound to confuse the party.

As the special session convened, the discord assumed serious dimensions. Throughout August 1837, Marcy had been apprehensive about the president's course. "I fear that there is not a sound state of things at Washington," he told his friend Prosper M. Wetmore.[13]

[10] *The Madisonian*, September 12, 14, 1837.
[11] For state responses to the Panic see James Roger Sharp, "Banking and Politics in the States: The Democratic Party after the Panic of 1837" (Ph.D. diss., University of California, Berkeley, 1966).
[12] Marcy to Van Buren, May 25, 1837, Van Buren Papers; Van Buren to Marcy, June 18, 1837, Gratz Collection.
[13] Marcy to Wetmore, August 18, 1837, Marcy Papers.

After reading a copy of Van Buren's special session message, Marcy dashed off a note to the president, asking how he, as a Democratic governor, was expected to follow the lead of the administration. "I confess that I shall be brought with great reluctance, if at all, to the immediate and full application of the doctrine of divorce . . . in the fiscal affairs of this state," he wrote angrily. "Yet I know full well the fate that awaits those who falter in the cause. Stragglers that fall behind the main body will be treated but little better than deserters."[14]

Shortly after writing this agonizing passage, Marcy had a two-hour conversation with the attorney general, who had recently arrived in Albany from the nation's capital. The governor was furious and asked Butler "if the men at Washington expected that I was to proclaim a *Divorce* between the Govt. of the State & the banks?" Butler said no. Not satisfied, Marcy then inquired, "What sort of supporters of Mr. V. B. shall we be if we repudiate his doctrines as applicable to the states?" To this, Butler made no reply.[15] Having vented some of his ire, Marcy rewrote his letter to Van Buren, deleting all but a few innocuous comments.[16] It is unfortunate that the governor chose to make this revision; his violent protest would have given the president dramatic proof of the problems facing local party organizations.

Although Marcy made no public announcement of his dissent, New York Democrats soon learned of the Regency's disenchantment with administration proposals. In his first public commentary on the special session message, the *Argus's* Edwin Croswell dismissed Van Buren's program as insignificant. The embattled editor praised the president's devotion to principle but thought there might be a "difference of views" on "minor questions." He then went on to define what he meant by minor. "We allude to the payment of . . . the last installment of the surplus revenue to the states, an issue of treasury notes, and the adoption of a system of collecting and disbursing the public moneys through the agency of government officers." Croswell was not being flippant or cavalier; essentially, he was trying to avoid taking a stand on the most important parts of Van Buren's legislative program. Such evasion was nearly as damning as outright criticism.[17]

[14] Marcy to Van Buren, September 13, 1837, Gratz Collection. Marcy wrote this draft between September 7 and 9.
[15] Marcy to Prosper M. Wetmore, September 9, 1837, Marcy Papers.
[16] Marcy to Van Buren, September 18, 1837, Van Buren Papers. See Marcy's comments on the deletions in Marcy to Wetmore, September 26, 1837, Marcy Papers.
[17] Albany *Argus*, September 6, 1837. See also Hermanus Bleecker to Van Buren, September 20, 1837, Van Buren Papers.

In Virginia, Thomas Ritchie followed an equally disturbing editorial policy. Like Croswell, he praised the spirit of the message and
saluted Van Buren's firmness, but then he began a long discourse on
the need for party unity, insisting that this was impossible so long as
the administration adhered to the independent Treasury scheme.[18] As
a leader of the Richmond Junto, Ritchie found himself in an awkward position. He had long worked for the Democratic party because
it in turn had supported Virginia's interests. The Panic seemed to
change all this. After the suspension of specie payments in May 1837,
the Virginia legislature reaffirmed its faith in the state banks by
granting them relief from the forfeiture law. Although desiring some
reform in the future, the majority of Virginia's politicians remained
committed to preserving the strong connection between the state
government and the banks.[19] Bound to uphold this policy, Ritchie
suddenly found himself at odds with the president, who now took
steps to withdraw government deposits and place them in an independent Treasury. To Ritchie, and to many other state leaders, this
move threatened to destroy public confidence in state banks and
seemed but the first step in a concerted attack on the entire credit
structure.

The president soon applied subtle pressure to overcome resistance
in New York and Virginia. Since his ties with Albany were much
stronger than those with Richmond, he naturally looked first to his
native state. On the day following submission of the special session
message, Silas Wright wrote to the Regency's Azariah Flagg, saying,
"The President requests me to ask you to tell Croswell that . . . it is
now time that the Argus should come out; that he thinks the message
such a document as he can support without equivocations." Wright
added that to have "Mr. Ritchie in opposition on the one side and
him [Croswell] non-comittal on the other . . . is a little too much."[20]
Van Buren undoubtedly issued similar statements through friends in
Virginia.[21]

The president's efforts had some effect. In Albany, Croswell at last
took more than a passing notice of the divorce bill, arguing on

[18] Richmond *Enquirer*, September 8, 1837.
[19] Sharp, "Banking and Politics in the States," pp. 314–34.
[20] Wright to Flagg, September 5, 1837, Flagg-Wright Papers.
[21] At this time Ritchie's brother-in-law, Richard E. Parker, fully supported Van
Buren and tried to change Ritchie's mind. See Parker to Van Buren, September
11, 1837, Van Buren Papers; Parker to William C. Rives, September 14, 1837,
Rives Papers; Ritchie to Thomas Green, September 20, 1837, in *Branch Historical Papers*, 4: 383–84. See also Amos Kendall to Thomas Ritchie, September 9,
1837, in Kendall, *Autobiography*, pp. 424–26.

September 9, 1837, that an independent Treasury was not hostile to all banks. Yet, the reluctant editor still showed a singular lack of enthusiasm for Van Buren's proposals. Later in the month he printed all Ritchie's objections to the divorce bill. By early October, Croswell felt compelled to explain his unusual practice of giving space to both the president's supporters and opponents. "Of course we shall not be held responsible," Croswell apologized, "for the views and positions of the respective litigants."[22]

For the most part, Ritchie said nothing, blaming his silence on lack of editorial space.[23] He, too, was trying to avoid widening the split in the party. Privately, Ritchie went through a period of intense soul searching. Although he shared with the Virginia Conservatives an abhorrence for the idea of separating bank from state, he remained concerned about Democratic unity. While Rives recruited converts for the Conservative cause, Ritchie searched for a means of compromise.

Thus at the very outset of the crucial struggle in Congress, Van Buren found his electoral base in jeopardy. He had lost the aid of his two most important state newspapers. For both the Albany *Argus* and the Richmond *Enquirer*, the financial crisis facing the states took precedence over the problems confronting the president. Furthermore, *The Madisonian* was undermining the influence of the Washington *Globe*. Bent on revenge, Blair began a personal vendetta that only aggravated the situation. Van Buren's sole remaining hope was that Congress would act swiftly and put an end to this bickering.

While the president tried in vain to solidify state support, his lieutenants mobilized Congress. In the House the venerable John Quincy Adams, watching Polk at work, wryly commented that the Speaker's promised impartiality was liable to be "between the two sides of his own party."[24] Adams's quip was close to the truth. Although Democrats outnumbered their opponents by a mere sixteen votes, they controlled eighteen of the thirty standing committees of the House. Furthermore, on the six crucial committees of Elections, Ways and Means, Foreign Affairs, Military Affairs, Public Lands, and Indian Affairs, Polk gave the administration a two-to-one majority. By contrast, the opposition dominated only the committees on Public Expenditures and Roads and Canals. Administration influence did not depend solely on a show of numerical strength. On the committee dealing with the District of Columbia, Van Buren's fol-

---

[22] Albany *Argus*, September 9, 11, 13, 20, 23, October 5, 1837.
[23] Richmond *Enquirer*, September 12, 15, October 3, 1837.
[24] Adams, *Diary*, 9: 366.

lowers had a bare five-to-four edge, yet all members of the opposition came from slaveholding states. Thus the president could count on this body to thwart any attempts to disturb slavery in the District.[25]

Statistics tell only part of the story. Democrats not only ruled key committees but also frequently ignored formalities. Massachusetts Congressman Richard Fletcher, a fledgling member of the Ways and Means Committee, gave his constituents a graphic account of the proceedings behind closed doors: "The chairman of the committee steps up to the White House, and there receives from the President, or the Secretary of the Treasury, such bills as they wished to have passed by the House. The chairman puts these bills into his pocket, takes them to the committee; without any examination, the majority of the committee approve them; the minority can do nothing; the bills are presented to the House, and received as the doings of the committee."[26] In the House Fletcher's remarks created a minor controversy and drew sharp rebuttal from Ways and Means chairman Churchill Cambreleng. It was Cambreleng's contention that his committee did make revisions in administration proposals. Significantly, he never mentioned to what extent his colleagues participated in these decisions.[27]

Democrats enjoyed even greater success in organizing the Senate, where they had a majority of sixteen votes.[28] On September 7, 1837, the opposition agreed to abandon the usual practice of choosing committee members by ballot, leaving the selection instead to its presiding officer, Vice President Richard M. Johnson. The following day, Johnson announced choices that clearly reflected Democratic preponderance; the administration controlled every one of the Senate's twenty-two standing committees. They enjoyed a two-to-one margin on fifteen, including the powerful committees on Finance, Foreign Relations, Commerce, Manufactures, Public Lands, the Judiciary, and the Post Office. Johnson named only a few key Whig senators to

[25] For a list of committee appointments see *Congressional Globe*, 25th Cong., 1st sess., 1837, 5: 18. The source for party affiliation is the Washington *Globe*, August 25, 1837. *The United States Magazine and Democratic Review* 4 (1838): 61–69, gives a more convenient tabulation of the *Globe*'s figures. Francis P. Blair's calculations do not take into account the Conservative defection, but they do represent the administration assessment of its strength in the House at the opening of the session.

[26] *National Intelligencer*, November 18, 1837.

[27] *Congressional Globe*, 25th Cong., 2d sess., 1837–1838, 6: 21–22.

[28] On party affiliations in the Senate see the Washington *Globe*, August 25, 1837, and the list in the *United States Magazine and Democratic Review* 4 (1838): 32. The actual majority during the session was only fourteen owing to the absence of Senators Cuthbert (Ga.) and Mouton (La.).

positions of importance and completely ignored John C. Calhoun.[29]

Under normal conditions, such efficient organization would have insured success, but these were not ordinary circumstances. For the first time since the administration of James Madison, the president had called Congress into extra session. Partisan committees might provide adequate machinery to work out details on minor legislation, but they could not compel adherence to a policy so radical as that embodied in the independent Treasury proposal.

The first signs of dissension came during the selection of the House printer. The administration expected to elect the firm of Blair and Rives, publishers of the Washington *Globe*, while the opposition backed Gales and Seaton, printers of the *National Intelligencer*. Voting began on September 5 and continued for the next three days. Six ballots made it obvious that the Democratic favorite could not command the necessary majority, and slowly the Conservative hopeful Thomas Allen, editor of *The Madisonian*, gained momentum. Rather than see Blair continue to live out of the public coffers, the Whigs threw their support to Allen, and on the twelfth ballot elected him printer. Blair's defeat disappointed Van Buren, for it indicated that Conservatives had enough power in the House to thwart the administration. Fewer than twenty Democratic congressmen originally voted for Allen but this was enough to prevent Blair's election.[30]

Disregarding this ominous sign, Van Buren's spokesmen turned to the specifics of the president's message. On September 8, Silas Wright informed the secretary of the treasury that the Senate Finance Committee was ready to deliberate. Wright hoped they might proceed "as rapidly as may be consistent with sound and discreet action, [to] expedite the business of the special session."[31] Within a week the New York senator presented the administration program to his colleagues.

Wright introduced five bills on the Senate floor, four of which were designed to meet the immediate needs of the government and provide relief to debtors. First, since the balance in the Treasury had

[29] U.S. Senate, *Journal of the Senate of the United States*, 25th Cong., 1st sess., 1837, pp. 27–28. The Senate gave no reason for the change in procedure, but it seems likely that the opposition saw that it had little chance of controlling committees and therefore agreed to suspend the normal balloting in order to save time.

[30] *Congressional Globe*, 25th Cong., 1st sess., 1837, 5: 10–16. There is no record of how individual members voted on each ballot. For opinions on the alleged cooperation between the Whig and Conservative presses see John Niles to Gideon Welles, September 8, 1837, Welles Papers; Francis P. Blair to Mrs. Blair, September 8, 1837, Blair-Lee Papers.

[31] Wright to Woodbury, September 8, 1837, Woodbury Papers.

drastically dwindled, the administration proposed that Congress postpone the fourth installment of surplus revenue. The only debate on this measure concerned the length of postponement. Van Buren favored an indefinite delay, but his lieutenants allowed an amendment by South Carolina's Francis Pickens, making payments due January 1, 1839.[32] In addition to insuring that states did not drain away vital funds, the president wanted to settle accounts with the former deposit banks. The Act of June 23, 1836, required him to remove all federal revenue from banks refusing to pay specie. The total suspension in May made this course difficult. Consequently, Van Buren asked Congress to establish a definite schedule for transfer of money to the Treasury. On September 13, 1837, Wright reported a bill requiring the secretary of the treasury to continue his withdrawal of revenue, but allowing the banks to pay in installments over the next eight months. Democrats agreed to extend this period of indulgence; on October 16, the House passed the bill.[33] Van Buren asked for similar leniency on the payment of custom-house bonds and his supporters again liberalized the period of grace before passing the bill.[34]

In light of the delayed payments, the administration thought it necessary to ask authority to issue Treasury notes to cover immediate expenses. Both Jackson and Cambreleng opposed this idea as a dangerous deviation from hard money principles, but Van Buren preferred it to a loan. Cambreleng finally relented and agreed to sponsor the president's plan. Under his leadership, the House passed the Treasury-note bill on October 9, 1837, by a vote of 127 to 98. The act empowered Woodbury to issue $10 million worth of interest-bearing notes.[35]

By willingly adopting these measures, Congress met the temporary needs of the government; it provided a source of income and made arrangements for eventual recovery of all deposits. On the president's recommendation, it also assisted the mercantile community in meeting its debts. Such expedients raised little opposition; they were but natural solutions to the pressing problems of the Panic.

Van Buren obviously hoped that the same sense of immediacy would influence debate on the divorce bill. He had tried to present

[32] *Congressional Globe*, 25th Cong., 1st sess., 1837, 5: 17, 30, 32, 70, 89–92.
[33] Ibid., pp. 22, 144–45.
[34] Ibid., pp. 30, 32, 38, 41, 43, 45, 123, 124, 138.
[35] Cambreleng to Abraham Van Buren, July 20, 1837, Jackson to Van Buren, September 14, 1837, Van Buren to Jackson, October 3, 1837, Levi Woodbury, Memoranda on loans or Treasury notes, September 1837, Van Buren Papers; *Congressional Globe*, 25th Cong., 1st sess., 1837, 5: 22–23, 38, 114–15, 119–21.

his plans as a remedy for the current crisis, not as a thoroughgoing institutional reform. He calculated that this appeal to the Jeffersonian ideal of simple government would counteract the novel aspects of the independent Treasury. In his message, he emphasized that because the system had actually been in effect since the suspension of specie payments, it was necessary only to assign "certain additional duties to existing establishments and officers." Levi Woodbury continued this theme in his report on finances. He suggested two possible schemes. One would merely expand the operations of collectors and postmasters, allowing them to receive, store, and disburse public funds; the other called for a new organization of subTreasuries. The first had the advantage of simplicity, while the second provided more safety by creating an intermediate agency capable of checking on collectors. Woodbury argued that both plans were appropriate because they required "but slight change in our existing laws or usages."[36]

The president had definite political reasons for preferring the first of these alternatives. By proposing only to modify present Treasury Department structure, he would avoid unnecessary enlargement of the civil service. Van Buren's advisers had anticipated objection on these grounds; ever since the first hint of the government's intentions, the opposition cried out against an increase of executive patronage. Van Buren countered this criticism by keeping things as simple as possible. The bill Wright introduced on September 14, 1837, merely imposed "additional duties as depositories, in certain cases, on public officers." Van Buren asked that officials of the Treasury, the Mint, and the Post Office be empowered to collect and disburse public funds without resort to any banks. As Woodbury later stated, there was no need "to appoint any number of 'new officers,'" nor would the bill require any additional physical facilities.[37]

No sooner had Wright presented this plan, than South Carolina's mercurial John C. Calhoun threw Democratic forces into disarray. In a move to advance his own presidential ambitions and thereby unite the South, Calhoun deserted his former Whig allies and announced support for administration fiscal policy. No one expected such a turn

[36] Richardson, *Messages and Papers*, 3: 335; U.S. Congress, *Senate Documents* (No. 2), 25th Cong., 1st sess., 1837, p. 12.
[37] John Brockenbrough to William C. Rives, May 20, 1837, Silas Wright to Van Buren, June 4, 22, 1837, John Niles to Van Buren, July 1, 1837, Van Buren Papers; *Congressional Globe*, 25th Cong., 1st sess., 1837, 5: 27; U.S. Congress, *House Documents* (No. 36), 25th Cong., 1st sess., 1837, pp. 1–2.

of events, and Van Buren's followers did not know quite how to proceed.[38] Wright could not spurn the assistance of so effective an orator, even though he must have suspected Calhoun's motives. Had the Nullifier been willing quietly to support the Democratic program, there would have been little cause for alarm. Unfortunately, he saw his position as one of leadership, exultantly telling friends that the president had "been forced by his situation and the terror of Jackson to play directly into our hands." Most other observers saw things differently. John Quincy Adams spoke of Calhoun's "bargain and sale of himself to Van Buren." South Carolina's William C. Preston complained that Calhoun abandoned him "without warning." Although thankful for the Nullifier's support, the Washington *Globe* regretted that "Some passages of his speech will be found tinged with the relics of prejudices engendered in the political conflicts through which Mr. C. has passed." Jackson was even less charitable and lashed out against his former antagonist, predicting that "Those that may repose confidence in him will, *surely*, be disappointed." The president remained silent.[39]

The new convert from South Carolina forced his allies into an untenable position. On September 16, 1837, Wright was trying to push the Treasury-note bill through the Senate, when Calhoun asked for a delay to express his views on the separation of bank and state. Over Wright's objection, the Senate postponed action on the pending legislation to allow Calhoun his say. Two days later, in a dramatic speech, Calhoun attacked a national bank and then called for a gradual exclusion of the notes of state banks in payment of government dues. Daniel Webster rose and asked the question then in everyone's mind—which bill did Calhoun seek to amend? The South

[38] For an opposite view see Charles M. Wiltse, *John C. Calhoun*, 3 vols. (Indianapolis, Ind., 1944–1951), 2: 343–61. Wiltse maintains that Van Buren, out of desperation, "joined the nullifiers." He bases his argument on the fact that Calhoun made his views known as early as July 12, 1837. This assumes that Van Buren was in a state of confusion at that time, when in fact he had already decided to introduce the divorce bill. When the Washington *Globe* listed the party affiliations of the members of Congress on August 25, 1837, it classed Calhoun as a member of the opposition. On Calhoun's motives, see the persuasive analysis in Gerald M. Capers, *John C. Calhoun—Opportunist: A Reappraisal* (Gainesville, Fla., 1960), p. 189.
[39] Calhoun to James Edward Calhoun, September 7, 1837, in Calhoun, *Correspondence*, p. 377; Adams, *Diary*, 9: 398; William C. Preston to Willie P. Mangum, October 4, 1837, in Mangum, *Papers*, 2: 508–10; Washington *Globe*, October 2, 1837; Jackson to William B. Lewis, October 19, 1837, in Jackson, *Correspondence*, 5: 516. Two years later Calhoun still assumed a defensive attitude about his political shift in 1837. See Calhoun to Virgil Maxcy, February 28, 1839, Galloway-Maxcy-Markoe Papers, Library of Congress.

Carolinian replied, the "one called the divorce between the Government and the banks."[40]

Although the Senate brushed aside Calhoun's amendment and passed the Treasury-note bill, the Nullifier raised an issue that administration spokesmen had tried to gloss over. In his message on September 4, Van Buren mentioned the advantages of limiting government transactions to specie, but he made no specific recommendations to this effect. Levi Woodbury followed a similarly cautious course, being careful not to speak out against a future reception of the notes of specie-paying banks. The administration was in a dilemma. So long as banks suspended payments, the president did not want to sanction their notes, but neither did he wish to appear hostile to local interests. In short, Van Buren wanted to take temporary political advantage of identification with hard money without committing himself to implementing a metallic currency. Administration spokesmen saw no need for legislation on the specie question. "As the law is," Silas Wright argued, "nothing but gold & silver is, or can be received whilst the Banks refuse payment. When they resume, it will be discressionary [sic] with Woodbury; he will probably instruct the Collectors, Receivers etc., to take nothing but coin or the bills of specie paying banks." Wright had never advocated a total reliance on gold and silver and felt that "no bill, directing the payment in coin can get through at this time."[41]

It is unlikely that the administration could have satisfied its critics with such an indefinite stand on the specie question. On the same day Calhoun offered his amendment, William C. Rives announced intentions of introducing a bill designating the type of funds "in which the public revenue should be received."[42] Once it became obvious that there was no hope of dodging the issue, Wright agreed to consider Calhoun's amendment in conjunction with the independent Treasury bill. He must have done so with reluctance, since the inclusion of a specie clause would make the measure all the more objectionable to the Conservatives, whose support was vital to Democratic success.

Before proceeding on the divorce bill, administration leaders

[40] *Congressional Globe*, 25th Cong., 1st sess., 1837, 5: 35–37; Thomas Hart Benton, *Abridgment of the Debates of Congress*, 16 vols. (New York, 1857–1863), 13: 363–67. Benton gives an account of the entire proceedings, which are somewhat unclear in the *Congressional Globe*.

[41] John Niles to Gideon Welles, September 15, 1837, Welles Papers. For Wright's views on a metallic currency see Wright to William L. Marcy, June 22, 1837, Gratz Collection. For a different interpretation of this letter see Garraty, *Silas Wright*, pp. 145–46.

[42] *Congressional Globe*, 25th Cong., 1st sess., 1837, 5: 36.

moved to head off anticipated pressure for a national bank. Henry Clay and Daniel Webster had given little indication that they would bring forward a bill on this subject, but Wright was nervous. The Senate had referred to his committee several memorials favoring a recharter; he used these as a pretext for sponsoring a resolution "that the prayer of the petitioners ought not to be granted." Clay objected to such a negative proposition. It reminded him of a tactic once used by John Randolph who, anticipating President Madison's war message, called on his colleagues in the House to rule "that it is inexpedient to declare war against Great Britain." After this brief moment of levity, Wright and his supporters overrode Whig attempts to shelve the entire matter and approved the committee's resolution by a straight party vote of thirty-one to fifteen. Rives and Tallmadge both supported the administration; the only Democrat to defect was Indiana's John Tipton.[43] This roll call put an end to administration fears about the power of Nicholas Biddle and his bank forces.

Democratic solidarity faded once the Senate turned to the question of separating the government from all banks. Debate on the measure ranged from the unstinting praise of Wright and Buchanan to the outright condemnation of Clay and Webster. In between lay the real source of friction; Rives and Tallmadge, though by no means friends of "Biddle's Monster," were not willing to see the state banks treated summarily.

As might be expected, senators usually began their orations with a history of the Panic, attempting to fix responsibility for precipitating the crisis. Clay and Webster traced all the distress back to the overthrow of the Second Bank of the United States and assailed Jacksonian policy as despotic and irresponsible. To Webster it had long been plain that Jackson's system was "radically vicious . . . its operations . . . all inconvenient, clumsy, and wholly inadequate to the proposed ends; and that, sooner or later, there must be an explosion."[44] By contrast, the Democrats saw the Panic as the inevitable result of natural fluctuations in the economy. "At successive periods the best and most · enterprising men of the country are crushed," observed Pennsylvania's James Buchanan. "They fall victims at the shrine of the insatiate and insatiable Moloch of extrava-

---

[43] Ibid., pp. 49, 73–76. See also John Tipton to Spear S. Tipton, October 1, 1837, in Nellie Armstrong Robertson and Dorothy Riker, eds., "The John Tipton Papers," *Indiana Historical Collections*, 24–26 (Indianapolis, Ind., 1942), 26: 447–48. The House passed a similar resolution on October 5, 1837, by a vote of 122 to 91 (*Congressional Globe*, 25th Cong., 1st sess., 5: 104–105).

[44] *Congressional Globe*, 25th Cong., 1st sess., 1837, 5: Appendix, 167–68, 179–80.

gant banking. It is an everlasting cycle. We are destined, I fear, again and again to pass through the same vicissitudes." This cyclical interpretation had the virtue of removing the Jacksonians from the center of attention. Government action could not arrest such a progression, but occasionally the administration might step in to smooth out problems. "I shall not stop to inquire," Buchanan added, "how much less gold and silver there would have been . . . had the specie circular never existed."[45]

The Conservatives argued along different lines. For obvious reasons they deemphasized the origins of the crisis. To dwell on the bank war would necessitate shouldering part of the blame, since their defection was of more recent origin. They could neither malign the banks to which they were attached, nor attack a policy they once supported. When Rives and Tallmadge did discuss factors leading to the Panic, they tended to focus on recent Democratic decisions. They argued that such measures as the specie circular destroyed the nation's confidence in banks.[46]

Discussion on the background of the crisis naturally led to debate on the administration's responsibility for providing a remedy. Daniel Webster advanced the most ambitious and comprehensive philosophy, maintaining that it was the constitutional duty of the government to regulate the country's medium of exchange. "I admit," he said, "that if the currency is not to be preserved by the Government of the United States, I know not how it is to be guarded against constantly occurring disorders and derangements." He accused Van Buren of attempting to abdicate responsibility for the nation's wellbeing and argued that the president's message, Wright's bill, and Calhoun's amendment "all, in effect, deny any such duty, disclaim all such power, and confine the constitutional obligation of Government to the mere regulation of the coins, and the care of its own revenues."[47] Rives and the Conservatives tended to support this argument for government regulation.

The day after Webster's forceful speech, Buchanan rose to challenge such latitudinarian doctrines. He denied that the administration should have any power to "regulate the banking system of this country." This task belonged to the states, and the most the government should do was to prevent banks from using Treasury Department funds as a basis for extravagant speculation.[48] Buchanan reiter-

[45] Ibid., p. 94.
[46] Ibid., pp. 157, 232.
[47] Ibid., pp. 159, 169.
[48] Ibid., p. 95.

ated Democratic faith in the virtues of a negative state. To their way of thinking, the independent Treasury would be beneficial because it would protect the government from convulsions when they occurred.

After much verbal sparring on the causes of the Panic and the duties of the government, the speakers suggested remedies for the disease. By adopting the resolution against a national bank, the Senate narrowed the alternatives to two—a reform of the state bank deposit system or an approval of Wright's bill. With the Whigs thus disarmed, Democrats fell to fighting among themselves. As anticipated, Rives and Tallmadge emerged as champions of local banking interests. Both charged the administration with unwarranted hostility to state institutions and maintained that the Panic was only temporary. After insisting that the deposit scheme had "not been fairly tried," each expressed his unqualified faith in the virtues of local banking. Both objected to the divorce bill because it increased executive patronage and separated the government from the people. The Conservative senators were not satisfied to rest their case here but insisted that isolation itself was inherently menacing. They tried to characterize the government's defensive reaction as a direct assault. In their eyes the administration was guilty of at once abandoning a position of beneficial influence over the economy while threatening to restrain state banks. To this catalog of grievances Rives added the charge that an independent Treasury would not provide adequate security to public revenue. He capped his treatise with an appeal to antibank rhetoric, maintaining that the confusion of presidential aims might well allow the opposition to recharter a national bank.[49]

Rives was not content merely to assail Democratic proposals; on September 19, 1837, he offered a bill designed to buttress the sagging deposit system. He proposed that Congress authorize receipt of the notes of specie-paying banks, so long as these institutions agreed to exclude gradually all small bills under twenty dollars. The government would thus maintain its deposits in the states. "The *sanctions* of this bill," according to Rives, "would exert a very considerable influence on the conduct of the banks." He remained convinced that Van Buren's aim was to separate the Treasury from the nation at large.[50]

Wright, Buchanan, and Calhoun rose to protect the independent Treasury from assault by the Conservatives. In a reasoned, judicious speech on October 2, 1837, Wright calmly reviewed all the arguments advanced during the special session. He stated that the govern-

[49] Ibid., pp. 156–64, 229–36.
[50] Ibid., p. 160.

ment's power over the currency was only incidental and then asked, "Is it not desirable, if it can be done with safety to all interests to be regarded, to relieve the Treasury, and the head of the fiscal department of this Government, from this always so delicate, and frequently so odious, an exercise of the power and influence of the public funds, upon the credit of the banks and the business of the country?" Wright implied that previous government involvement in the economy had been disastrous and therefore recommended a diminution of this influence. He denied that the divorce bill was inimical to state interests. By removing public money as a stimulant to speculation, the administration would contribute to the recovery of local banks. Wright admitted the error of entrusting a burgeoning surplus to the states and asked that Congress take remedial action. Finally, he repeated his belief that the states were the sole agency capable of reforming the fiscal structure; the federal government should not usurp their authority.[51]

Where Wright calmly outlined the nature, advantages, and effects of a separation of bank and state, Calhoun confined himself almost exclusively to a discourse on the salutary influence of hard money. The South Carolinian made little attempt to counter the objections of the Conservatives. Instead, he staunchly defended his own specie clause. Calhoun was a brilliant orator and undoubtedly attracted attention to the administration cause, but, because of his narrow and personal conception of the issues, he was often as much a liability as an asset. Moreover, his sudden shift of political allegiance made him a perfect target for opposition barbs, allowing Van Buren's opponents to strike indirectly at administration measures.[52]

When Calhoun finished, the Senate passed his specie clause by a narrow margin of twenty-four to twenty-three. Democrats then defeated Rives's proposal by four votes. With both of these controversial amendments resolved, Wright managed to bring the divorce bill to the floor. Administration lines held firm; by a vote of twenty-five to twenty-three, the Senate approved Van Buren's proposal to separate bank from state.[53]

Careful management produced the victory in the Senate. At the beginning of the session, administration leaders anticipated a majority of fourteen votes. By the time the Senate took up the indepen-

[51] Ibid., pp. 113–21.
[52] Ibid., pp. 121–26. For a different view of Calhoun's importance see Wiltse, *Calhoun*, 2: 352–56. Wiltse offers little evidence besides Calhoun's own statements.
[53] *Congressional Globe*, 25th Cong., 1st sess., 1837, 5: 96.

dent Treasury proposal, Conservative defections had reduced the Democratic advantage to a mere six votes. With such a small practical plurality, Wright had to exercise close control; the results of his efforts were impressive. Analysis of fifteen roll calls between September 14, 1837, and October 3, 1837, indicates that on these occasions the average administration senator missed only one vote. There was a total of only three Democratic absences when the Senate acted on the crucial questions of a bank recharter and the divorce bill. Good attendance is only valuable when coupled with party discipline; once again Wright proved a skillful leader. Democratic senators voted with the chairman of the Finance Committee 91 percent of the time.[54]

Democratic organization in the House was not nearly so effective as that in the Senate. Polk had made strong committee appointments that insured quick consideration of presidential recommendations, but he had only a small numerical majority to work with. The conservative defection threatened to block administration plans. "In the present state of parties in the House," observed New Hampshire's Franklin Pierce, "it is idle to expect any important legislative action at this session."[55] Despite such dire predictions, Churchill Cambreleng did manage to convince his colleagues to support most of Van Buren's program. On the divorce bill, however, Democrats ran into difficulty. Cambreleng introduced the measure with little fanfare on September 15, 1837, and tried to see it swiftly through the House. When the Senate sent over its version on October 5, he had it referred immediately to the Committee of the Whole, without mentioning the important addition of Calhoun's specie clause. In his desire to save time, he refrained from speaking on behalf of the measure, allowing South Carolina's Francis Pickens to make the first speech in support of Van Buren's scheme.[56]

Cambreleng soon regretted having relinquished his leadership. On

[54] These calculations are based on analysis of all but five of the recorded roll calls in the Senate prior to the passage of the divorce bill. Those votes excluded were lopsided Democratic victories and their inclusion would only increase the degree of party cohesion. The source for party affiliation is the *United States Magazine and Democratic Review* 4 (1838): 32. The most convenient listing of the roll calls is in the *Senate Journal*. I used the voting of Silas Wright as a model and compared all other Democrats to him. In no instance was there a case of excessive absenteeism except for Democrats Mouton (La.) and Cuthbert (Ga.). Both missed the entire session and therefore were not included in these figures.

[55] Pierce to John McNeil, September 7, 1837, Pierce Papers.

[56] *Congressional Globe*, 25th Cong., 1st sess., 1837, 5: 33, 105. On Cambreleng's motives, see his speech on October 13, 1837, in *Congressional Globe*, 25th Cong., 1st sess., 1837, 5: Appendix, 146.

October 10, 1837, Pickens rose to address the House at great length on the subject of the divorce of bank and state. A nullifier and staunch ally of Calhoun, he was expected to repeat the same arguments employed by his mentor in the Senate. Instead of giving a calm discourse on the advantages of an independent Treasury, Pickens delivered a tirade on the evils of banking and the dangers of irresponsible capitalism. For the most part, he ignored the provisions of the administration bill and poured forth a steady stream of invective that at times had little to do with finance. As if drawn by some ineluctable force, Pickens concluded with a violent attack on the North and a ringing defense of slavery: "The whole banking system there is a political substitute for the standing armies of Europe, without which the capitalists of the north would be compelled to submit to a loss of power. . . . We are not compelled to resort to those artificial institutions of society by which non-slave-holding regions seek to delude and deceive their victims. No, Sir, we avow to the world that we own our black population, and we will maintain that ownership, if needs be, to the last extremity."

Such an embittered sectional diatribe threw the House into confusion. Once Pickens sat down "there was a pause, as if everybody was afraid to encounter him."[57] He had interjected into a financial debate an issue calculated to raise the worst passions of the legislature. Over the next few days, no fewer than four congressmen responded at length to Pickens's critique. Massachusetts's William B. Calhoun gave the most reasoned reply. After stating his basic opposition to the independent Treasury bill, Calhoun deftly related this criticism to Pickens's rantings. "Let the gentleman from South Carolina proceed in his insurrectionary project against the labor and the institutions of the north. He looks for aid from the operation of this sub-Treasury scheme. It might aid him, it is true; but with whom, that is sound hearted, will that consideration recommend the scheme?"[58] By making his exposition on administration policy a vehicle for a polemic against the North, Pickens invited recriminations. To achieve success, the Democrats had to confine debate solely to economic issues; Pickens appealed to the forces of sectionalism, thereby complicating the campaign.

Amidst this confusion, Cambreleng delivered a belated defense of the divorce bill. Ignoring the whole question of slavery, he criticized those seeking to embarrass the government by opposing reform.

[57] *Congressional Globe*, 25th Cong., 1st sess., 1837, 5: Appendix, 178; Adams, *Diary*, 9: 399.
[58] *Congressional Globe*, 25th Cong., 1st sess., 1837, 5: Appendix, 303.

Where Wright and Buchanan urged moderation, Cambreleng threw caution to the winds and lashed out against proponents of all banks. He made no mention of any natural cycle of economic fluctuation, nor did he explicitly remove the government from complicity in precipitating the Panic. Democratic leaders in the Senate denied that it was the administration's duty to regulate the economy; at most, the government should set an example for the states. Cambreleng placed no such restrictions on federal responsibilities, but insisted that by receiving and maintaining a small surplus in specie, the Treasury would "be a regulator of trade far better than the foreign exchanges." Such a policy "would be a steady and salutary check, in preventing the excessive and unwarrantable issues" of bank credit.[59]

Cambreleng's deviation from official pronouncements is not difficult to explain. Of all the president's advisers, he alone tended to think in terms of economics more than politics. At the time of the debate on the specie circular, for instance, Cambreleng wanted Van Buren to consider the problem from a strictly financial standpoint. Prior to the special session, Cambreleng was the only member of the president's circle to oppose openly an issue of Treasury notes. At no time did he evince any sympathy for the state banks and apparently saw little reason to refrain from antagonizing local interests. When the banks suspended specie payments, Cambreleng, like Jackson, wanted the government to bring suit immediately; he felt that only a thorough purge would cleanse the system.[60] In the closing sections of his speech, Cambreleng referred to an idea that Wright and Buchanan studiously avoided. Both senators anticipated objection to the divorce bill as a radical scheme, and each tried to minimize the novel features of the president's plan. Cambreleng eschewed such subtlety. "We fear not the results of the experiment," he said in conclusion.[61]

Cambreleng's rather careless handling of the divorce bill only heightened confusion in the Democratic ranks. The Conservative defection was already in full swing. Since their unsuccessful efforts to defeat the bill in the Senate, Rives and Tallmadge had spent a majority of their time in the House giving aid and counsel to their friends. The Virginia senator saw his task as primarily one of obstruction. "We have done fully as much as I expected to be able to do, in checking bad measures," he told his wife, but then noted "we have

[59] Ibid., p. 149.
[60] On Cambreleng's previous financial views see Cambreleng to Van Buren, April 8. May 6, June 13, 1837, Cambreleng to Abraham Van Buren, May 30, 1837, Van Buren Papers; Cambreleng to Azariah Flagg, May 10, 1837, Flagg Papers; Cambreleng to Joel Poinsett, August 4, 1837, Poinsett Papers.
[61] *Congressional Globe*, 25th Cong., 1st sess., 1837, 5: Appendix, 151.

not yet strength enough to carry our own measures."[62] The major beneficiaries of Rives's assistance were Virginia's James Garland and South Carolina's Hugh Swinton Legaré. On September 18, 1837, Garland had introduced a measure, similar to that later proposed by Rives, calling for acceptance of notes of state banks and also providing for continuation of a system of local depositories.[63]

The administration tried to prevent Legaré from supporting the Conservative cause. The president thought the new congressman might listen to the arguments of an experienced politician. During the hectic week of debate on the divorce bill, Secretary of War Joel R. Poinsett paid a visit to Legaré and tried to persuade him not to risk political defeat by opposing the president. Legaré agreed to temper his remarks but refused to abandon his principles, maintaining that "the whole subject of banking & currency is too difficult & too unsettled to be made a party question." Poinsett returned empty-handed, convinced that Legaré remained committed to Rives.[64]

On October 13, 1837, Legaré made an eloquent and moving plea on behalf of state banks. Repeating many of the arguments popularized by Rives in the Senate, he blamed the administration for abandoning its duties toward the people. What should the nation think, he asked, of a government that did nothing in the face of widespread suffering? Turning to fellow Democrats, he thundered, "It is not enough to say you have no *power* . . . under the constitution, to regulate the currency. I admit that you have none. What then? Have you no *influence*—influence of example—influence of precept—influence of authority—influence of patronage—influence of connexion and custom in business, in the use of these very deposites?"[65]

With the Conservatives in open revolt and the Democrats in a state of disarray, there seemed little chance of success. On October 14, 1837, New York's John C. Clark suggested that the House postpone consideration of the divorce bill. Noting that "the subject matter of this bill is one on which there is, among the friends of the administration, a difference of opinion," he asked for more time so that he might consult his constituents. After all, he said, "Public opinion has not been sufficiently enlightened to draw any correct

[62] Rives to Mrs. Rives, September 25, 1837, Rives Family Papers; Francis P. Blair to Jackson, October 13, 1837, Jackson Papers; John Niles to Gideon Welles, October 14, 1837, Welles Papers.
[63] *Congressional Globe*, 25th Cong., 1st sess., 1837, 5: 39.
[64] Legaré to Poinsett, October 11, 1837, Poinsett Papers. Poinsett's penciled endorsement tells of the visit to Legaré and of the latter's decision to support Rives.
[65] *Congressional Globe*, 25th Cong., 1st sess., 1837, 5: Appendix, 238.

conclusion of its disposition." Then in mock amazement Clark observed that even the Albany *Argus* "had not . . . taken ground on this subject." This quip undoubtedly made Van Buren wince, for he was painfully aware of the Regency's disspirited response. After a brief flurry of activity, the House, by a vote of 120 to 107, agreed to Clark's resolution of postponement, thereby preventing any further consideration of the independent Treasury.[66]

It is not hard to determine the reason for this defeat in the House. Party discipline, normally impressive, broke down on the single question of the divorce bill. In spite of all the president's reassurances, his followers could not adjust to a fiscal proposal that asked them to protect the federal government but to do little for the states. Attendance was excellent during the special session; the average Democratic participation on roll calls was 87 percent. Analysis of the voting on thirty-one issues, including the divorce bill and a resolution to recharter a national bank, indicates that party members supported Cambreleng 90 percent of the time. Yet on the issue of the divorce bill, sixteen Democrats defected and seven abstained. Of the sixteen, six backed the party more than 75 percent of the time, and five voted with Cambreleng more than 50 percent of the time. Thus only five were outright deserters. Virginia's delegates created the most difficulty; five members out of fourteen abandoned Cambreleng on the independent Treasury proposal. Rives had done his work well. By contrast, Tallmadge's achievements were less impressive. Only one New York Democrat, out of a delegation of thirty, supported the Conservatives. Calhoun's heralded conversion had little effect on his fellow South Carolina congressmen. Not one supported the administration.[67]

As Congress adjourned and the legislators returned home for a brief vacation, Van Buren paused to assess the results of the special session. "I think I see my way quite clear through the difficulties that have beset my path," he wrote to a disappointed Andrew Jackson. "The Divorce Bill will pass at the next session, that is if I am right in believing that the people desire it."[68] Van Buren could take consolation in knowing that he had thwarted opposition efforts to recharter

[66] *Congressional Globe*, 25th Cong., 1st sess., 1837, 5: 140–41.

[67] These figures are based on analysis of Democratic voting on thirty-one recorded roll calls during the special session. There are omissions, but their inclusion would only increase the degree of party regularity. The source for party affiliation is the Washington *Globe*, August 25, 1837, as reprinted in the *United States Magazine and Democratic Review* 4 (1838): 61–69. I used Churchill Cambreleng as a model and compared all other Democrats to him.

[68] Van Buren to Jackson, October 17, 1837, Van Buren Papers.

a national bank.[69] He had also convinced Congress to provide for the temporary financial needs of the government.

Despite these rationalizations, the mood in Washington was hardly optimistic. Van Buren had gambled and lost. Compelled by the logic of circumstance and the dictates of previous Democratic policy, he had gone to the legislature in search of support, hopeful that his program would restore both national confidence and party harmony. He had come away emptyhanded. There was little reason to hope that Congress would be more receptive in the future. Instead of uniting the Democrats, the president's special session program divided them into warring camps and threatened to end their political control of the country.

[69] The British minister listed this as the most important accomplishment of the special session: Henry Fox to Lord Palmerston, October 20, 1837, PRO:FO: 5, Vol. 314, Pt. IV.

Chapter 6

Quest for Compromise

As soon as Congress adjourned, a sudden stillness settled over Washington. For the first time in more than six weeks, Capitol Hill was silent, the abandoned buildings warmed only by the heat of an Indian summer. Along Pennsylvania Avenue, departmental officers luxuriated in the calm, thankful for an opportunity to eliminate their backlog of paperwork. At the White House, the president summoned his cabinet to review the discouraging events of the past month.[1] Despite the legislature's recent rebuff, Van Buren had no intention of abandoning the independent Treasury; he had already risked too much in its behalf. This measure, more than any other, bore his personal imprint and showed his determination to meet the challenge raised by the Panic. He hoped that Congress would pass the divorce bill in December.[2] In planning for the coming campaign, the president seemed determined to appeal for compromise. Stunned by the Conservative revolt, he hoped to dispel the misunderstanding created by his proposals.

With this in mind, Secretary of the Treasury Levi Woodbury wrote to his friend Campbell P. White, a prominent New York banker, to explain the president's position. Woodbury argued that the administration had no intention of warring with state banks; both he and Van Buren had said so on several occasions. "How do you think the President or the Secretary of the Treasury ought to disclaim more distinctly than they did last September—that either of them was in favour of either an exclusive metallic currency or the suppression of all Banks?" "For God's sake," he implored, "give us the result of your own reflection on these points." White wasted little time in writing a reply. Such measures as those advanced at the special session were by their very nature "liable to be misinterpreted by our enemies and misunderstood by our friends"; he warned against giving the opposition similar ammunition in the future. After all, he said, "The divorce of Bank and State is a Manifesto from the highest authority in the Country proclaiming that the State Banks are unsafe as Depositories."[3] White's response typified the disagreement in Democratic ranks.

To complicate further the president's predicament, the Washington *Globe* now began attacking Democratic defectors, thereby hindering efforts at compromise. For most of the special session, Van Buren had managed to keep Blair in check. In editorials throughout September 1837 the vitriolic editor was remarkably tolerant, pointing out that an independent Treasury did not threaten the states. When he did lash out against the banks, he placed most of the blame on Nicholas Biddle.[4] Still, there were times when the *Globe* lapsed into its old style. At one point during the session Blair printed a statement that urged, "Let the people rally to *their own relief*—not to aid the banks in subduing the Government."[5] For many years Blair had been on the offensive, using his paper to champion the executive branch. Now he found it difficult to adjust to a new president, one whose methods were much more subtle.

The *Globe*'s treatment of the Conservatives provides the most startling evidence of Blair's restraint. Although Rives and Ritchie deviated dramatically from administration policy, Blair treated them leniently. To be sure, he took issue with Ritchie's objections to the divorce bill, but less than two weeks later he printed a dispassionate account of Rives's proposal to revive the deposit system. One White House visitor hinted that Blair was under presidential orders not to attack Virginia's Democrats.[6]

[1] Dickerson, MS Diary, October 16, 17, 1837.

[2] Van Buren to Jackson, October 17, 1837, Van Buren Papers; Levi Woodbury to Moses Dawson, October 30, 1837, Woodbury Papers.

[3] Woodbury to White, November 12, 19, 1837, White to Woodbury, November 21, 1837, Woodbury Papers. See also Gouverneur Kemble to Joel R. Poinsett, November 20, 1837, Poinsett Papers; Ransom Gillet to Francis P. Blair, November 25, 1837, Blair-Lee Papers.

[4] Washington *Globe*, September 9, 12, 16, 1837.

[5] Ibid., September 21, 1837.

[6] Ibid., September 9, 22, 1837; G. W. Gooch to William C. Rives, October 10, 1837, Rives Papers. On Van Buren's efforts to curb Blair's irresponsibility see Nathaniel Niles to William C. Rives, June 8, 1837, Rives Papers; Van Buren to Jackson, August 15, 1837, Van Buren Papers; Jackson to Blair, August 20, 1837, Jackson Papers; Memucan Hunt to R. A. Irion, August 4, 1836, in George P. Garrison, ed., "The Diplomatic Correspondence of the Republic of Texas," American Historical Association, *Annual Report for the Year 1907*, 2 vols. (Washington, D.C., 1908), 2: 246; hereafter cited as Garrison, *Texas Correspondence*.

Van Buren could not contain Blair for long. As the legislative debates wore on, and the damaging effects of the Conservative defection frustrated Democratic plans, Blair became incensed. Late one evening, near the end of the session, he sat writing to Jackson, pouring out venom in an all but illegible scrawl. "There is treachery in the man," said Blair of William C. Rives, "and . . . it has been brooding in him for more than a year past." "He may be trusted, as you trusted the Pirates at New Orleans." Blair believed it only a matter of time before Rives would "go over to the enemy . . . and abandon the Republicans forever."

This private catharsis presaged a violent attack on the Conservatives. In a stinging editorial, the *Globe* predicted that all these wavering Democrats would soon desert to the opposition; as far as Blair was concerned it was good riddance. Not content to rest his case here, he struck out against state banks, insisting that these avaricious corporations had no right to prey off public revenue. Blair warned that Americans would "hazard a dangerous issue if they adhere to a political league to establish a bank oligarchy in this country."[7] This outburst clearly shows that Blair and Van Buren were working at cross-purposes. While the *Globe* set upon state banks, the president searched for a way to appease the Conservatives.

The confusion of administration aims came at an unpropitious moment. By early November 1837, New York Democrats were fighting to preserve their hold on state offices. The Panic dealt a serious blow to the Regency by raising doubts about previous fiscal strategy. The success of Marcy's economic policy depended in part upon the actions of the national government. Washington would do incalculable damage if it undermined confidence in the governor's program of leniency. Van Buren realized this and tried to point out that an independent Treasury would not endanger local banks. As if to prove his good will, he proposed very moderate terms for the settlement of accounts with former government depositories. In short, the president hoped to avoid making his program an issue in state politics.

Despite the best of intentions, there was really no way for Van Buren to confine debate on an independent Treasury to a national forum. By taking a firm stand on separating bank from state and by asking the press to aid him in Congress, the president courted disaster. The very nature of the divorce bill made it a local as well as

---

[7] Blair to Jackson, October 13, 1837, Jackson Papers; Washington *Globe*, November 1, 1837. See also Washington *Globe*, October 21, 24, 26, 27, November 4, 11, 14, 21, 1837; Reuben Whitney to William C. Rives, October 29, 1837, Rives Papers; *The Madisonian*, November 3, 1837.

a national question. Although ostensibly encompassing only federal funds, the independent Treasury scheme implied that previous arrangements for keeping public revenue had failed—that state banks were unsafe. How could the states themselves ignore this imputation? In 1832, the Democrats had willingly accepted the bank veto because it benefited local corporations. Such acquiescence was simply not possible in 1837. There was no way to portray the divorce bill as a boon to the states. Blair committed the unpardonable sin of making this obvious for all to see.

The results of the New York elections in November 1837 demonstrated the impact of the Panic on New York politics. The Whigs scored a resounding victory, gaining sixty-seven seats in the assembly to assume a clear majority. Democrats retained control of the senate only because so few members stood for reelection. The only glimmer of hope came from New York City, where Tammany Hall and the leaders of the equal rights (Loco Foco) movement reconciled long-standing differences and joined in support of Van Buren's fiscal program. Still, the new allies were unable to deny the Whigs control of the city. As Marcy pointed out, the Loco Foco party, with its radical notions about capitalism and finance, was at best a "mischievous partner." Its endorsement of the independent Treasury made it difficult for Van Buren to portray his project as consistent with traditional Democratic principles.[8]

In the process of evaluating the debacle, New York's Democratic leaders came to the unanimous conclusion that Blair had irresponsibly maligned state banks. The former governor, Enos T. Throop, charged the *Globe* with quoting nonexistent passages from the special session message and claimed that it would be "impossible for our party to rise again" so long as Blair retained presidential favor. After conversations with Regency spokesmen, Silas Wright remarked, "The first thing to be done is to reform the Globe, by a change of both *name* & editor."[9]

The accusations of a single paper certainly did not bring about the Democratic downfall in New York. The Whigs won because Van Buren's followers could not resolve their differences and bore the

[8] Marcy to Prosper M. Wetmore, November 9, 1837, Marcy Papers. Leo J. Hershkowitz, "New York City, 1834–1840, A Study in Local Politics" (Ph.D. diss., New York University, 1960), traces the political fortunes of the Loco Foco party. On the fall election in 1837 see Jabez D. Hammond, *The History of Political Parties in the State of New York*, 2 vols. (Albany, N.Y., 1842), 2: 478–79.

[9] Throop to Van Buren, November 23, 1837, Benjamin F. Butler to Van Buren, November 28, 1837, Van Buren Papers.

stigma of the Panic. The controversy over Blair's editorials does reveal one salient aspect of the defeat—the deterioration of communications between Albany and Washington. Doubt and suspicion had replaced reason and understanding.

A similar spirit of despair prevailed in Virginia. Richard E. Parker wrote that Blair's denigration of the Conservatives made accommodation all but impossible. The editor must proceed with "the greatest prudence and caution in conducting a paper which is supposed to speak the sentiments of the executive." To combat the effects of the *Globe*'s pernicious editorials, Parker requested that he be employed as a personal emissary to convince members of the Virginia state legislature that Van Buren was willing to compromise. Parker added that a moderate annual message would certainly improve the situation.[10]

Parker's pleas and the stunning reversal in New York only increased Van Buren's determination to seek a compromise. On December 5, 1837, he sent his first annual message to the newly convened Twenty-fifth Congress. Deftly picking his way through the tangled financial issues of the day, Van Buren came quickly to the point. He saw no need to dwell on the alternate methods of collecting and disbursing the public revenue; on these he had been quite specific at the special session. Instead, he reasserted his faith in an independent Treasury and asked for congressional support. Having made his recommendations, he tried to appeal to the Conservatives by speaking kindly of state banking interests. Properly regulated, banks were "highly useful to the business of the country." This did not mean, however, that the federal government should manage them in any way. The connection between the public treasure and private corporations had been disastrous to both. Congress could best serve the banks and the nation by severing these ties and removing federal revenue as a stimulant to reckless speculation.

The president did more than sound a few friendly notes. After acknowledging the diversity of opinion prevalent at the previous session, he stated plainly that he would acquiesce, should Congress agree on a different mode of keeping public funds. By this, Van Buren did not mean to imply that he would sanction a recharter of a national bank. Rather, he suggested the possibility of keeping some money in state banks on "special deposit." Thomas Ritchie had first mentioned this plan in September as a means of ending the congres-

[10] Parker to Van Buren, November 14, 27, 1837, Van Buren to Parker, November 16 [?], 1837, Van Buren Papers.

sional impasse.[11] According to the Virginia editor, the Treasury could deposit funds in state banks in the government's account. The banks themselves would be prohibited from using this money as a basis for note issue. The administration could thus retain its ties with the states, but it would not contribute its funds to careless expansion of credit. Ritchie's ideas, although politically attractive, were not economically sound. There would be little incentive for the banks to store revenue they could not use.[12] Furthermore, the scheme entirely ignored the crucial question of whether the government should accept the notes of specie-paying banks.

In his attempts to please the Conservatives, the president made mention of special deposits but never as an alternative to the independent Treasury. Whereas Ritchie thought in terms of placing *all* government funds with the state banks, thereby resurrecting the defunct deposit act of 1836, Van Buren merely spoke of making "a temporary use of the State banks in *particular places* for the safe-keeping of portions of the revenue." The secretary of the treasury made this distinction even more explicit in his annual report on the nation's finances. Speaking of the recommended divorce of bank and state, he observed that "This change might judiciously *include* an authority to employ separate depositories, special or general, individual or corporate . . . if the amount in possession of any collecting officer *should generally exceed* what is well secured by official bonds."[13]

A masterful political document, Van Buren's message elicited praise from all segments of the party. Those who looked to the White House for strength and conviction were comforted by the president's reaffirmation of faith in an independent Treasury. New York's embattled Democrats greeted the president's pronouncements with unfeigned pleasure. "The age of reason is coming back again," commented Prosper M. Wetmore. Governor Marcy agreed and wrote Van Buren that the annual message far excelled its predecessor. A former Regency chieftain, Enos T. Throop, welcomed what he considered an end to the war on state banks. Even the Albany *Argus* broke a long silence to endorse the administration's stand; Croswell

---

[11] Richardson, *Messages and Papers*, 3: 379–82; Ritchie to William C. Rives, September 20, 1837, Ritchie to Thomas Green, September 20, 1837, in *Branch Historical Papers*, 3: 224–25, 4: 383–84.

[12] Albert Gallatin to William C. Rives, November 25, 1837, Gallatin Papers, New York Historical Society.

[13] Richardson, *Messages and Papers*, 3: 382; *House Documents* (No. 4), 25th Cong., 2d sess., 1837–1838, p. 16. Italics mine.

spoke glowingly of Van Buren's "deference for the opinion of others." In Virginia, readers of the influential Richmond *Enquirer* found to their surprise that Ritchie subscribed wholeheartedly to the principles of the annual report, applauding Van Buren's moderate tone and conciliatory language. Encouraged by the president's statements, the Conservatives in Congress seized upon special deposits as the middle course.[14] Van Buren had won the first battle; he had convinced the dissident elements of the party that he was amenable to compromise. Whether he could translate this spirit into effective legislation remained to be seen.

Wright, Cambreleng, and Polk faced more serious difficulties in December than they had in the fall. At the special session the aura of crisis had aided efforts to pass the presidential program. Van Buren had argued effectively that the government needed immediate assistance to escape financial chaos. His lieutenants, acting under specific instructions, had moved swiftly to present necessary legislation. There was no such urgency when Congress reconvened. Wright and Cambreleng now proceeded more cautiously, trying to anticipate the objections of their colleagues before making final legislative preparations. The New York senator went out of his way to seek advice on various sections of the divorce bill.[15] Owing to these deliberate precautions, there was a considerable delay between the submission of Van Buren's message and the introduction of the plan for an independent Treasury.

Congress did not remain idle in the interim. In September, both houses had silenced antislavery agitation on the grounds that it had little to do with the business of the special session. This ban proved ineffective three months later, when congressmen returned to Washington laden with bundles of memorials and petitions from their constituents. In the House, John Quincy Adams aimed a barrage at the administration, charging that the president sought war with Mexico to augment the power of the slave states. Congress had grown accustomed to the perennial outbursts of the elder statesman

---

[14] Washington *Globe*, December 6, 1837; Jackson to Francis P. Blair, December 14, 1837, Jackson Papers; Jackson to Van Buren, December 18, 1837, Marcy to Van Buren, December 8, 1837, Throop to Van Buren, December 6, 1837, Van Buren Papers; Wetmore to Marcy, December 6, 1837, Gratz Collection; John Niles to Gideon Welles, December 16, 1837, Welles Papers; James K. Polk to Andrew J. Donelson, December 12, 1837, Donelson Papers; William C. Preston to John Tyler, December 30, 1837, Tyler Papers, Library of Congress; Albany *Argus*, December 8, 1837; Richmond *Enquirer*, December 8, 1837.

[15] Wright to James Buchanan, December 29, 1837, Buchanan Papers, The Historical Society of Pennsylvania.

from Massachusetts, but it had not anticipated the sudden maneuvers of Senator John C. Calhoun. In response to the introduction of petitions by Vermont's Benjamin Swift, Calhoun decided to ask the Senate to put itself on record as upholding the interests of the South. Although Van Buren had already made extensive promises in his inaugural, these assurances failed to calm Calhoun's fears.

On December 27, 1837, Calhoun rose and asked his colleagues to approve six resolutions concerning slavery and the Constitution. In the first two, he merely expounded on the compact theory of government and on the idea of the states having jurisdiction "over their own domestic institutions." Neither resolution occasioned much controversy, and each passed on January 3, 1838, by sizable majorities.[16] In the third, he held that it was the duty of the government "to give, as far as may be practicable, increased stability and security to the domestic institutions of the States." The Senate refused to make such broad commitments; three days later, by a vote of thirty-one to eleven, it passed a modified version providing that the government is "bound so to exercise its powers, so as not to interfere with the stability and security of the domestic institutions of the States."[17] By agreeing to the fourth resolution, defining Southern interests, the Senate merely recognized slavery as a peculiar institution. So far, Calhoun had succeeded in gaining approval for some debatable, but not highly controversial, ideas.

During the following week, Calhoun's critics attacked the remaining two resolutions. Originally, the Nullifier had hoped to brand any interference with slavery in the territories or in the District of Columbia as "a direct and dangerous attack on the institutions of all the slaveholding States." James Buchanan and Henry Clay persuaded the Senate to pass a milder substitute stating that any interference would be "a just cause for alarm" and would tend "to disturb and endanger the Union." Finally, Calhoun wanted to censure those who would use antislavery arguments to oppose extension of the territories. The Senate tabled this resolution and later refused assent to a similar measure by William C. Preston.[18]

For more than two weeks, Calhoun occupied the Senate's time with his proposals. Administration spokesmen regretted the delay. "Our new ally Calhoun is rather a dangerous man," complained

[16] The vote on the first was thirty-one to thirteen and on the second, thirty-one to nine; *Congressional Globe*, 25th Cong., 2d sess., 1837–1838, 6: 74.

[17] For a comparison of the two texts see the resolutions as originally introduced and as finally passed: ibid., pp. 55, 98.

[18] Ibid., pp. 96, 98, 453.

Connecticut's John Niles. "He has drawn us into an abolition debate unnecessarily & which can do no good & may do harm." Calhoun was only partially successful in his quest for Senate sanction. His colleagues passed four of the original six resolutions and significantly modified the third and most important of these. That the Nullifier drew administration support for his efforts does not indicate that he had suddenly assumed a position of dominance in the party. Very few senators opposed Calhoun; they apparently wanted to end the fruitless debate as soon as possible. Even Calhoun's archenemy, Henry Clay, voted in favor of these resolves.[19]

With Congress preoccupied by the sectional debate, Van Buren tried to capitalize on the enthusiastic state response to his annual message. He hoped that local leaders now saw the necessity of endorsing administration policy. To his dismay, the spirit of accord, so prevalent in early December, suddenly vanished. Francis P. Blair was in part to blame. On the day after submission of the annual message, the Washington *Globe* assumed the task of interpreting the president's intentions. Blair wrote that Van Buren's willingness to abide by a congressional decision in no way amounted to sanction of a national bank. Not content to belabor the obvious, Blair went on to say that any "revival of the late connection with the State banks [is] entirely out of the question, not only with the PRESIDENT, but with Congress too."[20] Thus in a few strokes of the pen, he completely undercut all Van Buren's emphasis on the special deposit scheme.

The president's efforts to reestablish good relations with key state organizations failed because each side expected too much of the other. In Virginia, Thomas Ritchie was under attack from the Conservatives, who strongly supported Governor David Campbell's praise for state banks and criticism of administration policy. Ritchie reluctantly approved the governor's annual message but continued to trumpet special deposits as the only means of uniting the badly

---

[19] Niles to Gideon Welles, January 6, 11, 1838, Welles Papers. See also Felix Grundy to A. J. Donelson, January 18, 1838, Donelson Papers. For a different view of these proceedings see Charles M. Wiltse, *John C. Calhoun*, 3 vols. (Indianapolis, Ind., 1944–1951), 2: 369–76. Wiltse contends that Calhoun had the dominant position in the Democratic party and implies that he forced the administration to back these resolutions. Wiltse goes on to say that the Democrats' surrender on these issues indicated their willingness to follow Calhoun on financial questions. Wiltse makes a mistake in trying to use voting behavior on a nonparty issue to prove Calhoun's dominance in the Democratic ranks. He also sees the passage of these resolutions as a victory for Calhoun. Wiltse ignores the amendments and significant changes that seriously weakened Calhoun's propositions.

[20] Washington *Globe*, December 6, 8, 12, 1837.

splintered Democratic party. Ritchie seemed to think that Van Buren would, if necessary, abandon the independent Treasury in favor of such a compromise solution. Although the president welcomed all efforts at conciliation, he had risked too much on behalf of the divorce bill to discard it in favor of a plan that again gave all public funds to the states. Van Buren's quiet quarrel with Ritchie weakened Democratic strength in the Old Dominion. "We are suffering for want of an able and spirited press," moaned Virginia's Peter V. Daniel, "and yet I see no early remedy for this evil."[21]

Similar misunderstanding continued to plague Van Buren's relations with the Albany Regency. Although cheered by the conciliatory annual message, Governor Marcy worried about the effect of administration policy on New York politics. He dreaded preparing his own annual report, knowing that he must pass judgment on Van Buren's program. On January 2, 1838, the governor transmitted to the state legislature a document that clearly reflected his own indecision. He seemed torn between a desire to defend state banks and to acknowledge the worth of Van Buren's recommendations, and ended by doing both. After a cursory glance at the background of the Panic, Marcy turned to the question of whether the banks should bear responsibility for the financial crisis. He reproved those guilty of negligent and improvident management, but carefully pointed out that banks themselves were "indispensable to our prosperity." Marcy admitted that the speculative urge contributed to their undoing, but held that the banks only failed when forced to comply with the provisions of the deposit act of 1836. He then justified his own decision in obtaining a moratorium for defaulting institutions and urged a speedy resumption of specie payments.

Finally, after this lengthy discourse, the governor mentioned administration plans, confining his remarks to a single paragraph. He agreed that the general government had every right to collect and disburse its own funds. As to the specific mode of operation, Marcy was purposely vague, saying that either a sub-Treasury or a modified deposit system would be satisfactory. Before leaving this subject, he added the hope that whatever Congress enacted would "be of such character as will not affect injuriously the business concerns or the banking institutions of the country." Relieved at finally being rid of

[21] Peter V. Daniel to Van Buren, January 23, 1838, Van Buren Papers; Richmond *Enquirer*, January 25, 30, 1838; Howard Braverman, "The Economic and Political Background of the Conservative Revolt in Virginia," *Virginia Magazine of History and Biography* 60 (1952): 279–81.

this burden, Marcy commented that his message was but the "poor offspring of a reluctant mind."[22]

Washington detected none of this reticence; administration leaders lavishly praised Marcy's statements. The *Globe* regarded the message as a full and unqualified defense of the sub-Treasury. In a private note, Van Buren wrote that the document had "been received . . . with delight by all sincere democrats." Marcy was aghast at this response. Ignoring all portions of the message dealing with state banks, Van Buren and his advisers had singled out those few phrases that lent support to their cause. Marcy ruefully noted this misinterpretation. "The friends of the Genl. administration at Washington give me credit for a pretty full endorsement of the President. I meant to hang over the precipice but do not think I have plunged down it." He wished that the idea of a divorce of bank and state had never entered the president's mind. The proposal was ill-timed and would be held "responsible for all actual & imaginary evils."[23]

Thus, in the short space of six weeks, communications between Albany and Washington seriously deteriorated. Van Buren felt that Marcy's response to the annual report indicated the governor's willingness to take a positive stand on the most crucial of national issues. When Marcy spoke indulgently of the sub-Treasury, the president saw this as a vital endorsement. At the same time, Washington's insensitivity to New York's problems enabled the administration to misconstrue the governor's statements. Had Van Buren listened in the past to Marcy's protests, instead of dismissing them as irrelevant to national policy, he might have appreciated the real ambiguity of the governor's message.

Ignoring the plight of state leaders, Van Buren turned his attention to Congress, where Democratic forces were finally ready to consider his recommendations. In the Senate, Silas Wright quietly set about soliciting Conservative votes for the divorce bill. He thought that by including a section on special deposits, he could enlist the aid of Democratic dissidents and appease those who complained of a total economic separation between the government and the states. Wright went so far as to show drafts of his bill to William C. Rives, but he found the Virginia senator in no mood for

[22] State of New York, *Messages from the Governors*, ed. Charles Z. Lincoln, 11 vols. (Albany, N.Y., 1909), 3: 654–66; Marcy to Wetmore, December 7, 22, 31, 1837, Marcy Papers.
[23] Washington *Globe*, January 10, 1838; Marcy to Prosper M. Wetmore, January 22, 1838, Marcy Papers.

compromise. After private researches of his own, Rives was convinced that Ritchie's proposals were foolhardy. Despite this disappointment, Wright decided to retain the special deposit clause.[24]

On January 16, 1838, the New York senator introduced the independent Treasury bill. In principle, it differed little from its predecessor; the government would still collect and disburse its own funds. As a result of Calhoun's efforts, the bill now included a specie clause. Substantively, the new measure reflected the arguments and debates of the previous four months and had much less the appearance of emergency legislation. At the special session, the administration had tried in vain to sell its plan as a simple continuation of existing machinery. As a consequence, the president decided to incorporate those features that he formerly shunned for political reasons. First, he asked Congress to appoint new officials designated as "receivers general of public money." The president was apparently less worried about the problem of enlarging executive patronage. Second, Van Buren wanted four new agencies at St. Louis, Charleston, New York, and Boston. These, plus the Treasury at Washington and the Mint, would act as "sub-Treasuries," to receive and store funds transferred from the various collecting officers. This new structure would provide more safety and efficiency. In essence, the president now endorsed the more complicated plan outlined by Woodbury at the special session. Third, to offset criticism that an independent Treasury would create unproductive stockpiles of specie, Van Buren included a stipulation that the government should invest all surplus funds in excess of $4 million.

The most significant new feature of Wright's bill was the section on special deposits. Although Rives had displayed little enthusiasm for this idea, other Conservatives appeared more receptive. Richard Parker wrote that a large majority in Virginia's state legislature favored a combination of state banks and sub-Treasuries. According to Parker, the administration could still have its cherished divorce, so long as it made some provision for recognizing local interests.[25] Wright took these suggestions to heart; the twelfth section of the bill authorized the use of certain local banks to handle excessive accumulations of revenue. This did not meet all the demands of the Conservatives, since it applied only to a small portion of government funds.

[24] John Niles to Gideon Welles, January 6, 1838, Welles Papers; Albert Gallatin to Rives, November 25, 1837, Gallatin Papers.

[25] *Congressional Globe*, 25th Cong., 2d sess., 1837–1838, 6: 110–12; Parker to James Buchanan, January [?], 1838, Buchanan Papers, The Historical Society of Pennsylvania.

Still, Wright obviously hoped this provision would serve as a basis for bargaining. He was convinced that the bill must "pass in some form." Thomas Ritchie approved of Wright's efforts and told Rives, "The interest of the party depends upon your course. If you determine against that measure decidedly, I do not entertain the slightest hope that the party can be kept together."[26]

Rives refused to budge. He was not impressed by Ritchie's urgings nor by Wright's efforts at conciliation. Rather than negotiate on Van Buren's terms, Rives introduced his own substitute bill on February 2, 1838, thereby seriously diminishing chances for mediation. This measure authorized selection of twenty-five state banks as depositories for all government funds. In support of this legislation, Rives delivered a blistering attack on the administration, castigating the sub-Treasury bill and reiterating many of the arguments he had employed at the special session. He added one new twist, by charging Van Buren with desiring establishment of a "government bank." In September, Rives had complained that the president was abdicating his responsibility to control the economy. Now he contended that "the system organized by this bill is one of the most thorough centralization." Obviously, the Virginia senator had come to appreciate the potency of antibank rhetoric. Connecticut's John Niles thought the speech "a forced attempt to raise bugbears & scarecrows not fit to frighten old women & children."[27]

Before acting on either Wright's bill or Rives's substitute, the Senate fell into another bitter sectional debate. By now, Van Buren was beginning to realize that his ally from South Carolina was more a source of irritation than of strength. A veteran of numerous congressional battles, Calhoun proved a favorite target for the opposition, especially in view of his recent "conversion" to the Democratic cause. On February 15, 1838, he made a spirited defense of administration fiscal policy; four days later Henry Clay rose to reply. After a brief rebuttal of Calhoun's financial views, Clay launched into a brilliant philippic, assailing the Nullifier's past record and gleefully enumerating his inconsistencies. To Thomas Hart Benton, "The storm had been gathering since September," and "it burst in February." Calhoun retired to prepare himself for counterattack, reportedly by reading Demosthenes' *Oration on the Crown*. While Calhoun was in

[26] *Congressional Globe*, 25th Cong., 2d sess., 1837–1838, 6: 110; John Niles to Gideon Welles, January 30, 1838, Welles Papers; Ritchie to Rives, January 18 [?], 1838, Rives Papers.
[27] *Congressional Globe*, 25th Cong., 2d sess., 1837–1838, 6: 156–57, Appendix, 608–11; Niles to Gideon Welles, February 5, 1838, Welles Papers.

seclusion, the duel between Congressmen William Graves and Jonathan Cilley further increased tensions in the legislature. The confusion had not subsided when Calhoun responded to Clay. Before packed galleries, he delivered a magnificent speech that drew admiration from friend and foe alike.

Nothing could provide more excitement to a weary Congress than a battle between the giants. Debate on financial measures had grown sterile; as James Buchanan observed, "speakers generally now address empty chairs."[28] Clay and Calhoun relieved some of this tedium, and when Webster entered the fray, the cast was complete. For more than three weeks the atmosphere in the Senate chamber rang with the sounds of spirited oratory. Always at his best in defense of personal honor and prestige, Calhoun was in his element. Unfortunately for the Democrats, the Nullifier exhausted himself in this personal crusade. The titanic struggle subsided as quickly as it began, and the Senate somewhat reluctantly turned to more routine matters.

Not until the middle of March 1838 did debate resume on the sub-Treasury bill. On March 21 the Senate rejected Rives's substitute by a vote of twenty-nine to twenty. There were no surprises on the roll call; only three Democrats defected.[29] Although they defeated the Conservatives' project, Wright and his followers were not optimistic about chances for final passage of the sub-Treasury bill. Their fourteen vote majority was misleading; at least five Democrats would oppose the measure in any form. Both James Buchanan and Felix Grundy felt obliged to vote against the party because of instructions from their state legislatures. Neither wished to run the political risk of violating these dictates.[30] In addition, John Tipton (Indiana), Robert C. Nicholas (Louisiana), and John Ruggles (Maine) had

[28] Buchanan to Edward Buchanan, March 2, 1838, Buchanan Papers, The Historical Society of Pennsylvania. For accounts of this debate see Thomas Hart Benton, *Thirty Years View*, 2 vols. (New York, 1854–1856), 2: 97–101; Adams, *Diary*, 9: 505–506; Wiltse, *Calhoun*, 2: 378–84.

[29] *Congressional Globe*, 25th Cong., 2d sess., 1837–1838, 6: 250. These figures are based on the calculations of party strength published in the *United States Magazine and Democratic Review* 4 (1839): 174–76. This tabulation lists Rives and Tallmadge as members of the opposition and classifies Calhoun as an administration supporter.

[30] James Walker to James K. Polk, January 25, 1838, Polk to A. O. P. Nicholson, January 13, 1838, Polk Papers; John M. Niles to Gideon Welles, January 26, 1838, Welles Papers; A. M. Peltz to Buchanan, February 20, 1838, Buchanan Papers, The Historical Society of Pennsylvania; D. A. Smith to Nicholas Biddle, January 28, 1838, Biddle to Henry Clay, February 3, 1838, Clay to Biddle, February 5, 6, 20, 1838, C. S. Barker to Biddle, February 7, 8, 9, 14, 16, 1838, in Biddle, *Correspondence*, pp. 298–305.

previously indicated their support for the Conservatives.[31] The votes of Thomas Morris (Ohio) and Alfred Cuthbert (Georgia) were also questionable; each felt the bill required modification.[32] The defection of these seven Democrats would deadlock the issue. Van Buren anticipated such a situation and mentioned to Jackson that the vote of the vice president might well decide the fate of the sub-Treasury.[33]

Further confusion came on March 21, when one of the doubtful Democrats, Alfred Cuthbert, moved to strike out Calhoun's specie clause. Felix Grundy maneuvered the Senate into executive session, thereby giving the administration a chance to plan its next move. Van Buren now faced a dilemma. He preferred the bill with the specie clause, but the vote would be close. By striking the clause, he might well gain the support of Morris and Cuthbert. What went on in the next three days is unclear. On March 24 Cuthbert renewed his motion, and by a vote of thirty-one to twenty-one, the Senate deleted the specie provision from the sub-Treasury bill. Wright and Benton firmly supported Calhoun, but twelve other Democrats did not. What efforts, if any, these two stalwarts made to maintain discipline remains a mystery.

If administration spokesmen did give tacit agreement to the elimination of Calhoun's measure, they did so for only one reason—to pass the sub-Treasury bill.[34] At the beginning of the session, the president did not expect trouble in the Senate. He never anticipated the instructions from Tennessee, Ohio, and Pennsylvania.[35] Once he

[31] Nicholas and Tipton had both voted against the divorce bill at the special session, and Ruggles had abstained. Each eventually supported Rives's substitute bill; see *Congressional Globe*, 25th Cong., 1st sess., 1837, 5: 100; 25th Cong., 2d sess., 1837–1838, 6: 250.

[32] John Niles to Gideon Welles, January 26, 1838, March 23 [?], 1838, Welles Papers. Morris and Allen were acting under instructions from the state legislature in Ohio. The instructions were not binding: *Senate Documents* (No. 184), 25th Cong., 2d sess., 1837–1838.

[33] Van Buren to Jackson, March 17, 1838, Van Buren Papers.

[34] *Congressional Globe*, 25th Cong., 2d sess., 1837–1838, 5: 250–51, 259. John M. McFaul, "The Politics of Jacksonian Finance" (Ph.D. diss., University of California, Berkeley, 1964), pp. 199–200, suggests that Van Buren allowed striking of the clause for at least one, and possibly two, reasons. First, the bill without the clause would give the secretary of the treasury more control over state banks. There is little evidence to support this theory. If this had been the administration's true intent, they would have proposed a bill without a specie clause and then defeated Calhoun's attempt at amendment. Second, McFaul suggests that Van Buren may have been trying to weaken Calhoun's influence. This is a more attractive thesis but presumes that the president had an ample majority for such maneuvering.

[35] Tennessee passed instructions on January 23, 1838. Ohio approved its instructions on February 2, 1838, and Pennsylvania followed suit on February 16, 1838; *Senate Documents* (Nos. 170, 184, 210), 25th Cong., 2d sess., 1837–1838.

saw that Grundy, Buchanan, and Morris might defect, he began to worry and may have changed his mind about the wisdom of clinging to a clause that alienated so many senators. The president's primary aim was to pass Wright's bill; all other considerations were secondary. It is conceivable that to attain his objective, he allowed Democrats to undercut Calhoun.[36]

Whatever the reason for the Senate's actions on Cuthbert's motion, the president was not prepared for the developments of the next few days. With the objectionable hard money clause removed, Morris and Cuthbert rejoined the Democratic fold, giving the administration a sufficient majority. On March 26, 1838, the Senate passed the bill, twenty-seven to twenty-five. Upset at the loss of the specie clause, Calhoun voted with the opposition. Democratic leaders were astounded. To them the primary task was to enact the president's program. If this required compromise—so be it. Connecticut's John Niles bluntly summed up the party's discouragement and disgust. "The course of Calhoun has been unwise & foolish in the extreme, both as regards himself & the object he professes to have in view. His course will have the most injurious effect on himself, to say nothing about the gross apparent inconsistency of his conduct. It can hardly fail of making a general impression that no party can make any dependence on him."[37] When Calhoun deserted, Van Buren became concerned about the fate of the sub-Treasury in the House. According to James K. Polk, the Nullifier's actions would result in the loss of crucial Southern votes. In an attempt to prevent this from happening, the Democrats decided to push for passage of the bill originally reported to the House by the Ways and Means Committee. This version contained a specie clause. If the House defeated it, the administration would bring up the bill already approved by the Senate. As Polk exclaimed, "We must if possible pass some bill." The party could always resolve minor conflicts at a later date.[38]

Conditions in the House in the spring of 1838 were far different from those of the previous fall. At the special session the atmosphere was quite favorable. Deliberations promised to be short; there was little to distract the legislators from the pressing financial problems.

[36] Of course the converse may be true. Cuthbert's motion may have caught everyone by surprise, and the defeat of Calhoun's clause may have been purely accidental.

[37] *Congressional Globe*, 25th Cong., 2d sess., 1837–1838, 6: 264; Niles to Gideon Welles, March 26, 1838, Welles Papers.

[38] Polk to A. J. Donelson, March 26, 1838, Donelson Papers; Polk to Jackson, April 3, 1838, Jackson Papers; Silas Wright to Azariah Flagg, March 25, 1838, Flagg-Wright Papers.

The president had presented his recommendations in a clear and forthright manner, and the congressional committees moved quickly to bring bills to the floor for action. At the regular session, little of this efficiency prevailed. Congress now faced the normal flood of minor legislative problems and also had to deal with the threat of hostilities along the Canadian border. Antislavery agitation again disrupted proceedings, as did the torrent of antidueling petitions arising from the Graves-Cilley affair. John Quincy Adams thought "the session of Congress has already been long, and is growing tedious I believe to all the members." As debate dragged on, patience wore thin and tempers flared. Occasionally, discipline broke down altogether. "Yesterday there was an old fashioned *fist-fight* in the H. of R.," wrote William C. Rives. "This sort of thing has, of late, been so often exhibited on that theatre, that the occurrence does not seem to strike anyone here as out of the ordinary course."[39]

Amidst such confusion, Polk and his colleagues struggled to maintain order. At no time during the next three months were they ever confident of success. Although Polk believed that a majority favored the principle of separating bank from state, he feared that it might be impossible to reach agreement on specific details. Calhoun's crusade on behalf of the specie clause had complicated matters immensely. Since the vote promised to be close, Polk wanted to make sure that he had as much strength as possible. The Speaker of the House thought it best to wait, rather than press for immediate passage. A dispute over election results in Mississippi necessitated a new canvass; both seats involved administration supporters. Since there were three other temporary openings in Democratic districts, Polk hoped to gain as many as five affirmative votes.[40]

During this delay, Van Buren made another overture to the Richmond Junto. The *Enquirer* had recently disavowed Rives's congressional strategy and the president saw an opportunity to repair relations with the Old Dominion. In April 1838 Benjamin F. Butler formally announced his decision to retire from the cabinet.[41] Since Virginia had always complained that it deserved more national recog-

[39] Adams to Rev. William P. Lunt, June 7, 1838, MS Letterbook (1838), Adams Family Papers; *National Intelligencer*, May 5, 1838; Rives to Mrs. Rives, June 2, 1838, Rives Papers.
[40] Polk to Jackson, April 3, 1838, Jackson Papers; Polk to Andrew J. Donelson, April 22, June 11, 1838, Donelson Papers.
[41] Richmond *Enquirer*, February 6, 1838; Richard E. Parker to Van Buren, January 18, April 10, 1838, Butler to Van Buren, April 11, 1838, Van Buren to Jackson, April 15, 1838, Van Buren Papers; Van Buren to Butler, April 11, 1838, Butler Papers.

nition, the president decided to offer the vacant post to Ritchie's brother-in-law Richard E. Parker, a prominent lawyer and fervent advocate of administration fiscal policy. Although Van Buren had reason to believe that Parker would refuse, the request itself might prove politically advantageous. The president told Parker to feel free to show the bid to Ritchie. Parker subsequently declined, but the proposition helped convince Ritchie that the president still wanted to unite Virginia's Democrats.[42]

This reassurance came none too soon. The Whigs had just scored a stunning upset in the spring elections and threatened to dominate the next session of the legislature. In reaction to this setback, the Richmond *Enquirer* urged all Democrats to lay aside their differences and join in opposing the common enemy. Van Buren read this editorial with obvious delight, stating that although "Mr. Ritchie has done us much harm . . . he has entered upon a new campaign with great spirit." "I am confident," the president continued, that he "will do all in his power to recover the ground we have lost." As an afterthought, Van Buren observed that this ground "might easily have been retained had the Enquirer cooperated with us."[43]

Enthusiastic over Ritchie's apparent conversion, Van Buren now hoped that the editor would be of some assistance in convincing Congress to pass the sub-Treasury bill. Ritchie, on the other hand, believed that the long period of legislative inactivity meant that Van Buren had given up any plans for pressing the measure in the House. When this assumption later proved to be incorrect, Ritchie repeated all his objections to an independent Treasury and again brought forward his special deposit scheme as a compromise solution.[44] It was now obvious that Van Buren and Ritchie could not agree on financial matters. Each still hoped to convert the other, but neither expected to succeed. Ritchie approved of every aspect of administration policy save the most important one—the sub-Treasury. Van Buren maintained a courteous silence but undoubtedly shared the views of John Brockenbrough, who maintained that "our friend of

---

[42] Van Buren to Parker, April 29 [?], 1838 (misfiled under March 1837), Parker to Van Buren, April 10, May 2, 1838, Van Buren Papers; Parker to James Buchanan, April 21, 1838, Buchanan Papers, The Historical Society of Pennsylvania.

[43] Richmond *Enquirer*, May 4, 1838; Van Buren to Andrew Stevenson, May 16, 1838, Stevenson Papers. See also Levi Woodbury to George Bancroft, May 8, 1838, Woodbury Papers; Peter V. Daniel to Van Buren, May 23, 1838, Van Buren Papers.

[44] Ritchie to Rives, June 5, July 4, 1838, Rives Papers; Ritchie to Van Buren, July 2, 1838, Van Buren Papers; Richmond *Enquirer*, June 5, 15, 1838.

the *Enquirer* has . . . done infinite mischief to our party by the middle course he has taken."[45]

The decision to allow the sub-Treasury bill to lie idle in the House caused difficulties. In May 1838 the New York banks resumed specie payments, prompting other institutions across the country to follow suit over the next six months. This action created as many problems as it solved. The government had always favored resumption and welcomed the opportunity to recover some of its funds.[46] As of January 1, 1838, Woodbury calculated that out of a balance of thirty-six million dollars credited to the Treasury, only a million "was immediately available for general purposes." The rest had all but disappeared when the banks closed their doors in May 1837. Legislation at the special session had provided for return of this money, but the process had thus far been painfully slow. The administration was so unsure of income that it had to ask for another issue of Treasury notes.[47] Furthermore, a renewal of specie payments disproved the Conservatives' claim that Van Buren had fatally damaged state interests. Yet at the same time, this fiscal turnabout was bound to raise anew the cries for a return to the deposit system. The president could still argue that a connection between the government and the banks was inherently unhealthy, but he would no longer be able to point to a prostrate credit structure as an example of this malady.

The Whigs further complicated matters by using the congressional lull to embarrass Van Buren. As a target they selected the all-but-forgotten specie circular. The president's critics had long argued that the specie order precipitated the Panic by forcing banks to curtail credit. Van Buren had given serious thought to modifying the circular, but the onset of the crisis made any such action unprofitable. As far as the administration was concerned, the bank suspension had made the specie circular a dead letter.[48] It had served its purpose. Accordingly, Democratic senators raised little objection to Daniel Webster's call on March 24, 1838, for a repeal of the order. Webster

[45] Ritchie to J. H. Pleasants, March 31, 1839, in *Branch Historical Papers*, 3: 238; Brockenbrough to Andrew Stevenson, January 1, 1839, Stevenson Papers. See also Richard E. Parker to Francis P. Blair, November 5, 1838, Blair-Lee Papers.

[46] Benjamin F. Butler to Thomas W. Olcott, February 16, 1838, Olcott Papers; Azariah C. Flagg to Van Buren, April 12, 1838, Van Buren to Jackson, April 15, 1838, Van Buren Papers; Levi Woodbury to Campbell White, April 14, 1838, John Brockenbrough to Richard E. Parker, May 1, 1838, Woodbury Papers.

[47] Woodbury to Churchill Cambreleng, March 10, 14, 1838, Woodbury to Silas Wright, March [?], 1838 (filed under December 1838), Woodbury Papers.

[48] *Senate Documents* (No. 445), 25th Cong., 2d sess., 1837–1838, p. 15.

made no great public display, nor did he introduce a separate resolution, but sought simply to amend the sub-Treasury bill. By a vote of thirty-seven to fourteen, the Senate agreed to add this proviso in place of Calhoun's stricken specie clause. Wright voted in the negative but later expressed his approval of Webster's actions.[49] In this quiet manner the Senate laid to rest one of Andrew Jackson's most momentous pronouncements.

After witnessing the Senate's action, Henry Clay conceived an ingenious plan to ridicule the Democrats and advance the cause of state banks. The Senate rider rescinding the specie circular would not become effective until the House approved the sub-Treasury bill. Rather than have this repeal become a part of Van Buren's cherished project, Clay decided to press for approval of a joint resolution that would separate the question of the specie circular from that of the divorce bill. He could, thereby, publicize the defeat of one of the Democrats' vital policies. On April 30, 1838, he introduced a resolution making it unlawful for the secretary of the treasury to discriminate between the types of revenue receivable in public transactions. This was nothing more than a repetition of Webster's amendment and merely required that the government either extend the specie circular to all transactions or abandon it entirely.[50] Not satisfied with this simple provision, Clay added two clauses calling for the recognition of all state bank notes as legal currency. Any such action by Congress would greatly reduce the scope of executive authority and damage efforts to enact a sub-Treasury.

On May 21, 1838, Clay revealed his true intentions by proposing that Congress charter a national bank. The Kentucky senator's plan was obvious. If Congress required the government to receive local bank notes, it would give tremendous support to the dominant state institutions, such as Biddle's bank in Philadelphia. Once the legislature had diminished executive prerogative and control, it might feel bound to fill the vacuum by chartering a new national bank. In an effort to disguise his support of Biddle, Clay suggested that the new bank might be in New York City, with Albert Gallatin at its head.

If he expected an enthusiastic response, Clay was sorely disappointed. James Buchanan rose and thanked his Kentucky colleague for finally making the issue so clear, because "The two great parties

---

[49] *Congressional Globe*, 25th Cong., 2d sess., 1837–1838, 6: 259; *Senate Documents* (No. 445), 25th Cong., 2d sess., 1837–1838, pp. 1–39.

[50] *Congressional Globe*, 25th Cong., 2d sess., 1837–1838, p. 344. Webster bitterly took note of this in a letter to Biddle, May [?], 1838, in Biddle, *Correspondence*, pp. 310–11.

of the country would now know precisely where they stood."[51] Apparently, Buchanan spoke for the majority; five days later the Senate rendered Clay's resolutions ineffective by striking the last two sections dealing with bank notes and substituting Webster's original wording for the first clause. On May 30 the House added its approval. In effect, Congress made it necessary for the secretary of the treasury either to broaden or to cancel the specie circular. Yet as Clay ruefully noted: "the part of my resolution which directs the receipt of the notes of Specie paying Banks, in discharge of public dues, has been stricken out by a strictly party vote."[52] The congressional resolution of May 30, 1838, left the question of specie squarely up to the administration. Clay and Biddle wanted Congress to have this authority, but Democratic leaders had successfully frustrated this plan. Woodbury later allowed the temporary reception of state bank notes, but reserved the right to revoke this decision at any time.[53]

Despite Clay's failure, Nicholas Biddle rejoiced at the events in Congress. It had been a rather dismal spring for the Philadelphia financier. First, he had tried to persuade the administration to renew its connections with the Second Bank of the United States. "Now the present Bank is only the late Bank with no change except in the origin of its charter," he told John Forsyth. "Its whole machinery can be remounted in twenty-four hours." Forsyth replied that the government was willing to deal with Biddle's bank as it did with all other banks but would grant no special favors.[54] Then, when the New York banks resumed specie payments, Biddle began to feel both economic and political pressure. The Democratic press rejoiced at the prospect of recovery and used the occasion to castigate Biddle as the only roadblock to complete restoration of public confidence. In an effort to save face, Biddle grasped at the repeal of the specie circular as a signal that the government had repented its previous errors. He decided to resume payments, claiming that "The tide now has begun to turn, and the Bank has received today a triumph such as it never enjoyed in any part of its career."[55]

[51] *Congressional Globe*, 25th Cong., 2d sess., 1837–1838, 6: 396–97.
[52] Ibid., p. 412; Henry Clay to Colonel A. Hamilton, May 28, 1838, Henry Clay Papers, Library of Congress.
[53] Woodbury to Collectors, June 1, 1838, Letters to Collectors, National Archives.
[54] Biddle to Forsyth, April 30, 1838, in Biddle, *Correspondence*, pp. 307–309; Forsyth to Biddle, May 29, 1838, quoted in Thomas P. Govan, *Nicholas Biddle* (Chicago, 1959), p. 333.
[55] Washington *Globe*, May 4, 1838; Biddle to Samuel Jaudon, May 31, 1838, in Biddle, *Correspondence*, p. 311.

Having convinced himself that he had scored a victory over Van Buren, Biddle could not understand the administration's continued support for the sub-Treasury bill. He seemed to think it was somehow a plot to rob him of his moment of glory. In this frame of mind, Biddle decided to make every effort to defeat the president's program and sent representatives scurrying to Washington to sound out members of the Pennsylvania delegation. He then wrote to Congressman John Sergeant, asking for "a list marked with all those who you are sure will vote against it, & let me know also *how many votes you want in addition.* Perhaps we may prove to some of our Penna members, that their course is injurious to the state & to themselves."[56] We do not know what pressures Biddle brought to bear on Pennsylvania congressmen, but his efforts had little to do with the defeat of the divorce bill.

Cambreleng had now decided the time was right to press for the passage of the sub-Treasury, and on June 19, 1838, he reported the bill to the House. For the next week, supporters and critics battled day and night. The debate featured few new arguments, for both sides had made their positions clear at the special session. To the opposition, it seemed as though Van Buren's lieutenants were everywhere; the *National Intelligencer* compared the president's personal tactics with the "closettings" of James II. The test was crucial, and such key senators as Silas Wright were not above applying pressure to members of Congress.[57] Finally, on June 25, 1838, by invoking the previous question, Cambreleng brought the bill to a vote. The House defeated the measure 125 to 111.

The administration had done all within its power to win approval for the sub-Treasury bill. Only three Democrats abstained from the voting, and one of these would have supported the opposition. Again, the main reason for defeat was defection by Conservative Democrats, especially those in Virginia. Despite Democratic efforts at compromise, Rives and his supporters refused to accept anything short of a resurrection of the defunct deposit system. Van Buren welcomed the resumption of specie payments, but he was reluctant to entrust more

[56] Biddle to Samuel Jaudon, June 9, 1838, Biddle to Sergeant, June 15, 1838, in Biddle, *Correspondence*, pp. 313–14. For a different view see Govan, *Biddle*, pp. 333–35. Govan maintains that Clay duped the administration into voting for the repeal of the specie circular and that once Van Buren saw that he was "outwitted by Clay and Biddle" he reintroduced the sub-Treasury bill. This presumes that Clay's machinations were successful, which they were not, and that the president planned at one time to forego the divorce bill, which he did not.

[57] *National Intelligencer*, June 28, 1838; Wright to Azariah Flagg, June 21, 1838, Flagg-Wright Papers.

than a token amount of public revenue to the state banks, fearful that a complete renewal of deposits would touch off a new wave of inflation. The stalemate persisted.

The pattern of voting on the sub-Treasury bill was almost identical to that at the special session. Calhoun managed to swing four votes in South Carolina, but this was offset by an equal number of desertions in New York. Biddle's frantic pleas produced no discernible results; each member of the Pennsylvania delegation voted as he had at the special session and no Democrats defected.[58] In view of the strength of the opposition, Polk and Cambreleng decided not to proceed to the Senate bill.

In the wake of defeat, Democrats tried to rationalize that despite congressional intransigence, the sub-Treasury was already in operation. By now even this fact provided little consolation; administration spokesmen were smarting from a severe beating. Jackson lashed out against leadership in the House and stated that the president should have pressed the divorce bill earlier. By contrast, James Buchanan laid the blame squarely on the shoulders of John C. Calhoun for insisting on the specie feature and standing in the way of compromise.[59] Meanwhile, Nicholas Biddle was in a triumphant mood, claiming full responsibility for the congressional action and seeking a way to exploit Democratic disarray. He looked forward to the adjournment of the legislature, for then "the Administration, poor & dispirited, will be brought to reason as wild beasts are tamed by hunger. Remember that whatever you may read to the contrary, the repeal of the Specie Circular & the defeat of the Sub Treasury are the results, exclusively, of the course pursued by the Bank of the U.S."[60]

So elated was the Philadelphia financier that he decided the time was right to bring the government back into the orbit of the Bank of the United States. His main aim was to have the Treasury reinstate his institution as a "general depository."[61] Once he had the unrestricted custody and use of public funds, he could then renew his connections with various state banks and thereby assume a dominant

[58] *Congressional Globe*, 25th Cong., 2d sess., 1837–1838, 6: 478. I used the voting records of the special session as a guide to both party affiliation and Conservative allegiance. There were a total of sixteen Democratic defectors. The breakdown by state is as follows: Mass. (1), N.Y. (4), Va. (4), S.C. (2), Tenn. (1), Ky. (1), Ill. (2), Ohio (1).

[59] Jackson to Van Buren, July 6, 1838, Van Buren Papers; Jackson to Francis P. Blair, July 19, 1838, Buchanan to Jackson, July 21, 1838, Jackson Papers.

[60] Biddle to Samuel Jaudon, June 29, 1838, Biddle to Thomas Cooper, July 13, 1838, in Biddle, *Correspondence*, pp. 314–15, 316–17.

[61] Biddle to Samuel Jaudon, August 3, 1838, in ibid., pp. 318–21.

position in the nation's economy. Biddle knew that Van Buren would never consent to such an arrangement, so he hoped to reach his goal by covert means.

As the first step in this scheme, Biddle tried to take advantage of the administration's urgent need for funds. His bank owed the Treasury over $4 million for the purchase of the government's share of stock in the Second Bank of the United States. Biddle had agreed to pay this debt in three annual installments, beginning in the fall of 1838, and had given the government bonds to this effect. In April 1838 he tried to anticipate payments on these bonds, but Woodbury refused to agree to any transactions not in specie. At the same time, Van Buren, in search of revenue, asked Congress for authority to sell the bonds to cover expenses. Congress agreed but failed to make suitable arrangements to facilitate the sale. As a result, Woodbury could find no one to purchase the bonds and finally agreed to sell them to Biddle.[62]

After he concluded this transaction, Biddle thought he had Van Buren at his mercy. The Treasury was to receive $2 million for the first bond, and Woodbury agreed to place this payment on "special deposit" in Biddle's bank. With government funds again in his vaults, Biddle bragged of being "a depository of public money." "After all the nonsense of the last few years," he said, "the Govt. takes in payment of a bond, a credit in a bank which does not pay specie."[63] Actually, Biddle had won no great victory. The Treasury had not agreed to accept worthless bank paper but had insisted that the debt be discharged in legal currency. Furthermore, Biddle had already decided to resume specie payments. The money in his possession was to the credit of the Treasury and not the bank; it involved only the amount of the bond sale. Van Buren gave no indication that he would sanction any extension of this agreement to include other revenue or to enhance the power of the bank. In fact, the administration distrusted Biddle, and the banker himself hesitated to publicize these dealings.[64]

Throughout the spring and summer of 1838, Van Buren remained

---

[62] All these transactions are documented in Woodbury's report to Congress; *Senate Documents* (No. 31), 25th Cong., 3d sess., 1838–1839, pp. 1–52.

[63] Biddle to Samuel Jaudon, August 3, 1838, Biddle, *Correspondence*, pp. 318–21.

[64] Biddle to Samuel Jaudon, May 31, 1838, Biddle to R. M. Blatchford, July 31, 1838, in ibid., pp. 311–12, 317; Levi Woodbury to Silas Wright, August 23, 1838, Woodbury Papers; Woodbury to Van Buren, August 25, 1838, Van Buren Papers.

so preoccupied with these financial matters that he had little time to devote to state politics. The man who once prided himself on being able to master differences between various elements in the Democratic alliance now found it difficult to deal with state leaders. He chafed at their excessive concern with local problems, their myopic fears of the federal government, and their failure to appreciate the interests of the Union. Under the incessant pressure of the Panic, Van Buren strayed from his familiar role as political broker and increasingly acted as a national statesman. Ironically, he never articulated this transformation; he continued to conceive of his duty in terms of the traditional Democratic ideology that allowed little executive autonomy.

The New York gubernatorial election in November 1838 demonstrated the political results of the disaffection between the president and his key state leaders. Although administration fiscal policy promised to loom large in this contest, Governor William Marcy was hopelessly out of touch with Washington. On one occasion, during the height of Senate debate on the sub-Treasury bill, he complained that he knew more of proceedings in Parliament than of those in Congress. No one bothered to keep him informed of administration decisions. Once the Albany *Argus* had publicly sanctioned the divorce bill, Van Buren seemed to assume that the recovery in Albany was complete.[65]

Nothing could have been farther from the truth. Although he now spoke favorably of administration proposals, Croswell was at best a reluctant convert. He dutifully reported major congressional news but rarely spoke with enthusiasm about an independent Treasury. The *Argus* had the annoying habit of repeatedly referring to Democratic differences. During April and May 1838 Croswell did criticize Nicholas Biddle, but only in an effort to support state banks in their resumption of specie payments. Aside from occasional jabs at prominent Whig leaders, Croswell studiously avoided national politics; he seemed to tire of the party wars and lapsed into a tedious style.[66]

This further deterioration of communications severely hampered the Regency's efforts to defeat William H. Seward, the Whig candidate for governor. Already blamed for the continuing depression, Marcy bore the additional burden of administration policy. He found

[65] Marcy to Prosper M. Wetmore, March 27, 1838, Marcy Papers; Van Buren to Jackson, April 29, 1838, Van Buren Papers.
[66] Albany *Argus*, January 20, 30, February 3, 16, March 13, 30, April 20, 28, May 11, 29, 30, June 1, 22, 1838.

it extremely difficult to defend both state banks and an independent Treasury. Yet when he tried to deemphasize Van Buren's program, he received lectures on the necessity of party loyalty. The governor stood by helplessly as Senator Nathaniel P. Tallmadge led New York Conservatives into the Whig camp. In his dilemma, Marcy would have agreed with James K. Polk's observation about the effect of the Panic on relations between the states and the national administration. "We have heretofore been unused," the Tennessee congressman mused, "to political contests in which Federal parties have been made the test in state elections."[67]

Elated by the success of the previous year, the Whigs waged a vigorous campaign in the fall of 1838. Under the skillful direction of Thurlow Weed, they developed a statewide organization that rivaled the Regency in effective use of political propaganda. The Whigs capitalized on public discontent over the Panic and disenchantment with administration handling of the crisis on the Canadian border. Croswell countered with an assault on the character of William H. Seward, but even these lively editorials could not instill life into a dispirited party. On election day the Whigs swept the state and carried Seward into the governor's mansion. "The greatest excitement prevailed during the evening," wrote Philip Hone of the Whig celebration. "Masonic Hall was crammed full, and the street from Pearl to Duane a solid mass of Whigs, anxious at first and exulting afterward, but orderly the whole time. This election probably determines the question in this state, and Mr. Van Buren's chance for reelection may now be considered desperate."[68]

The Whig triumph came as a bitter disappointment to the president, especially in view of the earlier defeat of the Richmond Junto. The Albany-Richmond axis, long the nerve center of the Democratic party, now lay in ruins. No matter what small gains he might later make, Van Buren could not escape the fact that the alliance collapsed at its strongest point. At last the Whigs had undeniable proof of Democratic vulnerability. They would not forget the lesson.

Sometime after his unsuccessful bid for reelection, New York's William L. Marcy paused to reflect on the reasons for the downfall of his party. Dismissing the contention that the Whigs had won by

[67] Polk to Van Buren, May 29, 1837, Van Buren Papers.
[68] Philip Hone, *The Diary of Philip Hone, 1828–1851*, ed. Bayard Tuckerman, 2 vols. (New York, 1889), 1: 331; Albany *Argus*, October 2–November 1, 1838. On the election see Glyndon G. Van Deusen, *Thurlow Weed* (Boston, 1947), pp. 96–102; Ivor D. Spencer, *The Victor and the Spoils: A Life of William L. Marcy* (Providence, R.I., 1959), pp. 95–97.

fraud, the former governor blamed the administration for disrupting local political patterns. In a statement that might well have served as an epitaph for the Regency, Marcy concluded: "The Election was conducted chiefly with reference to the policy of the federal Gov. If we had had nothing but our own policy to vindicate I can not bring myself to doubt that we should have had a different result."[69]

[69] Marcy to Prosper M. Wetmore, December 11, 1838, Marcy Papers.

Chapter 7

The Hollow
Victory

CHARACTERISTICALLY, Van Buren masked his extreme disappointment at the results of the New York election. Ahead lay weeks of planning for the new session of Congress, leaving little time for political postmortems. The president stubbornly adhered to the sub-Treasury proposal, convinced that this reform alone could secure government revenue and end the speculation that had plunged the nation into depression. Although Congress had twice blocked passage of the divorce bill, Van Buren believed that the major disagreement was over administrative details and not the principle of separating bank from state. He remained open to compromise but made it clear to Virginia's Democrats that he would not approve a mere resurrection of the old deposit system.[1] On the eve of his third meeting with the legislature, the president received alarming news that upset all his calculations.

During the excitement of the New York canvass, Treasury department officials pored over the records of the New York customs house, checking on alleged shortages in the accounts of the former collector, Samuel Swartwout. To their amazement, they discovered that over eight years Swartwout had stolen $1,250,000 and had then fled abroad.[2] Try as they might, the Democrats could not ignore so monumental a scandal. Although a Whig, Swartwout was a Jackson appointee, a fact that Old Hickory's tormentors gleefully recalled. "You will have learned," lamented Churchill C. Cambreleng, "that my prophecy to Genl. Jackson about a certain officer has been super-abundantly fulfilled."[3] Van Buren, too, had reason to think back to 1829, when he had protested in vain against the appointment of Swartwout.

All these reflections were useless. With Congress due to convene in less than a month, the president realized that he could not avoid

mention of the shortage and would have to explain the administration's oft-stated contention that public revenue was safer in the
hands of collectors than in the vaults of state banks. Van Buren
decided not to sidestep the defalcation but to relate it directly to his
recommendation of the sub-Treasury. In his second annual message,
delivered December 3, 1838, he repeated the usual arguments in favor
of separating the Treasury from the banks and then turned to the
problem of the New York fraud. Van Buren stressed that the embez-
zlement took place over a period of years that included those when
the government was in league with the banks. The president was
trying to demonstrate that Swartwout's sins were in no way the
product of any one particular mode of handling federal funds. In
fact, the theft proved the necessity of an independent Treasury. "The
case is one which . . . furnishes the strongest motive for the establishment of a more severe and secure system for the safe-keeping and
disbursement of the public moneys than any that has heretofore
existed."[4]

Following the president's lead, Wright and Cambreleng introduced bills "more effectually to secure the public moneys in the
hands of officers and agents of the government, and to punish public
defaulters." Both men hoped that the legislature would agree to
establish definite regulations for collection of government dues. Although neither bill created a sub-Treasury, each sanctioned and
improved the temporary system that had been in operation since the
first bank suspension in May 1837. The Conservatives recognized this
as an attempt to sneak the divorce bill in through the back door. On
February 14, 1839, William C. Rives tried in vain to amend Wright's
bill and provide for a return to a state bank deposit system.[5]

The administration thwarted Conservative designs, but Van Buren
soon admitted that his own measures had little chance of success.[6]

[1] Van Buren to Jackson, June 17, 1838, Van Buren Papers; John Forsyth to
Nicholas Biddle, November 29, 1838, in Biddle, Correspondence, p. 336; Van
Buren to William C. Rives, July 21, 1838, Letterbook (1833–1839), Rives
Papers; Van Buren to Levi Woodbury, August 5, 1838, Woodbury Papers;
Washington Globe, July 23, 1838; Richmond Enquirer, August 10, 17, 1838.
[2] William L. Marcy to Prosper M. Wetmore, November 13, 1838, Marcy
Papers. For a description of the defalcation see Woodbury's report to Congress,
House Documents (No. 13), 25th Cong., 3d sess., 1838–1839, pp. 1–110.
[3] Cambreleng to Van Buren, October 30, November 12, 1838, Van Buren
Papers.
[4] Richardson, Messages and Papers, 3: 492.
[5] Congressional Globe, 25th Cong., 3d sess., 1838–1839, 7: 27, 57, 183.
[6] Van Buren to Jackson, January 8, 1839, Van Buren Papers (letter misdated
and misfiled under January 1838). See also William S. Fulton to Jackson, January
26, 1839, Jackson Papers.

"From present indications in the House of Representatives," observed Franklin Pierce, "I do not believe that any business of importance is to be transacted this session. Secretary Woodbury is at present the main object of attack, and there is little doubt that the two months to come will be wasted in partisan debate."[7] Pierce's prediction proved accurate. Although the Senate approved Wright's bill, Cambreleng could not force the House to a vote.[8] Instead of stimulating reform, the Swartwout debacle prompted relentless demands for a complete investigation of the Treasury Department. Democrats sat in stunned silence listening to the endless torrent of Whig invective. Finally, Cambreleng arose and tried to silence this abuse by moving to refer the Swartwout case to a select committee chosen by the Speaker. The administration was not to escape so easily. By a vote of 113 to 105, the opposition rejected Cambreleng's ploy, demanding that the entire House share in the selection of an investigatory body.

As the Democrats feared, the subsequent balloting gave the Whigs and Conservatives a two-to-one majority on the nine-man committee.[9] For the remainder of the session, this group paraded witnesses and bombarded the executive branch with calls for papers. On February 27, 1839, after weeks of prolonged publicity, it issued a lengthy report. The majority of the committee members concluded that Swartwout was guilty as charged but went on to assail the secretary of the treasury for shoddy administrative procedures and failure to institute an adequate system of inspections. Not content to rest here, the irate inquisitors launched into a withering attack on Democratic fiscal policy, contending that the "discontinuance of the use of banks as depositories" had permitted Swartwout to amass his fortune. In a futile effort to mitigate these charges, Van Buren's supporters published a minority report.[10]

At two A.M. on March 4, 1839, the final session of the Twenty-fifth Congress came to a close. The president was not disappointed to see the legislators leave. On three occasions he had pleaded for passage of the sub-Treasury; each time he had failed. "We have at last got rid of Congress," sighed Levi Woodbury, "and a most disreputable one in many respects it has been." The administration held out the hope that the next assembly might be more favorably constituted.[11]

[7] Pierce to John McNeil, January 2, 1839, Pierce Papers.
[8] *Congressional Globe*, 25th Cong., 3d sess., 1838–1839, 7: 197.
[9] Ibid., pp. 19, 124–27. I determined party affiliation on the select committee by referring to the voting records at the previous sessions of the 25th Congress.
[10] *House Reports* (No. 313), 25th Cong., 3d sess., 1838–1839, pp. 72, 262.
[11] Woodbury to Richard Rush, March 16, 1839, Woodbury Papers.

Once the legislature disbanded, Van Buren began to worry about the problem of government revenue. The longer the opposition persisted, the more he had to improvise. After the original suspensions in 1837, he had little choice but to order the withdrawal of deposits from defaulting banks and the collection of all dues by executive agents. Initially, this posed little difficulty; indeed, the administration cited its success as proof that sub-Treasuries would work. Yet some legislation was necessary, if only to provide adequate safeguards for this makeshift system. By constantly refusing to act, Congress created severe hardships for the Treasury. Woodbury had no guidelines to follow and fell back on some questionable expedients. Where collections in one district exceeded safe limits, he often found it necessary to store government funds in state banks. After the resumption of specie payments in 1838, he extended this practice. By 1839, the government had "special deposits" in fourteen banks.[12] Although the money remained in the government's account, this connection increasingly embarrassed the Democrats.

Consequently, the president asked his advisers about the propriety of concluding a contract with the banks. Such agreement would provide a measure of uniformity by establishing definite rules for the receipt and storage of excess funds. As usual, Silas Wright replied in a firm, frank manner. He realized the problems facing Woodbury, but he insisted that any formal compact with the banks would expose the president to serious criticism. The nation would assume that the administration had "voluntarily abandoned the independent treasury system." No matter how urgent the need for efficiency and security, the Democrats could not afford to acknowledge that "banks are indispensable agents in the management of the affairs of the Treasury." Wright therefore urged that Woodbury proceed with the utmost caution and that if Van Buren decided on a contract, it should be temporary and expire when Congress reconvened. Cambreleng generally argued along the same lines, adding that the proposal might be interpreted as a total capitulation to the demands of the Conservatives.[13]

Although Van Buren appreciated this sage political advice, he remained concerned about the indefinite relationship between the Treasury and the banks. He was so exasperated by congressional stubbornness that he thought fleetingly of establishing an indepen-

[12] *Senate Documents* (No. 2, Appendix, K. L.), 25th Cong., 3d sess., 1838–1839, pp. 52–53.
[13] Wright to Van Buren, March 23, 1839, Cambreleng to Van Buren, April 10, 1839, Woodbury Papers.

dent Treasury by executive order.[14] Since the legislature would not
meet for another eight months, there would be ample time to issue
the necessary directives, authorizing construction and operation of
the new sub-Treasuries. These agencies could then handle the surplus
now on "special deposit." Such a plan would admirably suit administration economic goals, but it was fraught with political risks. In
1833, Andrew Jackson had ignored Congress and removed government deposits from Biddle's bank. Few Democrats would forget the
storm that followed this decision. Already charged with exceeding his
constitutional prerogatives, Van Buren had no desire to fan the fires
of recrimination. He soon abandoned any thought of independent
action as a means of solving the problems left by Congress. By the
summer of 1839, danger signs warned of another depression, and
Woodbury cautioned the president not to involve the government in
the coming crisis.[15]

Since the resumption of specie payments in 1838, the nation's
economy had gained strength, erasing many of the memories of the
Panic. Foreign investors, eager to purchase American securities,
helped to create this welcomed turnabout. Once again, state governments devoted their attention to internal improvements, borrowing
abroad to finance new construction. Prices across the country re-
bounded from their 1837 lows. In Philadelphia, Nicholas Biddle took
advantage of the returning prosperity to continue his large-scale
speculation in cotton, hopeful of reaping a profit from the rising
market.

Early in 1839, a new rash of credit restrictions brought this recovery to a halt. A series of disastrous crop failures forced England to
purchase foreign foodstuffs, thereby placing an additional drain on
the country's bullion supply. Alarmed by dwindling reserves, the
Bank of England raised its interest rate, touching off a demand for
payment of outstanding debts. To complicate matters, British textile
manufacturers cut back sharply on production and sent the price of
cotton into a tailspin. The expanding American market felt the full
impact of this sudden international constriction. Biddle's bank was
hardest hit. With its assets frozen in cotton and the price of this
commodity in a steady decline, the bank tried to meet the demand
for specie by selling post notes and foreign drafts. Finally, in October

[14] William Gouge [?] to Van Buren, April 20, 1839, Woodbury Papers. This
letter is in Gouge's handwriting but may have been written at Woodbury's
request.
[15] Woodbury to Van Buren, July 27, 1839, Van Buren Papers; Washington
Globe, August 3, 4, 5, 1839.

1839, after months of such desperate expedients, the bank suspended. Soon institutions in the South and West followed suit. In all, nearly half of the nation's 850 banks discontinued specie payments. The failures were not nearly so widespread as those in 1837. The New York banks managed to survive, as did most of those in New England. Still, the depression was to continue for several years and in the end prove more ruinous.[16]

In the face of this crisis, the president moved with a vigor and determination that contrasted sharply with his defensive reactions two years earlier. The renewed onslaught of economic distress promised to work in his favor. It offered proof of what Democrats had long been saying—banks were unsafe. Whereas in 1837, Van Buren had to tread lightly for fear of a complete collapse of the entire fiscal structure, he could now publicly distinguish between the effects of wise and improvident management. Furthermore, he had the satisfaction of seeing New York hold firm while Biddle floundered.[17]

The president decided to renew his appeals for an independent Treasury, adding what he considered a timely argument. Formerly he had thought it best to proceed with caution, fearful of strengthening the Conservatives or of eroding his electoral base. Now he decided to try a bold, new tactic. In a long letter to Silas Wright, Van Buren outlined ideas for the approaching congressional session. He planned to devote a major share of his message to the sub-Treasury, reviewing all his previous arguments but then advancing on a new front. For the first time, Van Buren wanted to stress that passage of the divorce bill would help restrain overbanking and overtrading by "requiring short settlement with the banks." The president now felt that the time was right for the federal government to take some action to control the economy. Suddenly, as if recoiling from the implications of what he had just written, Van Buren lapsed into a lengthy discussion of Jeffersonian political theory, constantly reiterating the dangers of government intervention. "The wisest course," he intoned, "is to confine legislation to as few subjects as is consistent with the

---

[16] Douglass C. North, *The Economic Growth of the United States 1790 to 1860* (Englewood Cliffs, N.J., 1961), pp. 200–203; George Rogers Taylor, *The Transportation Revolution* (New York, 1951), pp. 344–45; Bray Hammond, *Banks and Politics in America from the Revolution to the Civil War* (Princeton, N.J., 1957), pp. 503–13. For a list of the banks that suspended see *Senate Documents* (No. 72), 26th Cong., 1st sess., 1839–1840, pp. 5–24.

[17] Levi Woodbury to David R. Porter, October 5, 1839, Van Buren to Woodbury, October 10, 1839, Campbell White to Woodbury, October 10, 1839, Woodbury Papers; Van Buren to Benjamin F. Butler, October 29, 1839, Butler Papers.

well being of a society & to leave as large a proportion of the affairs of man as is possible to their own management."[18]

Despite his constitutional doubts, Van Buren had good political reasons for favoring a new approach. The return of depression brought forth cries for a reform of the banking system, cries that would undoubtedly influence elections to the new Congress. This public outburst further damaged the faltering Conservative cause. Successful in thwarting administration measures, the Conservatives found it increasingly difficult to generate enthusiasm for a fiscal program that had little chance of passage. Subscriptions to *The Madisonian* dropped precipitously, placing the paper in financial jeopardy.[19] Early in 1838, William C. Rives tried to arrest this decline by severing all ties with the Democratic party and founding a new organization. As its battle cry, this dissident coalition adopted the slogan "armed neutrality," thereby signifying its independent intentions. Refreshing in theory, this plan proved politically impractical, as Rives discovered during his abortive bid for reelection to the Senate. All his high-flown rhetoric about the need to eradicate party discipline won him few converts; he eventually had to appeal for Whig votes. This marked the first step toward the disappearance of the Conservatives and their absorption by the Whigs.[20]

In the spring of 1839, Virginia Democrats prepared to exploit Conservative decay. Thomas Ritchie confidently predicted a recovery from the disastrous defeat of the previous year, so long as "friends at Washington" continued to refrain from placing "too many difficulties in our way."[21] When the legislative elections gave the Democrats a new lease on life, Richard E. Parker wrote to Washington, describing the rejuvenation and praising the *Enquirer*'s contribution. Significantly, these gains coincided with a lull in the administration's campaign for the sub-Treasury. When Van Buren later renewed his crusade, Ritchie once again dissented.[22] Although conditions in the Old Dominion were improving, the president still lacked the Junto's

[18] Van Buren to Silas Wright, September 21, 1839, Van Buren Papers.
[19] Thomas Allen to Rives, October 14, 1838, J. Garland to Rives, January 11, 1840, Rives Papers.
[20] Franklin Pierce to Asa Fowler, January 14, 1839, Pierce Papers; Nathaniel Tallmadge to Rives, February 20, 1839, Rives Papers; Richmond *Enquirer*, January 26, March 12, 1839; Howard Braverman, "The Economic and Political Background of the Conservative Revolt in Virginia," *Virginia Magazine of History and Biography* 60 (1952): 282–87.
[21] Ritchie to Van Buren, March 22, 1839, Van Buren Papers.
[22] Parker to Van Buren, June 4, 1839, Van Buren Papers; Parker to Francis P. Blair, May 27, 1839, Blair-Lee Papers; Ritchie to Andrew Stevenson, August 4, 1839, Stevenson Papers.

unqualified support. The return to the fold of the Albany *Argus* partially compensated for this weakness. With the Regency out of power, Croswell gravitated toward a strong administration line. In the fall of 1839, he printed, for the first time, a complete analysis of the sub-Treasury. Ironically, this conversion came on the eve of his ouster as a state printer.[23]

Politically, then, Van Buren had little to lose by pursuing an offensive strategy. He had already suffered serious setbacks in New York and Virginia; conditions could not deteriorate much further. No longer plagued by fears of Conservative inroads, the president could take advantage of the rising antibank tide to carry his earlier recommendations to their logical conclusion. As the Twenty-sixth Congress convened, Van Buren's managers took heart at what appeared to be a return to bipartisan normalcy. The Senate remained firmly under Democratic control. Although the elections reduced the president's House majority by more than half, they destroyed the Conservative bloc. All but four of Rives's former adherents either lost bids for reelection or joined the Whigs. Control of the House hinged on six disputed seats. The party that won these would have a majority; the months ahead promised a full measure of political suspense.[24]

Van Buren also faced the problem of finding a new Speaker. The previous spring, James K. Polk resigned to run for governor in Tennessee; the loss hampered Democratic efforts to organize the House.[25] To replace Polk, Van Buren selected John W. Jones, a Virginian with a strong proadministration voting record. This choice reflected the president's continuing effort to tip the delicate balance in the Old Dominion.

John C. Calhoun had other ideas. The fickle senator still nurtured dreams of an independent Southern party and wanted a Speaker who

[23] Albany *Argus*, December 10, 1838, March 12, September 16, 23, 30, October 2, 4, 5, 8, 9, 11, 15, 1839, January 14, 1840; Churchill C. Cambreleng to Van Buren, November 12, 1838, John A. Dix to Van Buren, January 2, 1840, Van Buren Papers; William L. Marcy to Prosper M. Wetmore, July 21, 1840, Marcy Papers.
[24] Analysis of the party affiliation listed in the *Biographical Directory of the American Congress*, comp. James L. Harrison (Washington, D.C., 1950), gives the Democrats an edge of 123–119 after resolution of the contested elections. This margin is two votes smaller than that forecasted by the administration prior to the opening of Congress; Levi Woodbury to Van Buren, August 18, 1839, Van Buren Papers; Washington *Globe*, November 30, 1839.
[25] For the details on Polk's decision to return to Tennessee see Charles G. Sellers, Jr., *James K. Polk: Jacksonian, 1795–1843* (Princeton, N.J., 1957), pp. 341–55.

would promote this cause.[26] Consequently, the Calhounites refused to accept Jones, turning instead to South Carolina's Francis W. Pickens. Inexplicably, Pickens was absent at the opening of the session, and so the insurgents shifted to Alabama's Dixon H. Lewis.[27] The growing disagreement between Calhoun and Van Buren disrupted the caucus. After hours of bitter quarreling, the feuding Democrats finally approved Jones by a slim one-vote margin. Dismayed at the turn of events, Calhoun's followers refused to abide by the caucus decision and thereby prevented Jones's election. On December 14, 1839, after six fruitless attempts to name a new Speaker, the House recessed. Two days later the struggle resumed. In the interim, the Democrats tried to regroup behind Lewis, but by now their forces were hopelessly splintered. There had been too many candidates and too little concord. Capitalizing on Democratic confusion, the Whigs dumped their first round choice, John Bell, and threw their support to Virginia's Robert M. T. Hunter, electing him on the eleventh ballot.[28]

Democrats tried to be optimistic about Hunter's victory. They told themselves that the new Speaker had always been a state rights advocate and a strong proponent of the sub-Treasury.[29] All this rationalizing could not erase the fact that the party had lost control of its key congressional post; the defeat promised to heighten confusion in an already chaotic assembly. "There is great disorder in the House every day," reported Franklin Pierce, "cries of Mr. Chairman —order—order—I claim the floor—go on—order—go ahead—I call the gentleman to order—the Gentleman is himself out of order—sit down—I rise to a question of order and the like were ringing out from every quarter of the hall."[30]

After weeks of aimless bickering, the legislature was hardly in a receptive mood. When Van Buren's message finally reached the floor, much of his subtle logic may well have been lost on a distracted audience. As planned, the president devoted a majority of his report to the problem of the sub-Treasury. He began with the usual justifi-

[26] Calhoun to Robert M. T. Hunter, June 1839, in Martha T. Hunter, *Memoir of Robert M. T. Hunter* (Washington, D.C., 1903), pp. 71–72.
[27] John C. Calhoun to Thomas G. Clemson, December 8, 1839, in Calhoun, *Correspondence,* p. 435.
[28] Francis P. Blair to Jackson, December 15, 1839, Jackson Papers; *Congressional Globe,* 26th Cong., 1st sess., 1839–1840, 8: 52–55; Sampson Butler to James Hammond, December 30, 1839, Hammond Papers, Library of Congress.
[29] William S. Fulton to Jackson, December 27, 1839, Jackson Papers; William L. Marcy to Van Buren, December 31, 1839, Van Buren Papers; Silas Wright to Azariah C. Flagg, December 16, 1839, Flagg-Wright Papers.
[30] Franklin Pierce to Asa Fowler, December 13, 1839, Pierce Papers.

cations for a separation of bank and state, referring briefly to the Swartwout scandal. The president then went on to cite the recent bank failures as proving the futility of again entrusting government funds to state depositories. In 1837, he had attributed the suspension more to the irresistible laws of nature than to the errors of individual bankers. Now he reversed this emphasis and brought both foreign capitalism and private corporations under attack. He was no longer vague on the need for a specie clause and called forthrightly for collection and disbursement in gold and silver.[31]

Near the end of his exposition, Van Buren mentioned that enactment of the sub-Treasury would assist in the reform of state banks. Although local agencies still bore the primary responsibility for overhaul of the banking structure, the president stated that "While the keeping of the public revenue in a separate and independent treasury and of collecting it in gold and silver will have a salutary influence on the system of paper credit with which all banks are connected, and thus aid those that are sound and well managed, it will at the same time sensibly check such as are otherwise by at once withholding the means of extravagance afforded by the public funds and restraining them from excessive issue of notes which they would be constantly called upon to redeem."[32] Attended though it was by serious qualifications, Van Buren's statement represented a dramatic step away from his former professions of laissez faire and his commitment to the principle of limited government. He still argued that federal influence should be subordinate to that of the states, but for the first time, he portrayed the sub-Treasury as a mechanism capable of reforming the nation's economy. By taking "strong ground," he hoped to break the long congressional deadlock.[33]

With the House still in a state of confusion, Democrats began their battle in the Senate. On January 6, 1840, Silas Wright introduced the sub-Treasury bill; it differed little from that presented two years earlier. Chances for passage seemed good, especially since William C. Rives had failed to win reelection and Nathaniel P. Tallmadge was temporarily absent. With the two Conservative spokesmen missing, Wright decided to push for quick approval.

During the ensuing debate, Democrats found themselves in an awkward situation. They were obliged to develop the president's

[31] Richardson, *Messages and Papers*, 3: 529–55.
[32] Ibid., p. 550.
[33] Van Buren to Hermanus Bleecker, January 2, 1840, Bleecker Papers, New York State Library; Van Buren to Benjamin F. Butler, November 25, 1839, Butler Papers.

arguments, but in so doing, they encountered severe criticism. After listening to his opponents fumble with novel theories, Henry Clay arose and charged that all the administration's hints about reforming the economy and curbing speculation amounted to this—the president secretly wanted to create a government bank and augment the power of the executive branch.[34] Van Buren's defenders futilely tried to disclaim this motive. In delivering the main speech in support of the sub-Treasury, James Buchanan denied that the executive branch should exercise any control over the economy. "The present administration has not had the slightest agency in creating the existing distress, and can do but little to arrest it, or prevent its recurrence. This is a duty which devolves upon the States." Yet in the next breath he pronounced that the divorce bill would "do some good in checking the extravagant spirit of speculation, which is the bane of the country."[35]

This glaring inconsistency exemplified the Democratic predicament. Swept along by the strong current of public protest, they tried to adopt a policy consonant with the national temper. Yet they found that innovation endangered their adherence to traditional Jeffersonian principles. The party had long prided itself on forging an effective coalition of state interests, bound together by agreement on the need to limit federal activity and allow local diversity. They took as their watchword the slogan from the masthead of the Washington Globe: "the world is governed too much." Now in response to a new wave of economic distress, Van Buren sought to increase the influence of the central government. Coming as it did amidst renewed Whig charges of executive despotism, this recommendation created more problems than it solved. No matter what mental gyrations the president might perform, he could not escape this dilemma.

Although stung by Clay's cutting remarks, the Democrats had more than enough votes to silence Whig opposition in the Senate. On January 23, 1840, they passed the divorce bill on a straight party vote, twenty-four to eighteen.[36] They were not so fortunate in the House. Lack of a clear-cut majority placed them in a much more precarious position, making it difficult to defeat Whig delaying tactics. The administration hoped that the new Speaker might expedite

[34] Congressional Globe, 26th Cong., 1st sess., 1839–1840, 8: Appendix, 124. See similar charges in The Madisonian, December 28, 1839. On administration response see Silas Wright to Van Buren, January 21, 1840, Van Buren Papers; Annual Report of the Secretary of the Treasury, Senate Documents (No. 2), 26th Cong., 1st sess., 1839–1840.

[35] Congressional Globe, 26th Cong., 1st sess., 1839–1840, 8: Appendix, 133.

[36] Congressional Globe, 26th Cong., 1st sess., 1839–1840, 8: 139–41.

Van Buren's program by appointing favorable committees, but on December 30, 1839, Hunter announced selections that clearly signaled an end to Democratic preponderance.[37] The Whigs took control of a majority of the standing committees, including those on the District of Columbia, Roads and Canals, and nearly every branch of public expenditures. Democrats retained the committee on Ways and Means, but only by a one-vote margin. They also missed the experienced leadership of the former chairman, Churchill Cambreleng, unsuccessful in his attempt at reelection. Of the fifteen committees that Van Buren's followers dominated, nearly half had Whig chairmen.[38]

One ray of hope came during the election of a printer to the House. The firm of Blair and Rives defeated its archrival, Gales and Seaton, by a vote of 110 to 92. Blair's victory was the first concrete sign of the deterioration of Conservative congressional strength. In 1837, the backers of Thomas Allen prevented a Democratic triumph; now they were nowhere to be seen. Van Buren believed this augured well for the sub-Treasury.[39] Still, the Whig entrenchment in the committee structure could prevent consideration of the divorce bill and place the Democrats permanently on the defensive.[40] With the fall presidential election rapidly approaching, Van Buren wanted to demonstrate that the sub-Treasury could protect government revenue and create economic stability. The longer Congress stalled, the less time the president had to prove his case.

Before they could proceed with confidence, Democratic leaders in the House wanted to make sure they had as many votes as possible. Of necessity, they decided to await the outcome of several election disputes, a delay that frustrated one influential observer. "I am sorry to see that our party has no head . . . in the House," wrote Andrew Jackson from the Hermitage. "It has truly sickened me to see the disgraceful proceedings of Congress & the want of unity in the Republican party to check & put such disgraceful proceedings to our country down."[41] Van Buren could do nothing to stem this criticism; until he knew his precise strength in the House, he could not press for legislative action.

On March 10, 1840, after nearly three months of debate, the House agreed to seat five Democrats from New Jersey instead of the

---

[37] Washington *Globe*, December 30, 1839.
[38] *Congressional Globe*, 26th Cong., 1st sess., 1839–1840, 8: 88–89.
[39] Van Buren to Jackson, February 2, 1840, Van Buren Papers.
[40] Washington *Globe*, April 13, 14, 17, May 19, 1840.
[41] Jackson to Francis P. Blair, February 15, 1840, Jackson Papers.

Whig claimants. This was the impetus that the administration needed. The following day, John W. Jones, the new chairman of the Ways and Means Committee, brought forward the sub-Treasury bill which had been lying on the table for some time.[42] Within two weeks, he guided it through committee and reported it on the House floor. Here, because of further Whig obstruction and more Democratic confusion, the measure languished for almost two months. Finally on May 20, 1840, debate began.[43] There were no new arguments, but there were new speakers; every fledgling legislator seemed determined to air his views on the state of the nation's economy.[44] Administration spokesmen could not persuade their colleagues to attend such repetitious and uninteresting debate. On many days, no more than half the House members appeared during discussions on the divorce bill.[45] Jones had to find a way out of the doldrums if he hoped to marshal sufficient support.

In mid-June the Democrats decided to seek a suspension of the rules so that they could cut off debate and bring the sub-Treasury to a vote. Their first attempt failed, but on June 26 the House voted 124 to 58 to end discussion no later than June 30.[46] Although the president's lieutenants were mobilizing for a final battle, the deliberateness of their preparations frustrated Andrew Jackson. The Old General wrote angrily to Blair demanding to know the reason for such lax discipline and claiming that delinquent Democrats should "be shot as deserters from their post on the lines of the enemy." Blair thought of publishing this letter as an exhortation to the faithful but on reflection decided to await the House vote.[47]

By setting a definite limit on debate, the administration hoped to rally its forces. The president succeeded beyond all expectations. On June 30, 1840, every Democrat save two answered to the roll call; seven members of the opposition were absent. The party invoked the previous question, ending last-ditch efforts at delay. Then the tally began. By a vote of 124 to 107, the House approved the bill. Only four Democrats defected and this loss was partially offset by a gain of two votes from Georgia. As anticipated, the outcome of the election

[42] Congressional Globe, 26th Cong., 1st sess., 1839–1840, 8: 257, 261–62.

[43] House Journal, 26th Cong., 1st sess., 1839–1840, pp. 691, 973.

[44] Francis P. Blair to Jackson, June 17–18, 1840, Jackson Papers.

[45] House Journal, 26th Cong., 1st sess., 1839–1840, pp. 1093, 1100, 1113, 1116–17, 1129, 1138, 1150, 1153, 1165. Francis P. Blair to Jackson, June 17–18, 1840, Jackson Papers.

[46] House Journal, 26th Cong., 1st sess., 1839–1840, pp. 1139–41, 1156–59.

[47] Jackson to Blair, June 27, 1840, Blair to Jackson, July 12, 1840, Jackson Papers; Jackson to Van Buren, June 27, 1840, Van Buren Papers.

disputes proved decisive. In the New Jersey delegation, for instance, all five newly seated congressmen supported Van Buren.[48] Had the party pushed ahead without resolving these contests, it would have jeopardized the final outcome of the divorce bill.

At three o'clock on the afternoon of July 3, 1840, Van Buren received the sub-Treasury bill from Congress. Rather than approve the measure immediately, he decided to wait a day and make his signature a part of the general holiday celebration. As luck would have it, July 4 dawned bright and clear, as "sweetly tempered as a day in May." At nine o'clock in the morning, crowds of citizens gathered along Pennsylvania Avenue, lofting banners and hickory poles in anticipation of a triumphal march through the streets of Washington. The flourishes of the Marine band heightened the festive atmosphere. It was as though the nation's capital had arisen from a long slumber and was once again reliving the thrill of an inauguration.[49]

A more somber mood prevailed in the White House. For the president, this was not a beginning, but an end—a climax to more than three years of bitterness and frustration. By approving the sub-Treasury bill he would complete a crusade begun nearly three years earlier. Yet now only four months remained until the election; Van Buren had little time to demonstrate the economic benefits of the bill resting on his desk. In November the Democrats would face an alliance hardened by recent congressional battles and encouraged by the collapse of Democratic solidarity. This prospect dampened the enthusiasm of those gathered to witness the signing of the "Second Declaration of Independence."

[48] *House Journal*, 26th Cong., 1st sess., 1839–1840, pp. 1170–75. See comments on Whig absenteeism and Democratic discipline in Kenneth Rayner to Willie P. Mangum, June 30, 1840, in Mangum, *Papers*, 3: 35–38.
[49] John Niles to Gideon Welles, July 4, 1840, Welles Papers; Washington *Globe*, July 6, 1840.

Chapter 8

Trouble along
the Border

THE president's untiring efforts to secure passage of the sub-Treasury all but obscured his concern for the explosive issue of slavery. For nearly two decades he had agonized over the sectional dilemma, basing his fortunes on the hope of founding a strong political coalition on a North-South axis. Van Buren believed that the Democratic party and the nation could avoid conflict only by stifling debate on slavery and respecting the dictates of the Constitution. He shared the predominant Southern desire to maintain silence on the peculiar institution. During his quest for the presidency, Van Buren repeatedly avowed his support for state rights, but to some Southerners, pledges alone proved little. These malcontents demanded more positive proof that Van Buren meant what he said; in 1836, the Texas revolution had provided them an opportunity to press their demands. Van Buren, the candidate, nervously studied the growing crisis, trying to keep clear of the pitfalls awaiting a Northern man with Southern principles. His actions in these crucial months prior to the election helped influence administration policy and set a pattern for his own presidential diplomacy.

The battle of San Jacinto on April 21, 1836, established Texas as an independent power and forced the United States to make a difficult choice. Enthusiasm for Sam Houston and his followers swept the country, triggering congressional demands that Jackson recognize the new regime. Although such a move was consonant with the president's impulsive nature and longstanding interest in Texas, it was diplomatically and politically dangerous. Premature recognition might well result in a war with Mexico. Furthermore, extreme elements in both the North and South seized Texas as a vehicle for expounding contradictory views on slavery.[1] As the Democratic nominee, Van Buren could not ignore this issue, not when such influential allies as Thomas Ritchie pleaded the Texan cause. "I can assure you," wrote the Virginia editor, calling for both recognition and annexation, "that the South counts upon you, in making every exertion to carry the measure against the prejudices of the Northern opposition." Fortunately, not all members of the Richmond Junto favored such bold action. Richard E. Parker warned that Van Buren might destroy the New York–Virginia alliance by speaking out on the Texas question.[2]

Heeding this advice, Van Buren sided with those congressional forces seeking delay. During the closing days of the session, William C. Rives and James Buchanan, both Van Buren supporters, consistently opposed recognition, arguing that the government lacked enough information about conditions in Texas. On June 18, 1836, the Senate approved a resolution leaving the matter to President Jackson's discretion. The independence of Texas should be acknowledged whenever he had sufficient proof that the new republic could stand alone. The president swiftly replied that he had received no news to warrant such a determination.[3] This exchange made it clear that Jackson would not act until after the election when Congress reconvened.[4]

As soon as the legislature adjourned, the president returned to the Hermitage for the summer. Although he reportedly favored both recognition and annexation, he decided to await the report of his executive agent, Henry Morfit, dispatched to investigate the situation in Texas. Meanwhile, Jackson made a fainthearted attempt to remain aloof from the conflict between Texas and Mexico.[5] At this time,

[1] For a discussion of the background of this problem see Justin H. Smith, *The Annexation of Texas* (New York, 1911); Stanley Siegel, *A Political History of the Texas Republic* (Austin, Texas, 1956); Joseph W. Schmitz, *Texan Statecraft, 1836–1845* (San Antonio, Texas, 1941); George P. Garrison, "The First Stage of the Movement for the Annexation of Texas," *American Historical Review* 10 (1904): 72–96.

[2] Ritchie to Van Buren, June 9, 1836, Parker to Van Buren, June 29, 1836, Van Buren Papers.

[3] *Congressional Globe*, 24th Cong., 1st sess., 1835–1836, 3: 488–89, 546–47, 565, 583.

[4] William B. Lewis to A. Pageot, July 6, 1836, in Jackson, *Correspondence*, 5: 413n.

[5] James Collinsworth and P. W. Grayson to David Burnet, July 15, 1836, in Garrison, *Texas Correspondence*, pp. 110–11; Jackson, endorsement on Stephen Austin to Jackson, April 15, 1836, Jackson to Amos Kendall, August 12, 1836, in Jackson, *Correspondence*, 5: 398, 420–21; Kendall to Jackson, July 30, 1836, Jackson Papers.

Van Buren was doing his best to keep the Texas question out of the election. For the most part, he succeeded, but Thomas Ritchie continued to prove an embarrassment.[6]

The excitement subsided temporarily. In November 1836 Jackson became dangerously ill. Hemorrhaging severely, he remained a virtual invalid for many weeks.[7] The task of preparing the annual message fell to the cabinet and several key advisers. The president's council decided not to discuss the Texas problem but instead notified the legislature that Jackson would submit a special report on the subject.[8]

Early in December, Van Buren had ample opportunity to visit the ailing chief executive and help in preparing the message on Texas. His words of caution evidently found their mark, for Jackson's next moves were uncharacteristically moderate. On December 8, 1836, the president asked Amos Kendall to prepare a paper on recognition. Jackson was determined to proceed cautiously. If Mexico acknowledged Texan independence, then the United States would be free to follow. This was, at best, a remote possibility; the president thought it advisable to tell Congress of the chaotic conditions in Texas and leave the rest up to them. The legislature alone had the power to declare war. Since immediate recognition might provoke hostilities with Mexico, Congress should make the decision. If both houses recommended acknowledging Texan independence, then Jackson was prepared to acquiesce. In essence, he wanted international or constitutional backing for so momentous a step.[9]

So pleased was Van Buren with the message of December 21 that one suspects he shared in its composition.[10] On the following day he

[6] Richmond *Enquirer*, July 5, 8, 12, 22, August 12, 1836.

[7] Jackson to Van Buren, October 2, 1836, Van Buren Papers; Jackson to Mrs. A. J. Donelson, November 27, 1836, Jackson to Maunsel White, December 2, 1836, in Jackson, *Correspondence*, 5: 439–41; William Wharton to Stephen Austin, December 31, 1836, in Garrison, *Texas Correspondence*, p. 167; Dickerson, MS Diary, November 29, 30, December 2, 1836.

[8] Richardson, *Messages and Papers*, 3: 238. See also John Niles to Gideon Welles, December 6, 1836, Welles Papers.

[9] Jackson to Kendall, December 8, 1836, in Jackson, *Correspondence*, 5: 441; Richardson, *Messages and Papers*, 3: 265–69. A draft of the message in Kendall's handwriting is in the Jackson Papers. Jackson's decision on recognition appears in its historical perspective in Richard W. Leopold, *The Growth of American Foreign Policy: A History* (New York, 1962), pp. 76–77.

[10] The Van Buren Papers contain superficial evidence suggesting the president-elect's role. Under the date of November [?], 1836, there is a memorandum in Jackson's handwriting, setting forth the various aspects of the recognition problem covered in the report of December 21. Whether these were questions to Van Buren, notations of Van Buren's opinions, or simply Jackson's views, it is impossible to say.

wrote to his son: "The President sent in a most interesting message today on the subject of Texas. The nullifiers or at least a branch of them will endeavor to prejudice me in the South in consequence of it." "The thinking and responsible portion of our people," however, "will sustain the views of the President."[11] Van Buren's critics also detected the New Yorker's influence. "The old chief is all for you," Samuel Swartwout wrote to the new Texas minister. "He has always been in your favor and . . . disposed to recommend the acknowledgement of your Independence but for some influences, which I regret to say will soon be in the ascendant as to endanger the objects you came for." "In plain words," added the irate collector, "*Mr. Van Buren, Mr. Forsyth & Mr. Butler are no friends of Texas.*"[12]

In Congress, Van Buren's followers continued their delaying action. When Mississippi's Senator Robert Walker introduced a resolution on January 11, 1837, stating that Texas had a stable government and should be recognized, he ran into immediate opposition from his own party. Early in February, the Senate, by a vote of thirty-one to twelve, refused to take up Walker's proposal. Both Wright and Buchanan sided with the majority. The Texan minister, William Wharton, blamed "the Van Buren party" for this intransigence. "They are afraid that the subject of annexation will be pressed immediately after recognition;—that annexation or no annexation will be made the test of the elections for Congress during the ensuing summer." When the Senate finally agreed to debate the question of recognition, there were only three days left in Jackson's term. Buchanan tried to table the entire matter. After this failed, he and Wright backed a substitute that would have again left recognition to executive discretion. In the House, Cambreleng employed similar obstructionist tactics. Clearly, Van Buren's closest congressional allies were trying to give the president-elect a free hand. Walker refused to be deterred, and on March 1 the Senate approved his resolution twenty-three to nineteen. Gratified by this legislative mandate, Jackson took advantage of his last day in office to nominate Alcée La Branche to be chargé d'affaires to the Republic of Texas.[13] "We see that 'Uncle Sam' has recognized our Independence," rejoiced Sam

[11] Van Buren to John Van Buren, December 22, 1836, Van Buren Papers.
[12] Swartwout to William Wharton, December 21, 1836, Republic of Texas, Diplomatic Correspondence, Texas State Archives.
[13] Wharton to Sam Houston, February 2, 1837, in Garrison, *Texas Correspondence*, p. 180; *Congressional Globe*, 24th Cong., 2d sess., 1836–1837, 4: 185, 263, 270; *Senate Executive Journal*, 4: 631. Note Jackson's wording regarding the prescriptive nature of the Senate's action.

Houston, adding that he would die a happy man if "we are annexed next session." He encouraged Samuel Swartwout to "start the tone in public meetings, and let it bear on the next election for Congress."[14]

Martin Van Buren thus fell heir to a policy not totally to his liking. The extension of recognition was bound to whet the appetites of some of his Southern associates. One Democratic stalwart even thanked the new chief executive for giving "negative support" to the Texan cause.[15] Van Buren ignored the solicitations; he tried to avoid any overt display of sympathy for the Texans, lest this jeopardize relations with Mexico.[16] With Congress no longer in session, the president turned to the more pressing problems of the economy.

As Van Buren absorbed himself in fiscal affairs, the Texas government began planning the next move. It felt annexation was the only cure for the internal anarchy in the new republic. "On the success of this measure," wrote the Texan secretary of state, R. A. Irion, "our permanent prosperity, and, perhaps, existence as an organized Government, mainly depends." Consequently, the Houston administration instructed its representative, Memucan Hunt, to bid for annexation as soon as possible. As added insurance, it dispatched a special agent to lobby among influential American politicians.

Hunt arrived in Washington near the end of June, and on July 6 he met Van Buren. The president was gracious, but noncommittal, and the interview produced a simple exchange of pleasantries. After this formal presentation, Hunt devoted himself exclusively to the task at hand. Prospects looked dim. In May, Forsyth had said that the United States would entertain no thoughts of annexation until Mexico recognized Texan independence. Up to this point, Hunt's observations seemed quite reliable. His dispatches clearly showed administration caution and the president's fear of war with Mexico. Perhaps inspired by Irion's pleas, Hunt threw himself into the cause; growing partisanship clouded his judgment. He now detected a move in the South, so strong "that the administration will be compelled to make the annexation of Texas a leading measure." According to his new analysis, even Van Buren's cabinet favored acquisition of Texas. Furthermore, Hunt felt the Panic had so shaken confidence in the

[14] Houston to Swartwout, March 22, 1837, Houston Papers, Barker Library, University of Texas. See also Houston to R. A. Irion, March 19, 1837, Irion Papers, Barker Library, University of Texas.

[15] Thomas Cooper to Van Buren, April 14, 1837, Van Buren Papers. See also James L. Clark to James Hammond, March 31, 1837, Hammond Papers.

[16] Fairfax Catlett to J. Pinckney Henderson, May 2, 1837, in Garrison, *Texas Correspondence*, p. 215.

Democratic party that the president would use Texas as a means to recruit new support.[17]

Having convinced himself that the political atmosphere was favorable, Hunt decided to act. On August 4, 1837, he formally requested that the United States annex the Republic of Texas. His note was a mixture of invective, propaganda, and bluff. He began by viciously attacking the Mexican government for its treatment of Texas. Then Hunt went into a lengthy justification of the revolt against Mexican rule, including a stirring account of Texan bravery at the Alamo and San Jacinto. After this passionate preamble, he listed the reasons why Texas should become part of the United States. The two nations shared ties of common ancestry, aspirations, and institutions. Texas had a viable regime, and chances were slight that Mexico could recapture the province. Furthermore, the new republic had vast natural resources and a strategic command of the Gulf of Mexico.

When he completed his emotional appeal, the Texan minister predicted the results should the Van Buren administration refuse. Any delay in approving the request would have serious consequences. Texas was already negotiating with major European powers and might soon conclude commercial treaties detrimental to American interests. Rejection would also make it difficult to resolve border tensions. Finally, Hunt argued that if the Van Buren administration did not respond quickly, it would prejudice any future chances for acquiring Texas. As if these reasons alone were not compelling, Hunt closed with another appeal to the American conscience, asking whether a nation like Mexico, "by a constant violation of the most solemn treaty obligations, by a series of the most licentious revolutions, by a most shameful prostitution of the lives, the liberties and the property of her people, and, in short, by every act of perfidy and cruelty recorded in the history of barbarians, has not thereby forfeited all claims to the respect of the Governments of civilized nations?"[18]

Hunt's note of August 4 was anything but a diplomatic triumph. It bordered on the bellicose and gave practically no consideration to the international problems involved in annexation. Worse yet, the Texan

[17] R. A. Irion to Memucan Hunt, June 26, 1837, Irion to John Mason, June 22, 1837, Hunt to Irion, July 11, 1837, in Garrison, *Texas Correspondence*, pp. 230–34, 236–41.
[18] Hunt to Forsyth, August 4, 1837, in *Diplomatic Correspondence of the United States: Inter-American Affairs, 1831–1860*, ed. William R. Manning, 12 vols. (Washington, D.C., 1932–1939), 12: 129–40; hereafter cited as Manning, *Inter-American Correspondence*.

minister picked the wrong moment to deliver his diatribe. Amos Kendall, whom Hunt reckoned a close supporter of annexation, was then absent from Washington. The president was completely preoccupied with preparations for the approaching special session. Given these circumstances, one must conclude that either Hunt was foolish or he intended the dispatch for a much wider audience. In a letter to Irion on August 10, Hunt suggested that should the administration prove unfriendly, it might be wise "to bring the consideration of the subject before Congress, whether the Executive may desire it or not." He even asked for a written appeal to a then-unnamed congressman, "soliciting him to present the within proposition and terms of annexation."[19] The Texan minister may have calculated that the president would oppose annexation, but that Congress at the special session would call for all relevant correspondence on the issue, thus triggering a major debate.

If Hunt expected immediate and enthusiastic administration response to his note of August 4, he was disappointed. Van Buren kept silent. While waiting impatiently for a reply, Hunt learned, to his dismay, that the secretary of state opposed annexation. The irate minister wrote an angry letter back to his superior, impugning Forsyth's character and calling him a "traitor to the most delicate and deepest interests of those to whom he is indebted for the very power and influence he is now attempting to exercise against them." Quite obviously, Hunt was groping for an alibi. He had been overly optimistic about the disposition of the president and was trying to prepare Irion for Van Buren's refusal. By assailing Forsyth, Hunt could minimize his own miscalculations.[20]

Four days after receiving the Texan bid, Van Buren raised the question of annexation at his weekly cabinet meeting. After little deliberation, he and his advisers decided to reject the proposition. Nevertheless, they waited more than two weeks before replying. Finally on August 25, 1837, Forsyth made what amounted to an unqualified refusal. He stated quite plainly that the government would not involve itself in a moral argument about the nature of Mexican rule. The United States was bound to Mexico by a treaty of

[19] Hunt to Irion, August 10, 1837, in Garrison, *Texas Correspondence*, p. 254.
[20] Hunt to Irion, August 11, 1837, in ibid., pp. 255–56; it is conceivable that Forsyth made private assurances favoring annexation. This would not have been out of character. Still, the Texas government should have been under no misapprehensions; its former representative in Washington, William Wharton, had previously indicated that Forsyth opposed even the recognition report (Wharton to Rusk, February 12, 1837, in ibid., p. 194).

amity; annexation of Texas might well be construed as a breach of this faith as well as a violation of neutrality. Furthermore, the American nation had never before been asked to annex a sovereign state. The constitutional objections to such acquisition were too great. In closing, the secretary of state dismissed Hunt's veiled threats of foreign influence by saying that the Van Buren administration would never object to Texas' establishing commercial ties with European powers.[21] Although the wording of the note was Forsyth's, the concern for neutrality and the Constitution were Van Buren's. Beset by financial crisis and party strife, the president wanted no part of such an explosive question.

Hunt refused to accept this setback without a reply. Shortly after the special session of Congress assembled, he dispatched a petulant communiqué, the apparent aim of which was to convince Van Buren of the administration's mistake. The Texan minister went so far as to venture that had Jackson been president, the United States would never have refused the Texas offer. Hunt concluded with an account of the evils that would follow in the wake of rejection.[22] Again he displayed a remarkable lack of tact.

Although sorely disappointed, the Texans had not given up hope. They had yet to press their case before Congress. When John Quincy Adams called for all correspondence relating to annexation, Hunt anticipated a lengthy and fruitful debate. The Texan minister felt that once these documents were made public, Congress might well pass a joint resolution asking Texas to set forth in detail the conditions under which it would agree to annexation. He hoped that both houses would then present the president with a mandate. Even the optimistic Hunt soon realized that such plans would have to wait until December; Congress was hopelessly preoccupied by economic matters.[23]

With the close of the special session in October 1837, the first act of the Texas drama came to a close. The government of the new republic remained unstable; it had failed to safeguard its sovereignty by gaining admission to the Union. Hunt still smarted over the rebuke suffered at the hands of the Van Buren administration—a

[21] Dickerson, MS Diary, August 8, 1837; Forsyth to Hunt, August 25, 1837, in Manning, *Inter-American Correspondence*, 12: 11–13.

[22] Hunt to Forsyth, September 12, 1837, in Manning, *Inter-American Correspondence*, 12: 140–45.

[23] Hunt to R. A. Irion, September 18, 1837, in Garrison, *Texas Correspondence*, pp. 258–59; *Congressional Globe*, 25th Cong., 1st sess., 1837, 5: 24–26, 117, 121.

rebuff made all the more painful by his own unrealistic evaluations of the political climate at Washington. He hoped to recover some ground at the next session when some observers predicted that Calhoun and the nullifiers would champion the Texan cause.[24] By the time Van Buren greeted Congress in December, Texas and annexation had become inextricably mixed with the problem of Mexican-American relations.

All the time Jackson and Van Buren struggled with the Texas question, they had to keep a watchful eye on developments in Mexico. The Texan revolt placed the United States in the difficult position of trying to maintain neutrality in a dispute in which its citizens overwhelmingly favored one side. This obvious partisanship made the Mexicans apprehensive and deepened their longstanding distrust of American policy.

The United States and Mexico had always regarded each other with suspicion. The government in Washington believed that internal instability made Mexico a troublesome and dangerous neighbor; the various regimes in Mexico City looked on the American nation as irresponsible and avaricious. By 1836, tensions reached a climax. The Mexicans suspected Jackson of giving secret aid to the insurgents in Texas. The president vehemently denied any such intentions, but the movements of General Edmund P. Gaines along the border did little to ease Mexican fears. It was against this background of doubt and hostility that the two countries tried to resolve a longstanding claims dispute.[25]

During the course of numerous internal struggles, Mexico had inflicted considerable damage on civilian property. In some instances the injured persons were United States citizens who for years had tried unsuccessfully to seek redress. During his second administration, Jackson tried to persuade the Mexican government to recognize the validity of these claims. Each time he met with delay. Finally in January 1836 the president instructed his new chargé d'affaires, Powhatan Ellis, to concentrate specifically on bringing these grievances to the attention of Mexican authorities. Although appreciating Mexico's domestic problems, Jackson felt they afforded "no sufficient apology for refusing or declining thus long to examine the claims." Ellis left for Mexico but could make little headway. The Mexicans,

---

[24] Caleb Cushing to [?], October 14, 1837, Carton 14, Cushing Papers, Library of Congress.

[25] For background on this see George L. Rives, *The United States and Mexico, 1821–1848*, 2 vols. (New York, 1913); James M. Callahan, *American Foreign Policy in Mexican Relations* (New York, 1932).

he felt, "look upon us as either too imbecile, or afraid to vindicate our just rights." Consequently he recommended more stringent action.[26]

While Ellis labored fruitlessly south of the border, the Jackson administration was finding it difficult to convince Mexico's special emissary, Manuel Gorostiza, that Gaines's actions were solely defensive. Jackson contended that the United States was justified in deploying troops to protect its citizens from attacks by hostile Mexican Indians. In October 1836 Gorostiza issued another in a long series of objections against such unilateral actions by American forces. He claimed that the Indian threat was imaginary and requested Jackson to recall Gaines. According to Gorostiza, "Mexico is outraged and ruined, from motives of mere precaution." When this plea proved futile, he asked for his passports and prepared to leave Washington.[27] Before departing, Gorostiza committed a serious breach of diplomatic privilege by writing a pamphlet containing extracts from official correspondence. This irresponsible action greatly increased tensions between the two nations.

At approximately the same time, Powhatan Ellis decided that it was senseless to continue negotiations with authorities in Mexico City. He had convinced the Mexican government that the United States was serious, but he failed to obtain satisfactory replies. Finally, his patience wore thin, and in December 1836 he requested his credentials.[28] Thus, while Jackson lay dangerously ill in Washington, the United States and Mexico simultaneously severed lines of communication.

Despite these ominous developments, the annual message of 1836 dealt with the Mexican problem in a relatively dispassionate manner. The president mentioned the failure to settle outstanding claims and the disagreement with Gorostiza, but then added: "I trust, however, by tempering firmness with courtesy, and acting with great forbearance upon every incident . . . to do and to obtain justice, and thus avoid the necessity of again bringing this subject to the view of Congress." In a dispatch to Ellis on December 10, Forsyth was

---

[26] John Forsyth to Ellis, January 29, 1836; Ellis to Forsyth, May 28, 1836, in *House Documents* (No. 351), 25th Cong., 2d sess., 1837–1838, pp. 160–62, 591–92.
[27] Asbury Dickens to Gorostiza, October 13, 1836, Gorostiza to Dickens, October 15, 1836, in ·Manning, *Inter-American Correspondence*, 8: 66–69, 369–75.
[28] Ellis to John Forsyth, October 25, November 10, 30, December 21, 1836, in Manning, *Inter-American Correspondence*, 8: 376, 378–79, 391, 401.

equally temperate. Although he discussed Gorostiza's pamphlet, he made no specific demand for reparation.[29]

This conciliatory spirit lasted only a few months. On February 6, 1837, Jackson told Congress of the stalemate in the claims controversy and stated that "in the eyes of all nations" Mexican actions would justify "immediate war." Before resorting to such methods, Jackson thought it appropriate to give Mexico "one more opportunity to atone for the past"; the president wanted this demand delivered from the decks of an American warship. Since Congress would soon adjourn, Jackson asked for authority to use force should this final mission fail.

Jackson's warlike message startled the Washington community.[30] At the opening of the session, he had expressed hope that the dispute might be settled amicably. Suddenly, he dashed off a note requesting contingent power to initiate reprisals. There had been no new developments or communications from Mexico to warrant such a change of heart; the State Department had for some time been aware of Mexican intransigence.

The president's dramatic about-face is not totally inexplicable. He had just recovered from his illness and was soon to leave the White House. Jackson wanted to end his public career on a high note; he planned to emulate Washington by delivering a farewell address. Yet even in these final months, the president's enemies would not relent. Congressmen Henry Wise and Balie Peyton had even concocted an investigation of the executive branch. Their committee promised to steal the spotlight from the retiring chief executive. While brooding over these developments, Jackson received a visit from Powhatan Ellis and learned firsthand of the failure of the Mexican mission. Four days later, the president made his unexpected presentation to the legislature.[31]

Satisfying though this strong declaration may have been to the beleaguered Old Hero, it caused serious problems for his successor. Van Buren did not want his hands tied at the outset of his administration. Should Congress approve Jackson's request, Van Buren

[29] Richardson, *Messages and Papers*, 3: 238; Forsyth to Ellis, December 10, 1836, in Manning, *Inter-American Correspondence*, 8: 71–75. It is possible that Ellis did not receive this note prior to his departure from Mexico in late December.

[30] Richardson, *Messages and Papers*, 3: 278–79; Henry Fox to Lord Palmerston, February 12, 1837 (No. 6), PRO:FO: 5, Vol. 314, Pt. II.

[31] Jackson to A. J. Donelson, January 9, 24, 31, 1837, Jackson to Benjamin C. Howard, February 2, 1837, in Jackson, *Correspondence*, 5: 449–50, 451–52, 456–57.

would have little diplomatic leeway. Although the president-elect refused to divulge his views on Mexico, there was little doubt that he opposed reprisals.[32] His close friend Thomas Ritchie expressed belief that Congress would consider "milder measures . . . than those which were suggested by the President's Message."[33]

The chairman of the Senate Foreign Relations Committee, James Buchanan, shared these views. In a lengthy report, unanimously adopted by all his committee colleagues, Buchanan admitted that the United States had cause for grievance but urged Congress to proceed cautiously. Although he defended Jackson's policies, Buchanan maintained "it was a matter of extreme delicacy for Congress to confer upon the executive the power of making reprisals upon a future contingency." He also ignored Jackson's suggestion that the next overture be accompanied by a military display. Buchanan agreed on the need for further negotiations, but if these failed, the president was to leave matters with the legislature. This statement implied that Van Buren would be able to approach the problem in his own way, without being committed to the use of force. Buchanan justified these moderate recommendations by saying that "whilst negotiations continued, it was not politic to use the language of menace." On February 27, the Senate unanimously approved the committee report. In the House, Van Buren's close associate, Churchill Cambreleng, prevented even so moderate a response to Jackson's message.[34]

As Van Buren took office, the British minister Henry Fox commented on administration reaction to the recent congressional decisions. "The President's government do not appear to be so much surprised, or displeased, as might have been expected at the temperate course pursued upon this occasion by Congress, in contradiction to the menacing tone of the executive message."[35] Indeed, Van Buren probably rejoiced at the rejection of warlike measures.

In accordance with the spirit of the Senate resolution, the new president decided to make one last attempt to reach agreement with Mexico. He had just received word that the government in Mexico City was confused by Jackson's belligerence. Still, Van Buren hoped a new mission might be effective.[36] Since both nations had broken

[32] Nathaniel P. Tallmadge to Van Buren, February 14, 1837, Van Buren to Tallmadge, February 14 [?], 1837, Van Buren Papers.

[33] Richmond *Enquirer*, February 11, 1837.

[34] *Congressional Globe*, 24th Cong., 2d sess., 1836–1837, 4: 218–19, 250–51, 257, 262–63, 271.

[35] Fox to Lord Palmerston, March 12, 1837 (No. 8), PRO:FO: 5, Vol. 314, Pt. III.

[36] R. R. Waldron to Levi Woodbury, March 10, 12, 1837, Woodbury Papers.

diplomatic ties, the president thought it proper to send an executive agent for the sole purpose of delivering American demands and waiting for a reply. For the task, he selected Robert Greenhow, a State Department official who had worked on the claims papers and was familiar with their contents.[37] Greenhow was to proceed to Mexico, present the American dispatches, wait one week, and then return.

The special emissary set out under unusual circumstances. He carried an official letter from the secretary of state, calling Mexico's attention to a list of fifty-seven outstanding claims and complaining of previous delays. Should Mexico fail to make suitable response, then, Forsyth contended, "the United States may be justified in the eyes of all nations for any measures they shall be compelled to take." In addition to this official remonstrance, Greenhow bore a private letter from Joel R. Poinsett to Mexican President Anastasio Bustamente. The secretary of war took the opportunity to express American desires for peace and friendship.[38] Apparently, no one in Washington worried about the contradiction between these two notes.

After a brief trip from Florida, Greenhow arrived in Vera Cruz on July 15, 1837, and left immediately for the Mexican capital. He obtained an interview with Minister of Foreign Affairs Luis Cuevas on July 20. At the same time he met Bustamente and delivered Poinsett's private greetings. Both the Mexican president and his minister immediately noticed the difference between Forsyth's warnings and Poinsett's assurances. Despite this shaky start, subsequent talks proceeded smoothly. Greenhow told Cuevas that the United States wanted the claims examined and acknowledged, but did not demand immediate reparation. In return, the Van Buren administration pledged to continue to respect Mexican territory. Discussions reached a minor impasse on the question of Gorostiza's conduct. The Mexican government found its minister's actions embarrassing, but it was not in a position to chastise publicly so influential an official. At the end of these meetings, Greenhow was impressed by Bustamente's sincerity but still wary of the political instability of the Mexican regime.[39]

---

[37] William B. Hodgson to William C. Rives, June 3, 1837, Rives Papers.
[38] Forsyth to Minister of Foreign Affairs, Republic of Mexico, May 27, 1837, Forsyth to Greenhow, May 27, 1837, in Manning, *Inter-American Correspondence*, 8: 79–83; Greenhow to Poinsett, August 14, 1837, Poinsett Papers in the Gilpin Collection.
[39] Bustamente to Poinsett, July 28, 1837, Greenhow to Poinsett, August 14, 1837, Poinsett Papers in the Gilpin Collection; Greenhow to Forsyth, August 10,

On July 29, 1837, Cuevas delivered his government's reply. In essence, Bustamente agreed to look seriously at the list of claims and to compare American documents with those in the Mexican Foreign Office. This would take some time, but Bustamente promised to transmit the Mexican decisions as soon as possible. Having fulfilled his instructions, Greenhow returned to the United States.[40]

Van Buren had again encountered delay but not total rejection. Originally he had given some thought to bringing the Mexican problem before the special session, but Bustamente's friendly attitude convinced the president to await the arrival of the new Mexican minister, Francisco Martinez.[41] Although Martinez reached Washington in mid-October, it was more than a month before he made any formal communication concerning the claims. Finally, on November 18, he broke silence and delivered the long-awaited Mexican answer. Instead of referring specifically to all fifty-seven cases, the note mentioned only eight, five of which never appeared on the list Forsyth had sent to Mexico in the summer.[42]

The president was now in a dilemma. Congress would soon reconvene, and he was obligated to report on the state of negotiations with Mexico. He could cite Bustamente's cooperative spirit as a hopeful sign, but then he would have a difficult time explaining Mexico's apparent unwillingness to act on specific claims. Furthermore, Congress was on record as favoring only one more mission. Although Van Buren was bound to mention the stalemate, he did so in a much more temperate manner than had his predecessor. He did not submit a special report but simply incorporated his views in the annual message. Where Jackson assailed Mexican sins and threatened war, Van Buren approached his subject cautiously. After reviewing all previous attempts at settlement, he solemnly told of the repeated disappointments. Significantly, he made no mention of Gorostiza's pamphlet but simply referred the entire matter to Congress, for them to "decide upon the time, the mode, and the measure of redress." Then, as if this language were in itself too extreme, he added:

1837, Dispatches from the United States Ministers to Mexico, 1823–1906, 9, National Archives.

[40] Cuevas to Forsyth, July 29, 1837, in Manning, *Inter-American Correspondence,* 8: 420–21.

[41] Mrs. Francis P. Blair to James Buchanan, June 2, 1837, Buchanan Papers, The Historical Society of Pennsylvania; Levi Woodbury to Silas Wright, June 5, 1837, Woodbury Papers.

[42] Martinez to John Forsyth, October 14, November 18, 1837, in *House Documents* (No. 3), 25th Cong., 2d sess., 1837–1838, pp. 117–32.

"Whatever may be your decision, it shall be faithfully executed, *confident that it will be characterized by that moderation and justice which will, I trust, under all circumstances govern the councils of our country.*"[43]

A chorus of criticism drowned out the president's emphasis on moderation. According to the *National Intelligencer*, Van Buren sought war with Mexico to divert attention from the Panic.[44] The primary proponent of this conspiracy theory was the indefatigable John Quincy Adams. In a speech to the House on December 12, 1837, he claimed that "The annexation of Texas and the proposed war with Mexico are one and the same thing."[45] Ever since the inauguration, the elder statesman believed that the administration was secretly fomenting tensions with Mexico in order to acquire Texas. To Adams, this entire project was designed to increase the power of slavery and to bind the North inseparably to the defense of Southern institutions.[46] In such a state of mind, he found it difficult to place any faith in the sincerity of Van Buren's request for calm, especially when the president's new ally, John C. Calhoun, was bent on pressing proslavery resolutions in the Senate.

Specifically, Adams complained that the administration had been dishonest. To prove his point, he referred to a resolution passed by the Mexican legislature on May 20, 1837, authorizing Bustamente to settle the claims dispute. Why had Van Buren ignored this document? Certainly it indicated Mexico's willingness to reach agreement.[47] Adams failed to mention that at the time of the annual message, the president had no official knowledge of the Mexican resolution. Martinez did not transmit this paper to the State Department until December 23, 1837.[48]

Adams's fears were largely groundless. Van Buren had no reason to provoke hostilities or to goad Congress to warlike measures. The

[43] Richardson, *Messages and Papers*, 3: 378–79. Italics mine. Significantly, most authors who quote Van Buren's message ignore this pacific passage.
[44] *National Intelligencer*, December 6, 1837.
[45] *Niles National Register*, 53: 267. The *Congressional Globe* did not print Adams's speech.
[46] Adams to Nicholas Biddle, March 30, 1837, Adams to Charles Francis Adams, April 4, 1837, Adams to Solomon Lincoln, November 13, 1837, Adams to William E. Channing, November 21, 1837, Adams MS Letterbook (1837), Adams Family Papers.
[47] *Congressional Globe*, 25th Cong., 2d sess., 1837–1838, 6: 54. For further discussion of this see Samuel Flagg Bemis, *John Quincy Adams and the Union* (New York, 1956). Bemis supports the conspiracy theory but cites little evidence aside from Adams's own statements; see p. 361.
[48] Martinez to Forsyth, December 23, 1837, in *House Documents* (No. 351), 25th Cong., 2d sess., 1837–1838, p. 9.

nation was in the midst of a severe depression, and the balance in the Treasury was dangerously low. The special session had opened deep splits in the party, and mention of slavery only widened these breaches. For this reason, Van Buren's congressional followers tried to soften Calhoun's proslavery resolutions. They had nothing to gain by fanning the fires of sectional controversy. Furthermore, a growing crisis on the northern frontier disrupted relations with England. Under these circumstances, Van Buren's sole aim was to maintain domestic and international peace. He had neither the appetite nor the resources for the annexation of Texas or war with Mexico.

Following the president's lead, the Democratic-dominated Senate Foreign Relations Committee delayed action on the Mexican question. During the next four months, James Buchanan made practically no effort to consider Van Buren's message. Finally, on April 11, 1838, when pressed by the ardent annexationist Robert Walker, Buchanan stated that the first step properly belonged to the House. It alone could authorize the funds necessary to sustain any military action. He advised delay until the "popular branch" of the legislature had its say.[49]

As Buchanan neatly dodged the opposition, Van Buren worked behind the scenes to reach an amicable agreement with Mexico. Since early in March 1838, Martinez had appeared more willing to negotiate. He now had concrete information on the list of claims, and his superiors seemed to be making a genuine effort to effect a reasonable settlement. Suddenly, on April 7, the Mexican minister suggested referral of the entire matter to arbitration by a third party.

Although intrigued, Van Buren hesitated when Martinez asked for a guarantee of American neutrality.[50] The president feared that Bustamente might be using this issue to frustrate negotiations. Would not another pledge of American neutrality be interpreted as an admission of previous sins? Before acting on the Mexican note, the president sought advice from the secretary of war. As a former minister to Mexico, Poinsett was familiar with that country's politics. He hastened to assure Van Buren that Bustamente was acting in good faith and that the question of neutrality need not prejudice a peaceful settlement.[51] On April 21, Van Buren agreed to the Mexican

[49] *Congressional Globe*, 25th Cong., 2d sess., 1837–1838, 6: 298–300, 301.

[50] Martinez to Forsyth, March 2, April 7, 1838, in *House Documents* (No. 351) 25th Cong., 2d sess., 1837–1838, pp. 16–17, 20–21.

[51] Van Buren to Poinsett, April [?] 8, 1838, Poinsett to Van Buren, April 8–9, 1838, Poinsett Papers.

proposal, adding briefly that his government had always followed and would continue to pursue a neutral course.[52] This exchange served as the basis for a subsequent convention, signed on September 11, 1838, setting forth the details of arbitration. Although final disposition did not come until two years later, the threat of hostilities had ceased.

During these early months in 1838, the Texas representatives eagerly watched developments in Congress. At the opening of the session, they hoped that the dispute with Mexico would aid their cause. American respect for the Mexican Treaty of 1832 had long been a major obstacle to annexation. Should open warfare erupt, the president might take the opportunity to acquire the former Mexican province. Van Buren's annual message quickly dampened these expectations. The Texas legation soon recognized that although the president referred the claims dispute to Congress, he did so in a manner calculated to evoke reason rather than anger.[53]

The anticipated debate on Texas never took place. Calhoun's colleague William C. Preston tried to bring an annexation resolution to a vote, but the Senate refused to cooperate.[54] Congress had grown wary of sectional agitation, especially since Calhoun had made such an issue with his proslavery resolutions. The nullifiers did not concede defeat, but with their champion silenced, there seemed little hope of rekindling the annexation fire.[55] Even the Texas government now appreciated this fact. Late in 1837, Irion admitted that Van Buren's outright rejection of the annexation proposal had radically altered sentiments in Texas.[56] In view of the continued congressional delay, and the rapprochement between Mexico and the United States, the Texan authorities saw little reason to agitate further. On October 12, 1838, they formally withdrew their request.[57]

As Van Buren discovered, the Jackson legacy contained diplomatic as well as political perils. The Old Hero's rash, intemperate personality put vigor in American policy but also undermined respect for the United States as a peaceful power. Upon taking office, Van Buren found it difficult to convince foreign envoys of his sincerity in desir-

[52] Forsyth to Martinez, April 21, 1838, in Manning, *Inter-American Correspondence*, 8: 85.
[53] P. W. Grayson to R. A. Irion, December 7, 1837, in Garrison, *Texas Correspondence*, pp. 273–74.
[54] *Congressional Globe*, 25th Cong., 2d sess., 1837–1838, 6: 76.
[55] Memucan Hunt to R. A. Irion, February 3, 1838, in Garrison, *Texas Correspondence*, p. 290.
[56] Irion to Hunt, December 31, 1837, in ibid., p. 279. See also Ashbel Smith to Barnard Bee, March 21, 1838, Smith Papers, Barker Library, University of Texas.
[57] Anson Jones to Aaron Vail, October 12, 1838, in Manning, *Inter-American Correspondence*, 12: 173–74.

ing to preserve neutrality. John Quincy Adams was not alone in suspecting a Southern plot to acquire slave territory; the Texans, too, counted on massive Southern pressure to aid their cause. Since Jackson had been avowedly friendly to the new republic, the Texans concluded that the Southern-oriented Van Buren would be even more receptive to the idea of annexation.

These calculations proved erroneous. The annexation of Texas might have made the South feel more secure, but Van Buren thought that the risks outweighed the rewards. He had helped found the party on a North-South axis, and he refused to abandon either pole to gratify the desires of the other. Like many Southerners, the president believed that the less said on slavery, the better. With the party under attack in Congress, he shied away from the Texas question, hoping to avoid renewal of the destructive sectional debate. "In short, it is not to be disguised," wrote Memucan Hunt, appraising the failure of Texan strategy, "that many of our friends as well as enemies in Congress dread the coming of the question at this time, on account of the desperate death-struggle, which they foresee, will enevitably ensue between the North and the South;—a struggle involving.the probability of a dissolution of this Union."[58]

[58] Memucan Hunt to R. A. Irion, January 31, 1838, in Garrison, *Texas Correspondence*, p. 287. See also J. W. Hampton to Ashbel Smith, October 9, 1837, Smith Papers.

Chapter 9

Neutrality
on Trial

THE president's actions during the Texas controversy reflect his determination to keep the United States on a peaceful, neutral course, a
goal he first set forth in his inaugural. Like his predecessors, he felt
bound by the precepts of Washington's Farewell Address. "Our
course of foreign policy has been so uniform and intelligible," Van
Buren told the sun-drenched crowd, "as to constitute a rule of
Executive conduct which leaves little to my discretion, unless, indeed, I were willing to run counter to the lights of experience." He
pledged to "cultivate the friendship" of world powers, but to "decline
alliances"; he promised to keep America's commercial relations on
"equal terms" with those of other nations.[1] A country so sprawling
and so intensely concerned with internal affairs ardently subscribed
to these traditional maxims. Having barely outgrown its infancy, the
nation welcomed relief from entanglement abroad.

Yet as Alexis de Tocqueville shrewdly observed, a democracy found
it difficult to "persevere in a fixed design, and work out its execution
in spite of serious obstacles." "These are qualities," he concluded,
"which more especially belong to an individual or an aristocracy." In
part this failing related to the American tendency to "obey impulse
rather than prudence, and to abandon a mature design for the
gratification of a momentary passion."[2] Should trouble erupt, the
administration at Washington was at the mercy of the federal system, reliant upon state authorities to deal with disturbances. The
military establishment was small; habitual aversion to a large standing army had seriously weakened the nation's defenses. The conten-
tiousness of American citizens, the lack of adequate civil discipline,
and the decentralization of society, all contributed to occasional
breaches of neutrality. One of the most serious incidents of this kind
occurred during Van Buren's first year as president, when a rebellion .

in Canada threatened to involve England and the United States in war. Ironically, the storm centered on the frontier in Van Buren's home state of New York.

Canadian dissatisfaction with British colonial rule reached a peak in the fall of 1837. William Lyon Mackenzie and Louis Jean Papineau led an uprising that spread throughout Upper and Lower Canada; sporadic and ill organized, these outbursts nevertheless constituted a definite threat to the British administration. British troops put an end to the fighting, but Mackenzie and Papineau escaped across the border and continued preaching their doctrines on American soil.

Imbued with the spirit of liberty and democracy, United States citizens formed an eager audience for the Canadian rebels. Mackenzie successfully recruited both men and supplies for reentry into Canada; the president was powerless to halt the spread of organizations sympathetic to the Canadian rebellion. He could invoke the neutrality act of 1818, but this was at best an imperfect piece of legislation. It was primarily punitive and geared to prevent only flagrant filibustering expeditions. During Monroe's administration, privateering posed the most serious challenge to peace. As a result, the neutrality law made no adequate provision for detecting and arresting land-based attacks on a friendly power contiguous to the United States. Furthermore, local juries often hesitated to indict those taking part in an apparent defense of the principles on which the United States was founded.

When he did act to enforce this statute, the president found his means quite limited. Those charged with immediate supervision of the law often gave in to local pressures. Military units could offer little assistance. At the time of the rebellion in Canada, the regular army numbered only eight thousand men. Over half were in the South fighting the Seminoles; the remainder manned sixty posts throughout the country. With an Indian war in Florida and unrest in Texas, the army naturally focused on the South and West. This left the Canadian frontier all but defenseless. Army commanders apparently thought nothing of staffing northern garrisons with the aged and infirm, freeing more able combatants for service elsewhere.[3]

---

[1] Richardson, *Messages and Papers*, 3: 319-20. See also statements in Van Buren's annual messages: pp. 373, 530, 603.

[2] Alexis de Tocqueville, *Democracy in America*, trans. Henry Reeve, ed. Phillips Bradley, 2 vols. (New York, 1945), 1: 235.

[3] Report of the Secretary of War, December 2, 1837, in *Senate Documents* (No. 1), 25th Cong., 2d sess., 1837-1838, pp. 171-211; Edmund P. Gaines to Joel R. Poinsett, March 18, 1837, Van Buren Papers.

In case of serious trouble, the chief executive could always call out the militia, but a levy of reserves created nothing but confusion. In addition to contending with the inevitable friction between regular and irregular forces, the president ran the risk of reviving public antipathy toward a large standing army. As Van Buren later discovered, any attempt to streamline or reform the militia resulted in widespread criticism. In view of his limited resources, the president had to rely almost exclusively upon state authorities to uphold the laws. If these officials failed in their duties, the nation suffered.

Late in November 1837, reports of the outbursts in Canada reached Washington.[4] At first the accounts were so vague that they created little concern, but by the time Congress reconvened, Van Buren realized the situation was serious. On December 7, he informed the governors and district attorneys in Michigan, New York, and Vermont of the disturbances, requesting them to arrest any persons making preparations "of a hostile nature against any foreign power in amity with the United States."[5] These instructions, if carried out to the letter, might have prevented further trouble.

The local response was neither as prompt nor as powerful as Van Buren expected. New York's Governor William L. Marcy, already at odds with Washington on domestic policy, thought the federal government must deal with foreign disturbances. Furthermore, he was ill and preoccupied with his annual report to the state legislature. Although aware of the gatherings along the border, Marcy apparently believed them harmless.[6]

Van Buren continued to receive distressing news from the frontier. The mayor of Buffalo wrote that Mackenzie had addressed a huge throng on the evening of December 15 and the following day had assembled men and arms for a foray into Canada. "The Civil Authorities," claimed the mayor, "have no adequate force to control these men, and unless the General Government should interfere, there is no way to prevent serious disturbances." After reading this communiqué, Van Buren directed the federal district attorney Nathaniel Benton to leave for the troubled region. At that moment, Benton was nearly 200 miles from Buffalo, but he vowed to start out immediately.

[4] Benjamin F. Butler to Van Buren, November 28, 1837, Van Buren Papers.
[5] John Forsyth to Daniel Kellog et al., December 7, 1837, John Forsyth to William L. Marcy et al., December 7, 1837, *House Documents* (No. 74), 25th Cong., 2d sess., 1837–1838, pp. 29–30.
[6] William L. Marcy to Prosper M. Wetmore, December 22, 31, 1837, Marcy Papers; Marcy to Sir Francis Head, December 21, 1837, in Ivor D. Spencer, *The Victor and the Spoils: A Life of William L. Marcy* (Providence, R.I., 1959), pp. 105–106. See also E. B. O'Callaghan to Caleb Cushing, February 7, 1838, Carton 16, Cushing Papers.

The intrepid law officer was unfamiliar with the Niagara region, and he took more than a week to prepare for the journey. During this time he convinced himself that the task was hopeless.[7] What one uninformed, fearful stranger could have done to quell a spontaneous uprising is best left to the imagination.

While Benton marshaled his courage for the coming ordeal, Mackenzie's followers took up fortified positions on Navy Island, a small land mass on the Canadian side of the Niagara River. Once established, they proclaimed a provisional government for Upper Canada and set about drilling their forces. By Christmas, the rebels boasted a garrison of 700 men and commanded twelve pieces of artillery. Their presence on Navy Island created a serious problem for both American and British authorities.[8] Despite these ominous developments, Van Buren gave no thought to calling out the militia; as yet, he had little concrete evidence that New York was incapable of dealing with the situation.[9]

Since the United States seemed oblivious to the developments on Navy Island, the British decided to intervene. As a target, they selected the steamship *Caroline*, a forty-six-ton vessel recently pressed into service to supply the rebel fortress. A raiding party set out on December 29, 1837, intending to attack the ship in Canadian waters, but it found the *Caroline* tied to the pier at Schlosser, New York. Ignoring the boundary line, the British commander led his men aboard the ship, set it aflame, and cast it adrift. The *Caroline* floated into midstream and sank before reaching the falls. In the ensuing confusion, one American was killed and several wounded.

Reports of the raid spread quickly. Each account tended to amplify and exaggerate the incident; George Templeton Strong registered the shock and dismay of the American public when he wrote: "It is infamous—forty unarmed American citizens butchered in cold blood, while sleeping, by a party of British assassins, and living and dead

[7] J. Trowbridge to Van Buren, December 14, 1837, Benton to Forsyth, December 18, 26, 1837, in *House Documents* (No. 74), 25th Cong., 2d sess., 1837–1838, pp. 30–31, 33–34, 43–44.
[8] Pierre Barker to Van Buren, December 23, 1837, ibid., pp. 42–43; N. Ganon to Van Buren, December 28, 1837, in Richardson, *Messages and Papers*, 3: 399–400; Rensselaer Van Rensselaer to Solomon Van Rensselaer, December 25, 1837, in Bonney, *Legacy*, 2: 68–69.
[9] Albert B. Corey, *The Crisis of 1830–1842 in Canadian-American Relations* (New Haven, Conn., 1941), p. 48, argues that Van Buren was under pressure to employ force. He cites one newspaper editorial in the New York *Morning Herald* and a letter from Charles J. Ingersoll. Neither is a reliable source. The *Herald* was a member of the "penny press," and Ingersoll wanted Van Buren to use the Canadian crisis as a pretext for a crusade to end British colonial rule in Canada. That Van Buren dismissed these arguments is not surprising.

sent together over Niagara." The president heard the news as he was preparing to entertain prominent Whig leaders at a White House banquet. He broke in on his guests and quickly pulled General Winfield Scott aside, saying, "Blood has been shed; you must go with all speed to the Niagara frontier."[10] Since local authorities had been unable to cope with the situation, Van Buren felt a presidential representative might command respect.

Recognizing the delicacy of the mission, Van Buren tried to prepare Scott for potential problems. If the general used the militia, he was not to arm border residents. No one could be certain they would not desert and join the rebels. Van Buren also stated that Scott had no legal authority to use force in restraining unneutral activity, but he wanted him to use his *"influence* to prevent such excesses." To impress Americans with the severity of the crisis, Van Buren issued a neutrality proclamation calling for strict adherence to the law.[11]

Simultaneously, the president requested the assistance of Congress, recommending a careful revision of the existing neutrality legislation. Three days later, on January 8, 1838, he informed the legislature that he had called out the militia and requested the necessary appropriations. The president added that he would seek reparation for destruction of the *Caroline*.[12] Van Buren's firm, decisive actions contrasted sharply with the dilatory manner in which his predecessor had dealt with the question of neutrality in the dispute between Mexico and Texas.

Even this forthright response did not allay the fears of the British minister. Henry Fox appreciated Van Buren's "earnest and decided measures" and felt that Scott would exert a moderating influence on the frontier. As the weeks passed, however, Fox grew increasingly disgruntled over congressional apathy. The legislature made little effort to act on the president's urgent message; Fox felt that neither house was responding "as frankly or as expediently as we had a right to expect."

Congress delayed for several reasons. At the beginning of the

---

[10] George Templeton Strong, *The Diary of George Templeton Strong, 1835–1875*, ed. Allan Nevins and Milton Halsey Thomas, 4 vols. (New York, 1952), 1: 81; Winfield Scott, *Memoirs of Lieut-General Scott*, 2 vols. (New York, 1864), 1: 307.

[11] Joel R. Poinsett to Winfield Scott, January 5, 1838, Van Buren Proclamation, January 5, 1838, in Richardson, *Messages and Papers*, 3: 403, 481; Corey, *Crisis in Canadian-American Relations*, p. 46. Corey mistakenly places Van Buren's first neutrality proclamation in November 1837. As a result, his interpretation of the president's initial response to insurgent activity is open to challenge.

[12] Richardson, *Messages and Papers*, 3: 399, 401.

session, Van Buren had given top priority to fiscal reform, and his managers busily prepared the sub-Treasury bill. It was also at this moment that John C. Calhoun insisted on taking up precious time with his proslavery resolutions. The Mexican claims dispute added greatly to the confusion. "We are in the midst of a Florida war," complained Levi Woodbury, "a quasi Mexican war—& almost a Canadian war. Beside these, we have our domestic difficulties as to the currency—the keeping of the public money—and numerous other less exciting topics." By the end of January, Congress finally approved a bill authorizing expenditures of $625,000 for defense of the frontier.[13]

Meanwhile, Scott had reached Buffalo and assumed command of all regular units. Accompanied by Governor Marcy, he began a hurried inspection of various outposts, exhorting citizens to observe the law. Scott soon obtained an interview with the leader of forces on Navy Island; undoubtedly disheartened by the ruthless efficiency of the British army, the rebels agreed to abandon their fort. After this meeting, Scott continued his tour of the frontier. Resplendent in his full dress uniform, the general took every possible opportunity to strut up and down before American troops.[14] Although these parades contained all the elements of a comic opera, they served a useful purpose. For the first time, Canadian authorities had evidence of Van Buren's desire to preserve order.[15]

The Scott mission had a similar effect on Washington. Henry Fox now conceded that state authorities had come to their senses, and he was much more optimistic about the possibility of avoiding conflict. For his part, Van Buren made it quite clear that he had no intention of leading the nation into war.[16]

A restoration of calm in Buffalo and Washington by no means solved all the difficulties. Although able to ease tensions, Scott could not halt the spread of clandestine organizations. There was a lull in activity but no decline in sympathy for the Canadian cause. In part, the problem stemmed from the lawless nature of the frontier. Bands

[13] Fox to Lord Palmerston, January 13, 1838 (No. 3), PRO:FO: 5, Vol. 322; Woodbury to Richard Rush, January 8, 1838, Woodbury Papers; *Statutes at Large*, 5: 209–10.

[14] Scott, *Memoirs*, 1: 309–10. See also Scott to Joel Poinsett, January 28, 1838, Poinsett Papers. For a fuller description of Scott's activities see Charles W. Elliott, *Winfield Scott: The Soldier and the Man* (New York, 1937).

[15] Sir John Colborne to Sir George Arthur, March 24, 1838, in Charles R. Sanderson, ed., *The Arthur Papers*, 3 vols. (Toronto, 1943–1959), 1: 65–66; hereafter cited as Arthur, *Papers*.

[16] Fox to Palmerston, January 21, 1838 (No. 4), PRO:FO: 5, Vol. 322; Van Buren to James A. Hamilton, January 23, 1838, Van Buren Papers.

of desperadoes roamed the countryside, eager to enlist under any banner. The Canadian rebels had also won the support of influential New Yorkers. Van Buren found it hard to convince this element of society that he seriously desired peace. For many years, he had been identified with Jackson's bellicose policies. Loyal Democrats in New York assumed the president's defense of neutrality to be a momentary whim, brought on by the coincidence of the *Caroline* crisis and the Panic. They fully expected that at some future date Van Buren would express sympathy for the rebels, in effect condoning their activity.[17]

Continued congressional delay in revising the neutrality law added to the British minister's frustration. He could not understand why antipathies generated by party rivalry should jeopardize a measure of obvious international import. The Senate had acted promptly enough, passing a suitable bill on January 18, but in the House, Van Buren's opponents mounted a strong counterattack. Benjamin C. Howard, Democratic chairman of the House Committee on Foreign Affairs, argued that failure to act quickly could lead to further bloodshed. This line of reasoning proved ineffective; the opposition charged that Van Buren sought to expand the power of the executive branch. Trying to ward off this criticism, Howard claimed that a new law would reduce the need to call out militia in the future.

Howard labored under several handicaps. While he fought for passage of the neutrality bill, Clay and Calhoun staged a brilliant forensic battle in the Senate. Before the culmination of this debate, the Graves-Cilley duel threw the legislature into an uproar. Such distractions made it extremely difficult for the administration to exercise discipline. Its first attempt ended in failure on February 24.[18] Fox was incredulous. Unfamiliar with normal party strife, he charged the opposition with secretly favoring the rebel cause.[19]

On March 1, 1838, Howard dispelled some of Fox's qualms by introducing a new bill. After more than a week of feverish activity, both houses consented to a compromise, and on March 10, Van

[17] See, for instance, Lieutenant Colonel W. J. Wyatt to Joel R. Poinsett, February 17, 1838, Poinsett Papers in the Gilpin Collection; comments on the course of the Albany *Argus* in *National Intelligencer*, January 9, 1838; Adeline Van Rensselaer to R. Van Rensselaer, December 23, 1837, in Bonney, *Legacy*, 2: 66–68; Thomas Hart Benton, *Thirty Years View*, 2 vols. (New York, 1854–1856), 2: 208.
[18] *Senate Journal*, 25th Cong., 2d sess., 1837–1838, pp. 121, 149, 151; *Congressional Globe*, 25th Cong., 2d sess., 1837–1838, 6: 184–87, 191–93, 199.
[19] Fox to Lord Palmerston, February 26, 1838 (No. 12), PRO:FO: 5, Vol. 322.

Buren added his signature. The new neutrality act was to run for two years and focused specifically on the problems of frontier warfare. It empowered civil authorities to seize arms, ammunitions, vehicles, and vessels involved in any expedition attempting to cross the border. The president still could not prevent the organization of an expeditionary force.[20]

Although deficient in some respects, the act of 1838 had a significant psychological impact. It provided proof of the president's determination to preserve American neutrality. Where Jackson had been content to make a few private statements in support of a neutral course, Van Buren issued an official proclamation and then convinced Congress to revise existing laws. "The President and his government," Fox now conceded, "are . . . beginning to act with more honesty than heretofore." Still, the minister did not expect any dramatic transformation because he felt there was as yet "no power within the United States, capable of restraining the people from rushing in mass across the frontier for the purposes of plunder and devastation."[21]

The passage of the neutrality act offered temporary relief to both sides. There was no immediate threat on the frontier, but doubt still existed whether Van Buren's decisiveness could overcome local disrespect for the laws. London took no chances. Fox spent the next few months gathering information on American defenses and trying to determine if the Van Buren administration was secretly preparing for war.[22] Taking advantage of the lull, the president prepared a formal protest on the destruction of the *Caroline*. On March 12, 1838, he sent all necessary documents to the American minister, Andrew Stevenson. Van Buren was inclined to believe American accounts, but even if these proved false, he thought there was still no justification for the invasion of United States territory.[23]

Although obliged to demand reparation, the president wanted

---

[20] *Congressional Globe*, 25th Cong., 2d sess., 1837–1838, 6: 203, 205–206, 214–15, 223, 230–31; *Statutes at Large*, 5: 212–14.
[21] Fox to Sir Francis Head, March 11, 1838, in Arthur, *Papers*, 1: 60. See also Fox to Palmerston, March 13, 1838 (No. 16), PRO:FO: 5, Vol. 322; Fox to Sir Charles Paget, March 15, 1838 (No. 26), PRO:FO: 5, Vol. 323, Pt. II; Woodbury to Richard Rush, May 11, 1838, Woodbury Papers.
[22] Palmerston to Fox, April 4, 1838, PRO:FO: 115, Vol. 68, Pt. II; Fox to Sir William Gray, May 9, 1838, Gray to Fox, May 11, 1838, PRO:FO: 5, Vol. 323, Pt. II.
[23] John Forsyth to Andrew Stevenson, March 12, 1838, in *Diplomatic Correspondence of the United States: Canadian Relations, 1784–1860*, ed. William R. Manning, 4 vols. (Washington, D.C., 1940–1945), 3: 48–51; hereafter cited as Manning, *Canadian Correspondence*.

nothing to disrupt Anglo-American efforts to solve the border crisis. He sent his son John as a personal courier to transmit an appeal to Lord Palmerston. In a remarkably candid fashion, Van Buren expressed hopes for peace, stating that this "would be the case if the wishes of the men in power in both countries were alone to be consulted." Thus the president admitted the delicacy of his position. Palmerston received this letter shortly after Stevenson's formal protest concerning the *Caroline*.[24] With concrete evidence of Van Buren's good will, Palmerston decided not to respond immediately to the American note, even though his advisers had long since determined that the United States stood in the wrong. By refusing to make an issue of the *Caroline* affair, Van Buren and Palmerston avoided a direct confrontation. In such a tense atmosphere, neither country could afford a diplomatic incident.[25]

Late in the spring of 1838, American citizens threatened to disrupt this mutual understanding. Early on the morning of May 29, a band of rebels boarded the British steamboat *Sir Robert Peel*, near Clayton, New York, driving off the passengers and burning the ship. Clearly a retaliation for the *Caroline*, this act of violence inflamed tempers on both sides of the border. Acting with unusual speed, Governor William Marcy left immediately for the scene and helped impress New Yorkers with the need for order.[26] Van Buren sent General Alexander Macomb to take command of army regulars and again publicly declared his disapproval of acts of lawlessness. Meanwhile, the secretary of war cooperated completely with British authorities, providing them with details on the disposition of American troops. This interchange allowed local military commanders to use available force to best advantage.[27]

Fox approved of Van Buren's stand but distrusted American mo-

---

[24] Van Buren to Palmerston, May 16, 1838, Van Buren Papers; Van Buren to Andrew Stevenson, May 16, 1838, Stevenson Papers; Stevenson to Palmerston, May 22, 1838, in Manning, *Canadian Correspondence*, 3: 449–56.

[25] See opinions of the British law officers in Palmerston to Fox, March 6, 1838 (No. 5), PRO:FO: 115, Vol. 68, Pt. I; Palmerston to Stevenson, June 6, 1838, in Manning, *Canadian Correspondence*, 3: 469. The *Caroline* affair was not specifically settled until 1842.

[26] Marcy to Joel R. Poinsett, June 3, 1838, Gratz Collection; Marcy to Prosper M. Wetmore, June 7–11, 1838, Marcy Papers; Marcy to Edwin Croswell, June 2, 1838, Van Buren Papers; Albany *Argus*, June 16, 17, 1838.

[27] John Forsyth to Henry Fox, June 12, 1838, in Manning, *Canadian Correspondence*, 3: 56; Poinsett to Van Buren, June 19, 1838, Letters from the Secretary of War to the President, National Archives; Fox to Poinsett, June 22, 1838, Poinsett Papers; Van Buren to the House of Representatives, June 20, 1838, in Richardson, *Messages and Papers*, 3: 478–79.

tives. Although he believed that "the U.S. Government are now . . . sincere in their desire to perform the duties of neutrality," he suspected that the administration had secret designs on Canada. To Fox, the solution to current difficulties was for Britain to strengthen the army in Canada. Military might alone could dissuade rebel elements from further aggression.[28]

The burning of the *Sir Robert Peel* proved to be an isolated incident, but it indicated the persistence of sympathy for the rebel cause. In the fall of 1838 the administration received news of renewed activity along the shores of Lake Ontario. Again the president issued strong instructions to civil and military personnel to be on the alert for possible violations of the law. Van Buren saw that Fox received all incoming messages; the British minister in turn passed this information on to Canadian authorities.[29] The commander of northern forces, General Macomb, discounted these reports, feeling that they exaggerated rebel strength.[30] Such nonchalance prompted Fox to remark that "In this country, it is not the Govt. that governs, as we have already sufficiently witnessed."[31]

Macomb's inertia stemmed from an increasing preoccupation with New York's internal affairs. Loyal Democrats already fighting for their political lives convinced the general that a military display might embarrass the party in the approaching campaign. Mackenzie's cause was much too popular. Thus, while Van Buren sent another strong warning to state governors, Macomb sat idly by, waiting for the end of the canvass before taking any action. As the general told one visitor, "The hands of the Government were, in a manner, bound until after the coming elections."[32]

Macomb, quite obviously, underestimated the potential threat in New York state. Early in November, Ogdensburg and Watertown teemed with recruits. Less than a week after the New York elections, an armed force crossed the St. Lawrence and moved toward the Canadian town of Prescott. British troops soon surrounded the at-

[28] Fox to Sir George Arthur, June 26; 1838, in Arthur, *Papers*, 1: 210–11. See also Fox to Palmerston, June 24, 1838 (No. 29), PRO:FO: 5, Vol. 323, Pt. II.

[29] Fox to Lord Palmerston, October 2, 1838 (No. 30), PRO:FO: 5, Vol. 323, Pt. II; Fox to Sir George Arthur, October 4, 1838, Sir John Colborne to Arthur, October 21, 1838, Arthur to Lord Fitzroy Somerset, October 30, 1838, Arthur to Fox, October 31, 1838, in Arthur, *Papers*, 1: 294–95, 310–12, 335–37.

[30] Fox to Lord Palmerston, October 18, 1838 (No. 33), PRO:FO: 5, Vol. 323, Pt. II; Fox to Sir George Arthur, October 21, 1838, in Arthur, *Papers*, 1: 312–13.

[31] Fox to Sir George Arthur, October 28, 1838, in Arthur, *Papers*, 1: 330.

[32] J. T. Jones to Sir George Arthur, November 5, 1838, in ibid., 1: 349.

tackers and on November 17 obtained their surrender. Once more Canadian defenses provided the most effective deterrent to invasion from the United States.

As this battle took place, Van Buren was appealing to the British for a cooperative effort to halt filibustering expeditions. On November 15, he admitted the "utter impracticability of placing a frontier, extending nearly one thousand miles, in a military attitude sufficiently imposing and effective to prevent such enterprises." The president added that the United States would not retaliate for injuries inflicted on its citizens, should they take part in raids on Canadian territory. Van Buren continued this theme a week later in his neutrality proclamation of November 21, 1838. After hearing the news of Prescott, he warned that Americans crossing the border would be left to their own fate. Fox appreciated these admonitions, but argued that "The president can of course only threaten the criminals with the enforcement of such laws as exist; and it has become every day more manifest and certain, that the existing laws do not enable the Government of the United States to fulfill its national duties toward the Crown of Great Britain."[33]

With the renewal of bloodshed on the frontier, Van Buren's forthcoming annual message suddenly took on added significance. Several close New York associates advised the president that a strong defense of neutrality might further damage the party. They beseeched him to avoid any criticism of the rebel cause.[34] Turning a deaf ear to these pleas, Van Buren stated that "it is utterly impossible to prevent the young . . . from embarking in those enterprises, so long as their conduct is indirectly applauded by public expressions of sympathy." In his report to Congress, the president condemned those "misguided or deluded persons" who participated in "criminal assaults upon the peace and order of a neighboring country." He understood why Americans might sympathize with an apparent struggle for freedom, but such sentiments should never jeopardize the security of a foreign power. After fully discussing the dangers inherent in filibustering, Van Buren pledged adherence to the laws. "Whether they are sufficient," he said, "to meet the actual state of things on the Canadian frontier it is for Congress to decide." In his

[33] Forsyth to Fox, November 15, 1838, in Manning, *Canadian Correspondence*, 3: 57–59; Richardson, *Messages and Papers*, 3: 482–83; Fox to Lord Palmerston, November 24, 1838 (No. 35), PRO:FO: 5, Vol. 323, Pt. III.

[34] Azariah C. Flagg to Van Buren, November 23, 1838, Edwin Croswell to Van Buren, November 25, 1838, Van Buren Papers; Ransom Gillet to Francis P. Blair, November 14, 1838, Blair-Lee Papers.

own subtle way, the president suggested that both houses might reappraise their work of the previous session.[35]

This declaration finally convinced Fox that Van Buren was not playing a double game. After the submission of the annual message, the British minister wrote that "the President's Government is sincerely striving, as far as so weak and feeble a Government can be said to strive at anything,—to fulfill its natural duties." Fox took further encouragement when Winfield Scott relieved the ineffectual Macomb.[36]

Portions of the Democratic party greeted Van Buren's statements with less enthusiasm. They bridled at the friendly Whig response to the president's message. As an assistant editor of the Washington *Globe* put it: "It may be that our executive may have exhibited too much solicitude to preserve peace."[37] Similar attitudes prevailed on the frontier; to his dismay, Scott found that some of the most vocal sympathizers were recipients of federal patronage. This tended to give the impression that the administration condoned rebel militance.[38]

Once again, Scott's arrival helped to restore quiet. The defeat at Prescott had dampened the enthusiasm of Mackenzie's followers, and the general found his task much easier than anticipated. In Washington, Van Buren had finally succeeded in convincing Fox that the United States sincerely desired peace. Considering the obstacles, this was no mean accomplishment. Although the British still believed that their defenses were the only effective barrier to aggression, the president, by gaining Fox's confidence, insured Anglo-American cooperation in future crises. Understanding came none too soon. Within a matter of months, a serious confrontation along the Maine frontier again threatened to plunge the two nations into war.

The rebellion in the Canadian provinces overshadowed the continuing controversy over the northeast boundary. The United States and Great Britain had ostensibly resolved this problem in 1783. Later

[35] Van Buren to Flagg, November 28, 1838, Flagg Papers, Columbia University Library; Richardson, *Messages and Papers*, 3: 486–87.
[36] Fox to Sir George Arthur, December 6, 1838, Fox to Lieutenant Colonel Farquharson, December 7, 1838, in Arthur, *Papers*, 1: 420–23, 426; Fox to Palmerston, December 4, 1838 (No. 40), PRO:FO: 5, Vol. 323, Pt. III. See also Palmerston to Stevenson, December 8, 1838, Van Buren Papers.
[37] W. E. Moore to William Lyon Mackenzie, December 12, 1838, in Mackenzie, *The Lives and Opinions of Benj'n Franklin Butler and Jesse Hoyt* (Boston, 1845), pp. 289–90.
[38] Scott to Joel R. Poinsett, December 16, 1838, January 12, February 4, 1839, Poinsett Papers. See also Woodbury to Jesse Hoyt, November 17, 1838, Woodbury Papers.

generations found that the Treaty of Paris left in doubt the exact location of the line separating Maine from Canada, and both sides laid claim to portions of the St. John Valley. The Treaty of Ghent authorized a new survey, but the commissioners could not agree on a line conforming to that described in 1783.[39]

For the next two decades, diplomats on both sides of the Atlantic tried to reach a settlement. Since attempts to draw an acceptable boundary had failed, it seemed only reasonable to divide the territory between the two disputants. Maine repeatedly balked at such a procedure. State leaders feared that the national government would bargain away valuable land to appease the British and insisted on a survey as the only basis for agreement. The region in question presumably belonged to Maine, and Washington could do little without the state's concurrence. This deadlock posed no threat to peace so long as the area around the St. John River lay vacant.

By the 1830's citizens of both Maine and New Brunswick began casting longing glances at the 7 million acres of virgin land. To the Americans, the timber and fertile soil held out the promise of prosperity. To the Canadians, the basin offered a strategic winter link between the icebound St. Lawrence and the seaport of Halifax. In the spring of 1835, the British prepared to construct a railroad between New Brunswick and Quebec. Two years later the Van Buren administration learned of these plans and protested the projected railway as "an encroachment upon the territory in dispute between the United States and Great Britain." London subsequently agreed to abandon construction.[40]

Throughout the Canadian rebellion, England and the United States continued to search for a means to settle the boundary controversy. The British remained convinced that a convention alone could reasonably divide the territory.[41] Van Buren privately agreed that further surveys were useless and in the spring of 1838 made another attempt to sway stubborn Maine authorities. Again he met with complete refusal. Not only did Governor Edward Kent decline to

[39] For background on this subject see James M. Callahan, *American Foreign Policy in Canadian Relations* (New York, 1937); Thomas Le Duc, "The Maine Frontier and the Northeast Boundary Controversy," *American Historical Review* 53 (1947): 30–41.

[40] John Forsyth to Henry Fox, March 23, 1837, in Manning, *Canadian Correspondence*, 3: 23–26; Fox to Lord Palmerston, March 29, 1837 (No. 9), PRO:FO: 5, Vol. 314, Pt. III; Fox to Forsyth, August 24, 1837, PRO:FO: 5, Vol. 314, Pt. V.

[41] Palmerston to Fox, November 19, 1837 (No. 14), PRO:FO: 5, Vol. 313, Pt. II.

consider a convention, he even threatened that if Congress did not authorize a survey, the state would run its own line. Angered by this response, the president reminded Kent that the federal government was not so callous as to ignore the interests of Maine.[42]

Fox was thoroughly disgusted with Maine's obstinance, though this was not the first time he had experienced the frustrations of dealing with a democratic nation. He had come to realize that the power of the central government over the states was "at all times indistinct, debatable and undefined." Furthermore, Fox believed that politics complicated matters immensely. He found it most difficult to deal "with a Party that is not always the master of its own ground." Although Fox complained of the lack of progress in negotiations, he worried more about the possibility of armed encounters in the St. John Valley.[43] With the state and national governments at loggerheads, any Anglo-American incident might mushroom into full-scale fighting.

By the end of 1838, there were signs of impending clashes in the disputed area. Maine had gradually extended its roads northward, making it easier to explore the region. With improved transportation, the state began a series of geological and agricultural surveys. Each study publicized the potential of the undeveloped land. In New Brunswick, Canadian officials had yet to abandon the idea of a winter road. Furthermore, the new lieutenant governor of New Brunswick, Sir John Harvey, considered it his duty to police the St. John region; since his patrols met with no opposition, he assumed that Americans recognized the right of England to exercise jurisdiction pending eventual settlement of the boundary.[44]

In early January 1839, the Maine legislature decided to clear the disputed region of trespassers. It chose Rufus MacIntire, a state land agent, to lead an expedition in search of the law breakers. For days the party combed the area around the Aroostook River, looking for poachers. Exhausted by his searches, MacIntire gladly accepted the hospitality of a local settler. He awoke the next morning to find the cabin surrounded by the very culprits he had so fearlessly sought; MacIntire offered little resistance as the outlaws bundled him off to a

---

[42] John Forsyth to Edward Kent, March 1, 1838, Kent to Van Buren, April 28, 1838, Fox to Forsyth, May 1, 1838, Forsyth to Kent, May 8, 1838, in Richardson, *Messages and Papers*, 3: 442–59, 470–73, 474–75.
[43] Fox to Palmerston, November 24, 1837 (No. 21), PRO:FO: 5, Vol. 314, Pt. V.
[44] Le Duc, "Maine Frontier," pp. 36–41; Harvey to Fox, March 6, 1839, Fox to Palmerston, March 7, 1839 (No. 8), PRO:FO: 5, Vol. 331, Pt. II.

New Brunswick jail. A member of MacIntire's party rushed back to Augusta with news of the dramatic capture.[45]

Meanwhile in Frederickton, New Brunswick, Sir John Harvey received the first details on the MacIntire expedition. Believing that Maine was making an unauthorized incursion into territory under his command, he issued a proclamation calling for a withdrawal of American forces. Harvey also announced he would use British troops, if necessary.[46] To the south, Maine's Governor John Fairfield excitedly pored over accounts of MacIntire's arrest. Although the new governor had spent the last three years in Congress, he had not become immune to the war fever raging in Maine. His first reaction was to reinforce the remnants of the MacIntire party. After dispatching 300 troops, Fairfield asked the local commander of regular forces, Major R. M. Kirby, for assistance. Kirby sympathized with Fairfield's predicament but hesitated to take any steps that might provoke hostilities. Up to this point, there was still no immediate cause for alarm.

When Fairfield received word of Harvey's proclamation, the fireworks began. The governor bristled at the British claim of jurisdiction and promptly gathered another 1,000 men to send into the field; he then asked the legislature for money and authority to call out 10,000 state militia. Aghast at this unexpected bellicosity, Major Kirby refused to put any of his regular forces under Fairfield's command.[47] This failed to sway the determined governor, who now resolved to find a military solution to what had once been a diplomatic problem. Only after making these extensive preparations did Fairfield send any information to the president.[48]

A year earlier, Van Buren had been plagued by a lack of local response; now he had to deal with an excited governor who seemed ready to instigate a needless war. After an emergency cabinet meeting on February 24, the president made a full report to Congress on the situation in Maine. He reviewed the relevant negotiations, denying that New Brunswick had any basis for claiming responsibility for the St. John region. At the same time, Van Buren chided Maine for not

[45] For a more complete description see David Lowenthal, "The Maine Press and the Aroostook War," *Canadian Historical Review* 32 (1951): 315–36.
[46] Harvey, Proclamation, February 13, 1839, in *House Documents* (No. 270), 25th Cong., 3d sess., 1838–1839, p. 18.
[47] Fairfield to Maine Legislature, February 15, 18, 1839, in ibid., pp. 9–12; Kirby to Fairfield, February 14, 18, 1839, Fairfield Papers, Library of Congress.
[48] Fairfield to Van Buren, February 18, 1839, in *House Documents* (No. 270), 25th Cong., 3d sess., 1838–1839, pp. 6–7.

informing New Brunswick of the MacIntire expedition. The president urged both Fairfield and Harvey to recall their troops and disband the militia. Since Congress was scheduled to adjourn in a few weeks, Van Buren also requested contingent authority to act should the crisis worsen.[49]

Van Buren then took independent action to resolve the dispute. Frustrated in the past by legislative delays and state objections, the president appealed directly to the British minister, proposing a joint memorandum calling for immediate withdrawal of all forces from the Aroostook Valley. So long in the making, Anglo-American cooperation now paid off handsomely. Fox applauded Van Buren's message to Congress and on February 27 signed the memorandum.[50] He then sent a communiqué to Harvey requesting the lieutenant governor to "refrain from any further action until time shall have been afforded her Majesty's govt. to attempt adjustment of the difference by friendly means."[51] The British minister had evidently changed his mind about the need for force.

There was still a threat to peace so long as Fairfield relished a military showdown. The governor was in an angry mood. "Should you go *against* us upon this occasion—or not espouse our cause with *warmth* and *earnestness* and with a true *American feeling,*" he threatened the president, "God only knows what the result would be politically."[52] Distasteful though this crude letter must have been, Van Buren realized that simple transmission of the joint memorandum would not suffice. Again the president turned to Winfield Scott, ordering the general to proceed to Augusta and deliver the document in person. Scott was to impress Fairfield with the need for calm; under no circumstances was he to enter the disputed territory. If New Brunswick tried to take possession of the region, Van Buren would issue new instructions.[53]

[49] Benjamin F. Butler to Mrs. Butler, February 23, 25, 1839, Butler Papers, New York State Library; Richardson, *Messages and Papers*, 3: 516–17.
[50] Fox to Palmerston, February 23, 1839 (No. 7), PRO:FO: 5, Vol. 331, Pt. I. Fox-Forsyth Memorandum, February 27, 1839, in Manning, *Canadian Correspondence*, 3: 65–66.
[51] Fox to Harvey, February 27, 1839, PRO:FO: 5, Vol. 331, Pt. II; Fox to Sir George Arthur, February 28, 1839, in Arthur, *Papers*, 2: 68–69.
[52] Fairfield to Van Buren, February 22, 1839, Van Buren Papers. Italics in the original.
[53] Joel Poinsett to Scott, February 28, 1839, in *House Documents* (No. 169), 26th Cong., 1st sess., 1839–1840, p. 2. The definite restrictions set forth in this letter indicate that, contrary to what Scott later claimed, Van Buren did not give the general "carte blanche" (Scott, *Memoirs*, 2: 334).

As Scott made his way to Augusta, the northeast frontier seemed ready to explode. The Maine press roundly denounced Van Buren's message to Congress as an abandonment of all that was dear to the state.[54] Despite the president's appeal, the troops assembled at Bangor refused to disband.[55] Congress added to the excitement by preparing the nation for war. On March 9, 1839, both houses passed a bill granting Van Buren authority to call out 50,000 militia and spend up to $10 million for defense of the frontier.[56] "A greater parade of preparation need scarcely have been made," wrote Henry Fox, "if Great Britain had declared a desire to reconquer the United States as British colonies." He was careful to add, however, that Van Buren's "friendly feelings toward England will go far to strip the Act of the offensive and mischievous character which it would otherwise have borne."[57]

These circumstances combined to make Scott's assignment all the more difficult. His main task was to prevent the governor or the legislature from rushing pellmell into war. Fairfield had taken a strong stand throughout the crisis; undignified retreat might only goad the angry assembly to ignore him and take over the troops itself. Scott had to allow Fairfield to withdraw gracefully. For some time after his arrival in Augusta, the presidential envoy sat and listened without making any open moves. Privately, he made contact with Sir John Harvey in Frederickton. Fox's letters had found their mark; Harvey wanted peace.[58]

After several days of talks, Scott convinced Fairfield to support the president. Now the two had to find a way to make the legislature agree. To satisfy public opinion, Fairfield sent a message to the assembly, repudiating the Anglo-American memorandum; the document was of little use, since local commanders had already ignored its provisions. Significantly, Fairfield made no appeal to the war spirit but hinted at the possibility of a peaceful solution. In the meantime, Scott had written to Harvey, proposing a settlement along lines

---

[54] For a summary of the press opinion see Lowenthal, "Maine Press and the Aroostook War."

[55] J. R. Rogers to Fairfield, March 1, 1839, Fairfield Papers.

[56] Congressional Globe, 25th Cong., 3d sess., 1838–1839, 7: 217–19, 224–29; Statutes at Large, 5: 355–56. For a description of the hurried manner in which the Democrats prepared this bill see Benjamin Howard to Andrew Stevenson, March 8, 1839, Stevenson Papers.

[57] Fox to Palmerston, March 7, 1839 (No. 8), PRO:FO: 5, Vol. 331, Pt. II. On Van Buren's peaceful intentions see Washington Globe, March 4, 1839.

[58] Harvey to Fox, March 6, 1839, PRO:FO: 5, Vol. 331, Pt. II; Harvey to Fairfield, March 7, 1839, PRO:FO: 5, Vol. 331, Pt. III.

remarkably similar to those contained in the abandoned memorandum.[59]

When he received Harvey's informal assurances that agreement was possible, Scott then dispatched a formal proposal. On March 21, he suggested that New Brunswick disavow any intention of occupying the contested area; Maine would then give serious consideration to removing all but a token civil force. Scott attached a private note to this declaration, assuring Harvey that if New Brunswick complied, Maine's acquiescence would be a mere formality. To protect Fairfield, Scott made sure that he kept the copies of this correspondence. He did not want the legislature to discover that their governor had been a party to all stages of the negotiations.[60]

As planned, both Harvey and the Maine assembly cooperated. On March 23, 1839, the legislature agreed to withdraw troops if New Brunswick would reciprocate. The same day in Frederickton, Harvey formally consented to the conditions of Scott's note.[61] These official acts confirmed what had been apparent for several days—there would be no war.

Back in Washington, the president heaved a sigh of relief. He had narrowly averted a dangerous confrontation. Both sides now appreciated that there was little sense in resorting to force to solve the boundary dispute. Van Buren allowed tempers to cool before he made any further overtures. When he did resume negotiations, he was unable to reach a solution, for Maine's precarious political situation made agreement difficult. A change of administrations on both sides of the Atlantic would be required before Webster and Ashburton finally resolved the question in 1842.

Van Buren's record as a statesman is an impressive one, especially when one considers the handicaps under which he operated. The Panic of 1837 demanded his full attention; dissension within the Democratic ranks proved a continual source of irritation and deprived him of crucial state support. Despite these preoccupations, the president acted swiftly and surely in times of international crisis. In dealing with Great Britain, Texas, and Mexico, Van Buren pursued a

[59] Fairfield to Anna Fairfield, March 15, 1839, Fairfield Papers; Scott to Joel R. Poinsett, March 8, 11, 13, 1839, Scott to Harvey, March 9, 1839, in *House Documents* (No. 169), 26th Cong., 1st sess., 1839–1840, pp. 4–8.

[60] Harvey to Scott, March 12, 1839, Scott, Declaration, March 21, 1839, Scott to Harvey, March 21, 1839, in *House Documents* (No. 169), 26th Cong., 1st sess., 1839–1840, pp. 9–10, 13–15; Scott to Joel R. Poinsett, May 24, 1839, Poinsett Papers.

[61] Harvey, Declaration, March 23, 1839, Fairfield Declaration, March 25, 1839, in *House Documents* (No. 169), 26th Cong., 1st sess., 1839–1840, p. 17.

consistent course; at no time did he indulge in the irresponsible behavior that so often marred the diplomacy of his predecessor.

Van Buren's image was his own worst enemy. Foreign emissaries found it hard to place faith in administration pronouncements. Time after time, the Texan representatives speculated that Van Buren would drop all pretenses and approve annexation. For nearly two years, Henry Fox suspected that the president secretly sympathized with the Canadian rebels. Party leaders were no less incredulous. Loyal members of New York's Democracy thought Van Buren's espousal of neutrality to be only a temporary expedient. The president struggled to surmount these prejudices. One false step might have discredited his reputation. By acting fairly and honestly, he convinced Mexico to settle the claims dispute. In a similar fashion, he won the admiration of Henry Fox, at a time when close Anglo-American cooperation was essential to the maintenance of peace.

Van Buren found it much more difficult to win the support of his countrymen. There were no mass media to transmit executive appeals for neutrality. He had to rely upon the cooperation of local party organizations, the press, and the federal bureaucracy. The Panic of 1837 weakened these channels of communication. In foreign as well as domestic affairs, he discovered the shortcomings of the federal system and the cruel restrictions of limited government. To his credit, Van Buren tried to overcome these obstacles. On three different occasions, he employed General Winfield Scott as a personal representative to publicize administration policy, enforce executive decisions, and circumvent local obstinance. In 1839, when faced with a serious disturbance on the Maine boundary, the president took extraordinary steps to meet the crisis. Realizing that lengthy congressional debate would only further increase tensions, Van Buren quietly reached an executive agreement with Great Britain that served as a basis for ending the threat of hostilities. In the growing political tumult, these measures passed unnoticed.

Chapter 10

Disillusion
and Defeat

No idle spectator to the disintegration of Democratic unity, Martin Van Buren tried desperately to suppress conflict and restore order. This was not an easy task. The Panic, the crises in foreign affairs, and countless administrative burdens demanded his continuous attention, leaving him little time for local problems. Furthermore, he no longer had adequate communications with state advisers. Deprived of a power base in his native state, bereft of wise counsel in Virginia, Van Buren labored under severe handicaps in his attempt to rally Democratic forces for the coming presidential campaign.[1]

Even had he been free to devote his full energies to party affairs, Van Buren still might not have appreciated the fundamental change taking place in American politics. Since 1828, administration officials had spent more time worrying about internal dissension than about opposition challenges. The defection of John C. Calhoun, the desertion of Hugh Lawson White, and the Conservative revolt caused more anxiety than the violent denunciations of Whig orators. Concerned by these splits in Democratic ranks, Van Buren did not recognize the emergence of a new national party. For a time, there was no need for alarm; throughout Jackson's first administration, the Whigs remained a loosely knit organization that seemed to exist for the sole purpose of bedeviling Old Hickory. Henry Clay, Daniel Webster, and John Quincy Adams led the congressional fight against executive tyranny. Despite such distinguished and vocal leadership, the Whigs were slow to mount a serious threat to the ruling party. Gradually during Jackson's second term, they gained momentum, scoring impressive victories in such Democratic strongholds as Pennsylvania, Virginia, North Carolina, and Tennessee. Although building loyal state followings, the Whigs failed to develop a coordinated national organization. Their ill-starred, multicandidate campaign of

1836 could not prevent Jackson from passing the crown to his chosen successor.

The Panic of 1837 changed all this. The nation entered an economic crisis so extreme as to erase all memories of previous financial disorders. Had the blow been short and sharp, the Democrats might have recovered, but the depression continued without letup for more than a year. When relief came, it was only temporary; in 1839, the economy suffered a relapse and a second wave of bank failures. The Panic was truly a national experience and stimulated widespread interest in politics.

The Whigs were ready to take full advantage of the tremendous excitement generated during this period. As the party out of power, the Whigs had everything to gain by appealing to emotion rather than reason. They now expanded their local network to rival that established by the Jacksonians a decade earlier. In New York, Thurlow Weed's smooth, efficient machine served as a glowing example of the effectiveness of this new substructure. Thaddeus Stevens presided over a similar organization in nearby Pennsylvania. Although less stable, his alliance of anti-Masons and Whigs proved capable of ending Democratic rule in the Keystone State. Similar groups in Ohio, Tennessee, Kentucky, and Virginia attested to the return of two-party politics throughout the country. Prepared to contest Democratic superiority on the state level and eager to exploit public distress over the Panic, the Whigs entered the campaign of 1840 full of hope and enthusiasm. The prospect of a lively canvass and a close presidential race brought voters to the polls in unprecedented numbers.[2]

Too long preoccupied with their own problems, the Democrats were not nearly so adaptable to shifting political winds. There was really no way for them to capitalize on the Panic. At best they might convince the electorate that the depression was but part of a natural economic cycle and thus not of partisan origin. Frustrated, divided, and constantly on the defensive, the president and his party never

---

[1] This chapter makes no attempt to provide a complete account of the election of 1840. For an excellent narrative that gives an analysis of both campaign rhetoric and election statistics see Robert Gray Gunderson, *The Log Cabin Campaign* (Lexington, Ky., 1957).

[2] On the development of Whig organization see ibid., pp. 29–40, 148–60; Glyndon G. Van Deusen, *Thurlow Weed* (Boston, 1947), pp. 86–113. For a complete analysis of the nation's return to two-party politics see Richard P. McCormick, *The Second American Party System* (Chapel Hill, N.C., 1966). Although McCormick accounts for the tremendous turnout in 1840 in terms of political organization, he does not sufficiently emphasize the effect of the Panic of 1837 in stimulating voter interest.

understood the significance of the log cabin campaign. They believed that all the furor was a temporary aberration and assumed that the voters would recover their senses in time for the balloting.

Van Buren himself overlooked the implications of Whig election strategy. During political trials over the past decade, he had developed a rather stereotyped view of the opposition. In 1835, after hearing of the proceedings in a Virginia election, he told William C. Rives that "if the absurd stories to which you refer (and which are indeed true specimens of Whig electioneering) have been to any extent successful . . . you stand more in need of the *schoolmaster* than the politician."[3] Van Buren never abandoned this view; he thought the log cabin and hard cider mania sheer folly—the madness of profligate opportunists rather than a new means of appealing to an expanding electorate. He refused to believe that a campaign so devoid of principle could possibly succeed.

Instead of searching for an emotional theme to revive the spirit of the party and relieve public concern for the depression, the president concentrated on correcting the defects of Democratic machinery. Taking the Whig triumph in his native state as a personal loss, Van Buren set out to resurrect the Regency. Once before, in 1825, Van Buren had engineered a dramatic turnabout in his native state. He felt that the redemption of New York would inject new life into the Democratic alliance and establish a pattern for recovery across the nation.

With this in mind, he wrote to the Regency's Azariah C. Flagg, stressing the need for a regrouping of New York's Democratic forces. Van Buren wanted to assume personal control of this task and promised to provide a complete blueprint for victory. In the meantime, Flagg was to make every possible effort to alert the faithful. The president then reflected momentarily on the reason for recent defeats in New York. Accustomed to success, Democrats had grown complacent, relying solely on the press and a few scattered meetings to maintain themselves in power. It was the Whigs who had carefully checked the local constituencies, attempting to sway doubtful voters. Vowing not to be outmaneuvered again, Van Buren asked for the names of representatives in various counties; he personally would send material to each and every one. The president closed by asking Flagg for any additional comments that might prove helpful.

Answering promptly, Flagg agreed wholeheartedly with Van Buren's recommendations. He suggested that since the Regency no

[3] Van Buren to Rives, April 10, 1835, MS Letterbook (1833–1839), Rives Papers.

longer worked effectively, the party should form a state central committee to direct the campaign. Flagg also requested the assistance of New York's congressmen; Democratic members of the legislature could help immensely by directing preparations in their own districts.

After discussing these organizational details, Flagg urged that the party establish a new paper to supplement the Albany *Argus*. Croswell had become so bound up with bank interests that he had been unable "to devote his time constantly to the editorial department of the Argus." To make matters worse, the paper frequently faced the charge of inconsistency. Whenever Croswell published a defense of the sub-Treasury system, the opposition gleefully dug back into its files and reprinted those *Argus* editorials from 1837 and 1838 that objected to administration policy. A new paper would not operate under such handicaps. It could adopt a strict Jeffersonian tone and discuss Van Buren's program without embarrassment or fear of contradiction. In closing, Flagg observed that had the *Argus* pursued a proper course over the past three years, it might have prevented a Whig takeover in New York.[4] The president agreed that a new press was essential, wryly commenting that it was bound to succeed because Croswell was so enthusiastic about the project. In keeping with the new journal's Jeffersonian image, Van Buren proposed to name it either *The Rough Hewer* or *The Working Man*. Thinking about these alternatives for a while, he decided that the latter had too much "clap-trap about it."[5] Although Van Buren would soon issue an executive order creating a ten-hour workday on federally sponsored public projects, he still did not consider himself the champion of labor.[6]

Despite the best of intentions, the president took a great deal of time to perfect his plans for the campaign. The renewal of debate on the sub-Treasury and the confusion attending selection of a new House Speaker prevented him from amplifying his suggestions. Finally, in February 1840 Van Buren completed the draft of a document entitled "Thoughts on the Approaching Election in New York." Originally intended as "hints" for state officials, these presidential ruminations ran to seventy-five pages.[7]

[4] Van Buren to Flagg, November 25 [?], 1839, Flagg Papers, Columbia University Library; Flagg to Van Buren, December 20, 1839, Flagg Papers, New York Public Library.

[5] Van Buren to Flagg, December 28, 1839, Flagg Papers, Columbia University Library.

[6] Richardson, *Messages and Papers*, 3: 602.

[7] Silas Wright to Azariah C. Flagg, January 26, February 8, 1840, Flagg-Wright Papers.

If New York Democrats expected a bold new battle plan, they were sorely disappointed. They received not a rousing call to arms but a lecture on the virtues of organization and a discourse on traditional political principles. The president began by declaring that only a vigorous canvass of local constituencies could bring victory. The Whigs had scored temporary triumphs because they had adopted painstaking procedures, checking registration lists and courting doubtful voters. The Democrats must reassert themselves and regain the ascendancy. Van Buren argued that the task was by no means hopeless, since the majority of the American people naturally favored the Democratic cause.

Although recognizing the need to restore effective electoral machinery, Van Buren placed primary emphasis on guarding against vote frauds. The Whig victories in New York, Pennsylvania, and Ohio proved the existence of a fearful opposition plot to destroy the purity of elections, seize power by force, and establish an oligarchy. To combat this scheme, the Democrats must immediately create committees of vigilance and press for state legislation to guard against repetition of such criminal acts.

The president believed that these practical efforts would succeed only if the electorate understood the basic issues involved in the coming contest. A clear statement would stimulate discussion and generate enthusiasm; Van Buren took it upon himself to lay down the guidelines for such a presentation. To comprehend the opposition challenge, voters must first be aware of the origins of the American party system.

In a lengthy historical analysis, the president traced the founding of political parties to the administration of John Adams. Van Buren argued that the Federalists had consistently supported a national bank, worked toward an Anglo-monarchal system of government, and opposed extension of the suffrage. The Whigs, as true descendants of the Federalists, continued to subscribe to these theories and manifest antidemocratic tendencies. By contrast, the Democrats believed wholeheartedly in the dignity of the common man, state rights, and simple government. If only the voters could grasp these distinctions, perhaps they would come to their senses. "We have only to awake," wrote Van Buren, quoting Jefferson, "and snap the Lilliputian cords which have been entangling us."[8]

---

[8] Van Buren, "Thoughts on the Approaching Election in New York," March [?], 1840, Van Buren Papers. Gunderson, *The Log Cabin Campaign*, pp. 86–87, suggests that this was written by Kendall. The draft in the Van Buren Papers is in the president's handwriting.

These remarkable notes indicate Van Buren's approach to the election of 1840. He sensed that the nation was in a state of political flux, but instead of searching for new methods, he clung tenaciously to old ideas. Van Buren talked of the recent Whig victories in New York, Pennsylvania, and Ohio. Rather than use these as examples of superior Whig tactics, he cited them as evidence of widespread fraud, as if this revelation, once made public, would magically restore the Democrats to power. The president seemed to realize that the public was excited and eager to engage in partisan debate. Yet he shunned relevant issues, confining himself to a description of Whig lineage. Not once in the course of his narrative did he refer to the Panic or the sub-Treasury. Nor did he allude to his bold call for a reform of the banking structure.

On the contrary, the president groped for the familiar, resorting to the tried and true appeals that had worked so well in the past. In 1822 he had sounded the alarm, pointing to the smouldering ruins of Federalism and warning that continued Republican apathy might touch off a new political holocaust. Such admonitions had ideally suited a majority party suffering only from want of discipline. By conjuring up the specter of Federalist tryanny, Van Buren had helped combat the heresies of amalgamation. In 1840, the political system had changed. The Whigs now constituted a second major party, capable of challenging administration power throughout the country. To those Democrats entrusted with the task of meeting this challenge, the president's suggestions must have seemed totally unrealistic.

After making arrangements to have his instructions printed and then distributed in New York, the president turned his attention to the forthcoming Democratic national convention, scheduled to meet in Baltimore early in May 1840. Here would be an excellent opportunity to unite the party in defense of traditional principles. Not all Van Buren's advisers looked forward to the Baltimore meeting with such enthusiasm. For several months, Silas Wright had tried to convince the president that a convention would only add to the confusion existing in the Democratic ranks. Van Buren listened patiently but felt that cancellation might anger those states that had already chosen delegates.[9]

Wright worried primarily about an incipient quarrel over the choice of a vice-presidential nominee. In 1836, the Democrats had selected Richard M. Johnson as Van Buren's running mate. A sena-

---

[9] Silas Wright to Azariah Flagg, January 26, 1840, Flagg-Wright Papers.

tor and military hero, Johnson seemingly had all the necessary qualities of a successful candidate, but his private life left something to be
desired. The acknowledged father of two illegitimate mulatto children, Johnson became the subject of a continuous barrage of abuse.
Even after his mistress died in 1833, the stories continued to circu-
late. Six years later, administration leaders still complained about the
vice president's morality.[10]

A number of prominent Democrats coveted the second spot on the
ticket. Early in 1839 the secretary of state dropped hints about his
availability.[11] He obviously believed that he could bolster the sagging
Southern wing of the party. Regarding Forsyth as both a personal
enemy and a political liability, James Buchanan worked behind the
scenes to promote the candidacy of Alabama's Senator William R.
King.[12]

These covert maneuvers constituted but one aspect of the vice-
presidential controversy. By far the most serious disagreement arose
between Van Buren and his predecessor. The storm had been brew-
ing for several years. Upon his retirement to the Hermitage in 1837,
Andrew Jackson ceased to have the dominant voice in Democratic
politics. Soon after taking office, Van Buren made it clear that the
West no longer would occupy the paramount position in the alliance.
In selecting a cabinet, the new president looked first to the South and
then to the North to fill vacancies. He did bring Tennessee's Felix
Grundy into the council, but only because he could not find someone
more suitable. Although Van Buren always kept Jackson informed of
administration decisions, he rarely sought Old Hickory's advice before acting. During preparations for the special session, Van Buren
relied primarily upon the counsel of associates in Virginia and New
York, frequently ignoring the pointed suggestions of Jackson and
Kendall.

At times, Jackson reacted bitterly to his growing isolation. He
privately disagreed with Van Buren's fiscal program, feeling that the
president treated banking interests too gently. When his hints had
no apparent effect, Jackson wrote angrily to Kendall, "Had my voice

[10] Amos Kendall to Van Buren, August 22, 1839, Van Buren Papers.
[11] Judge Catron to Jackson, January 4, 1839 [?], Jackson Papers; Francis Smith
to Nathaniel Niles, January 8, 1839, Niles Papers, Library of Congress; George
Plitt to James Buchanan, April 23, 1839, Buchanan Papers, The Historical
Society of Pennsylvania.
[12] Buchanan to Jonas R. McClintock, March 11, 1839, George Plitt to
Buchanan, March 14, 1839, William R. King to Buchanan, June 20, 1839,
Buchanan Papers, The Historical Society of Pennsylvania; Buchanan to Mrs.
Francis P. Blair, May 15, 1839, Blair-Lee Papers.

been heard, I would have brought suit against every bank that dishonored the Govt. draft upon it & adopted every energetic means to have met the debts of the Govt. regardless of the cries of Bankers, stockholders, speculators & gamblers."[13] Jackson's hostility spread to his close associates. In 1839 Van Buren planned a trip to the Southwest, intending to visit Tennessee along the way. James K. Polk argued vehemently that such a move would have disastrous political consequences and might defeat his bid for governor. With state elections in the offing, the Whigs would charge that Polk was nothing but a presidential puppet. Hearing of these objections, Van Buren contemplated canceling his whole tour. When the Maine boundary dispute erupted in March 1839, the president took advantage of the incident to retract all plans for a swing through the Southwest.[14]

This undercurrent of controversy came to the surface in 1840. Faced with the possibility of a Democratic defeat, Jackson spoke out, stating explicitly his own private formula for victory. It was imperative that the party draft a vice-presidential nominee who would appeal to the Western voters. The only suitable candidate was James K. Polk. After several letters to Blair failed to produce results, Jackson wrote directly to Van Buren, expressing the belief that Johnson could not possibly carry the West; Democrats must unite behind Polk before the Baltimore convention.[15]

Van Buren was annoyed. For months he had been trying to revive the party; while he labored to coordinate the efforts of all Democratic groups, Jackson seemed to worry only about Tennessee and the West. Van Buren was not oblivious to the political importance of this region. Twice he had come to the support of Western demands for a more liberal policy in the sale of public lands.[16] Despite this displeasure, Van Buren could not afford an open break. Responding politely, he stated that since there were so many candidates for the vice-presidency, he must remain neutral. To back any one hopeful would only create turmoil. Van Buren praised Polk's abilities but

[13] Jackson to Kendall, March 23, 1838, Jackson-Kendall Papers.
[14] Polk to Jackson, January 29, 1839, Francis P. Blair to Jackson, February 8, 1839, Jackson Papers; Jackson to Van Buren, March 4, 1839, Van Buren to Jackson, February 17, March 23, 1839, Van Buren Papers.
[15] Jackson to Blair, November [?], 1839, February 15, 1840, Jackson Papers; Jackson to Van Buren, February 17, 1840, Van Buren Papers.
[16] Richardson, *Messages and Papers*, 3: 389, 536–37; Roy M. Robbins, *Our Landed Heritage: The Public Domain, 1776–1936* (Princeton, N.J., 1942), p. 76; James P. Shenton, *Robert John Walker* (New York, 1961), p. 25; Joseph H. Parks, *Felix Grundy* (Baton Rouge, La., 1940), pp. 288–94; Thomas Hart Benton, *Thirty Years View*, 2 vols. (New York, 1854–1856), 2: 125–28.

then quickly shifted to a defense of Johnson. "Old Tecumseh" would rival Harrison's martial image. Furthermore, Johnson already had strong followings in New York and Pennsylvania; any move to replace him on the ticket would cost the party dearly in those states.[17]

Jackson accepted the need for presidential neutrality, but refused to recognize Johnson's strong points. "I shall add no more," he wrote disgustedly, "but barely remark that if Johnson is selected, the democracy when too late will see their error."[18] Van Buren was busy preparing for the convention and let these complaints pass without comment.

On May 5, 1840, the Democrats assembled in Baltimore's Music Hall to hold their third national nominating convention. Outside, a throng of Whig celebrants wildly shouted the praises of their candidates, William Henry Harrison and John Tyler. The blare of band music and the din of the jeering crowd did nothing to improve Democratic dispositions.[19] Four years earlier, Jackson's followers had come to the same city in high spirits to nominate a man who seemed perfectly qualified to preside over the alliance and heal political wounds. Then the Panic came, and with disconcerting swiftness the coalition collapsed. The Whigs marched into office, gleefully predicting triumphs to come. All these memories contributed to make the atmosphere in Baltimore one of sober determination. As the delegates dutifully cast their ballots for Martin Van Buren, they must have wondered whether so colorless a man could rekindle party spirit.

Fearful of creating any further dissension in their already battered ranks, the Democrats shied away from an open battle on the vice-presidential nomination. Rather than choose any one of the hopefuls, they adopted an ambiguous resolution leaving the selection to the states. Hopefully, the statement continued, "their opinions shall become so concentrated as to secure the choice of a vice-president by the electoral colleges."[20] In short, the convention adopted Van Buren's policy of neutrality.[21]

Although perhaps dictated by immediate political circumstances, this evasive tactic only contributed to the confusion and ill feeling. Jackson reacted to the convention's decision by claiming that Johnson's supporters were false friends, bent on dividing the party; he

[17] Van Buren to Jackson, April [?], 1840, in Jackson, *Correspondence*, 6: 55–56.
[18] Jackson to Van Buren, April 29, 1840, Van Buren Papers.
[19] Gunderson, *The Log Cabin Campaign*, pp. 78–79.
[20] *Niles National Register*, 58: 150.
[21] On Van Buren's motives see Joel R. Poinsett to Joseph Johnson, March 12, 1840, Poinsett Papers in the Gilpin Collection.

reminded Van Buren that Polk would not wait in the wings forever.[22] Still, the president made no move. By the middle of June 1840, Forsyth, Polk, and King all withdrew their names, leaving Johnson as the lone contender.[23] This by no means solved all problems; Forsyth, in a characteristic display of impetuosity, let it be known that he was withdrawing under protest.[24] Jackson resigned himself to Johnson's candidacy but continually expressed doubts about prospects in Tennessee and Kentucky.[25] Thus, while the Whigs busily sent speakers throughout the country, whipping up public sentiment, administration spokesmen fell to arguing among themselves. It was as if the Democrats were all but oblivious to the opposition campaign.

This confusion came at a most inopportune time, just when the Whigs had begun a vicious congressional assault. During debate on a routine appropriation bill, Pennsylvania's demagogic Charles Ogle gained the floor of the House and delivered a rambling oration on the "Regal Splendor of the President's Palace," during which he guided his listeners on a tour of the White House. For three days, Ogle let his imagination run wild, depicting life in the sumptuous "Asiatic mansion" and assailing Van Buren as a dandy and a spendthrift. This lampoon soon became standard fare in Whig journals across the land.[26]

Ogle's invective represented a new twist in the opposition's continuing antiexecutive tirades. Since Jackson first incurred congressional displeasure, Whig leaders had lashed out against executive usurpation. This was more than just a reaction to Old Hickory's personality; a legislature accustomed to ruling the Washington community resented presidential interference. Van Buren fell heir to this animosity. During debate on the sub-Treasury, he repeatedly encountered charges that the measure was designed to increase his personal power. The Whigs rarely missed an opportunity to appeal to the lingering American fear of despotism. In December 1839, when Van Buren departed from the familiar grounds of state rights and called for more government control of the economy, Henry Clay stood ready to level a withering blast at the executive branch. Ogle merely

---

[22] Jackson to Van Buren, May 21, 1840, Van Buren Papers.

[23] Gunderson, *The Log Cabin Campaign*, p. 83.

[24] Forsyth, Letter in the Washington *Globe*, May 8, 1840; Jackson to Van Buren, May 21, 1840, Van Buren to Jackson, June 17, 1840, Van Buren Papers.

[25] Jackson to Van Buren, June 27, July 31, 1840, Van Buren to Jackson, July 16, 1840, Van Buren Papers.

[26] *Congressional Globe*, 26th Cong., 1st sess., 1839–1840, 8: 327, 331; for a description of this speech see Gunderson, *The Log Cabin Campaign*, pp. 102–107. It is ironic that Van Buren should have been charged with extravagance at a time when he was trying so hard to reduce government expenditures.

elaborated on the familiar theme by charging that the president was extravagant as well as tyrannical. In the midst of a bleak depression, such propaganda had a devastating effect. Moreover, Ogle's rantings coincided with accusations that Van Buren was trying to preserve his position by raising a standing army. For the furor that this charge created, the president had only himself to blame.

The rebellion in Canada and the disturbance in Maine had cast serious doubt on the adequacy of the nation's defenses. To correct existing deficiencies, Secretary of War Joel R. Poinsett urged a reform of the state militia structure. In particular, he objected to the lack of a consistent method of drilling the militiamen. "This instruction . . . without which it is impossible to form the soldier," Poinsett told Congress on March 20, 1840, "cannot be given in a day's training by officers as ignorant of these branches of the service as the soldiers themselves." The key to preparedness lay in a thorough, uniform training program. Poinsett realized that it would be too costly to apply these methods to all the country's 4 million citizen soldiers, and that it would be inefficient to instruct only the officers. Instead, he advocated creation of a new militia organization. Every male between the ages of twenty and forty-five would be required to enroll in his home district. The aggregate of all men thus enlisted would constitute the "mass" of the militia. From this body, the states would then choose 100,000 men for service in the "active or moveable force." This select component would drill several times a year under supervision of the federal government. Annually, one quarter would retire to the reserves, to be replaced by a new levy from the mass.[27]

Although perfectly logical in conception, Poinsett's plan was susceptible to misconstruction and distortion. The secretary had deliberately left blank the number of days during which the active force would drill. Obviously, he wanted Congress to fix this annual requirement. Unfortunately, he created the impression that the president wanted blanket authority over the militia. The sections of the bill specifying the exact location of yearly training sites were very vague; in establishing district commands, Poinsett had lumped together several states.[28] His critics were quick to charge that local troops might well be liable for extensive drilling away from home. The very term "active or moveable force" had an ominous ring.

A scheme that seemed to threaten a majority of the nation's eligible voters was bound to provoke widespread political turmoil. As

[27] *House Documents* (No. 153), 26th Cong., 1st sess., 1839–1840, pp. 1–17.
[28] Ibid., sections 14, 17, 36.

one commentator later said to Poinsett, "No plan was ever so misrepresented as yours. While every other subject such as finance, Banks etc. connected with the general government has been thoroughly discussed for years past before proper assemblies, that of *organizing the militia* was comparatively a new one and . . . [one about] which the public mind was least informed."[29] Less than six weeks after Poinsett's report to Congress, Virginia's Richard E. Parker wrote that the militia proposal had wreaked havoc in the recent state elections. "There is no describing, to you," he explained to James Buchanan, "the effect it produced upon those, who were told that they would immediately have to find their own arms . . . & be marched wheresoever the President pleased." Furthermore, the prospect of being "trained for an unlimited period under *Regular* officers" gave rise to extensive protests. "We have . . . evidence," Parker concluded, "that we lost more than a dozen counties & many votes in others, by Mr. Poinsett's project for training the militia."[30]

Alarmed at the vociferous response, administration tacticians tried to correct their mistake. The Washington *Globe* maintained that the new plan was no different from the one already in effect; men would not have to march outside their home states. As if realizing that these untruths might not prove persuasive, Blair added that Poinsett's proposal was by no means as comprehensive as that suggested by the Whig candidate William Henry Harrison.[31]

These feeble excuses in no way dampened the excitement. Seeing that only a wholesale retraction could relieve administration embarrassment, Poinsett decided to take all the blame himself. "I have derived an impression," he told Azariah C. Flagg, "that it is thought expedient . . . to show that the President was ignorant of the details of the militia bill and is not therefore answerable for them."[32]

The Virginia Democratic committee soon gave Poinsett his chance to apologize, by asking the administration to clarify its views on militia reorganization. In an open letter to Thomas Ritchie, Poinsett stated that the president had no specific knowledge of the particulars of the project sent to Congress.[33] Without even waiting for publica-

[29] Bedford Brown to Poinsett, September 23, 1840, Poinsett Papers in the Gilpin Collection.

[30] Parker to Buchanan, May 4, 1840, Buchanan Papers, The Historical Society of Pennsylvania.

[31] Washington *Globe*, April 27, May 1, 2, June 6, 1840.

[32] Poinsett to Flagg, May 5, 1840, Flagg Papers, New York Public Library; Flagg to Poinsett, May 10, 1840, Poinsett Papers in the Gilpin Collection.

[33] Ritchie to Poinsett, May 29, 1840, Poinsett to Ritchie, June 4, 1840, Poinsett Papers; Ritchie to Van Buren, June 2, 1840, Van Buren Papers; Poinsett to Ritchie, June 5, 1840, in Richmond *Enquirer*, June 12, 1840.

tion of Poinsett's apologia, the Albany *Argus* printed an identical explanation, absolving Van Buren of all responsibility.[34]

For a time, this ploy sufficed. Yet the Whigs now had an excellent campaign weapon, and they meant to use it to full advantage.[35] By mid-summer, continued complaints from state leaders convinced the president to make a personal statement. In reply to anxious queries from Virginia, Van Buren claimed that he had no personal knowledge of the details of Poinsett's reforms, adding that the "heads of departments act for Congress and not for the President." Van Buren further said that under the present circumstances, he could not constitutionally sanction any such thoroughgoing changes in the militia. Before closing, he denied that it had ever been his intention to raise a standing army. "If I had been charged with the design of establishing among you at public expense, a menagerie of two hundred thousand wild beasts, it would not have surprised me more, nor would it, in my judgment, have been one jot more preposterous."[36] Even this strong disclaimer failed to stem the criticism that continued unabated for the remainder of the campaign.[37]

This dispute provides an excellent example of Whig tactics and Democratic insensitivity. As in the past, Van Buren's opponents based their attack on the theme of executive usurpation. Ironically, Poinsett anticipated this stratagem in first recommending militia reform to Congress. He argued that proposed changes would obviate the need for placing a large standing army at the disposal of the chief executive.[38]

Clearly, the secretary of war and the president had not expected this controversy to extend beyond Capitol Hill. They ignored the capabilities of the new opposition network. Local Whig organizations, eager for material, spread the alarm throughout the countryside. To an electorate already incensed by the Panic, it seemed as though Van Buren was resorting to desperate expedients to keep his party together. Had the president understood that his opponents

[34] Albany *Argus*, June 5, 1840.
[35] James Graham to William A. Graham, May 20, 1840, in Graham, *Papers*, 2: 91–93; Millard Fillmore to Thurlow Weed, September 6, 1840, in Fillmore, *Papers*, 11: 213.
[36] Van Buren to John B. Carey et al., July 31, 1840, copy in the Van Buren Papers.
[37] Bedford Brown to Van Buren, August 30, 1840, Mahlon Dickerson to Van Buren, September 11, 1840, Peter V. Daniel to Van Buren, September 28, 1840, Garrett D. Wall to Van Buren, November 5, 1840, Jackson to Van Buren, November 20, 1840, Van Buren Papers; Albany *Argus*, August 15, September 8, October 15, 1840.
[38] *House Documents* (No. 153), 26th Cong., 1st sess., 1839–1840, p. 3.

could now appeal effectively to a mass electorate, he might have been more careful in his legislative proposals. By advocating reform of the military establishment during the height of an emotional upheaval, the administration showed that it was unaware of the changing political climate. Even when it became obvious that the Whigs had used this issue to good advantage, the president still reacted with characteristic detachment, writing a lengthy letter to justify his course. He seemed to think that logic and reason were sufficient to counter opposition calumnies. Once again, he failed to see that the times demanded new election procedures.

Van Buren's response to the militia issue typified his behavior in the closing months of the campaign. Throughout the sultry spring and summer months, he sat in the White House patiently directing local preparations and providing Democratic electoral committees with a steady stream of documents. The president continued to pay particular attention to New York; no detail seemed to escape his notice. He even solicited the names of likely readers for Amos Kendall's *Extra Globe*.[39] Repeatedly, in his appeals for vigorous canvassing, Van Buren warned of the need for vigilance. "Depend upon it," he cautioned Azariah C. Flagg, "that unless the most energetic measures are taken in advance to prevent frauds . . . we shall suffer severely from them."[40] Whenever the Whigs turned their attack to a new topic, Van Buren and his advisers calmly set about composing a suitable refutation.[41]

Although they repelled opposition sallies, the Democrats made little attempt to develop a theme that might divert attention from the Panic. For a time, they toyed with the issue of abolition, trying to cast Harrison as a covert accomplice in the antislavery cause.[42] This tactic proved dangerous, especially since Van Buren had always opposed open agitation on so sensitive a question. Clearly, the Democrats were on the defensive, a party without a dynamic appeal. Despite his political acumen and administrative ability, Van Buren simply did not have the magnetic personality that might erase memories of prolonged depression. His previous political career had attested to the success of cautious diplomacy and shrewd management.

[39] Van Buren to Azariah C. Flagg, May [?], 1840, Flagg Papers, Columbia University Library.

[40] Van Buren to Flagg, May [?], July [?], 1840, Flagg Papers, Columbia University Library.

[41] William L. Marcy to Prosper M. Wetmore, September 21, 1840, Marcy Papers.

[42] Washington *Globe*, March 7, 14, 21, May 13, 26, June 9, 27, August 25, September 21, November 5, 1840; Albany *Argus*, July 27, August 20, 1840.

These qualities, so essential to Van Buren the politician, did not assist Van Buren the president. The air of secrecy that had always surrounded his actions lent credence to the spurious charges of Whig propagandists.

While the president remained in the capital conscientiously answering the normal flood of campaign inquiries, his opponent broke all tradition and took to the stump. Harrison was by no means a stunning orator, but his appearance on the platform helped create a new bond between the voter and the candidate. Here was a man willing to go to the people, to converse with them in simple, understandable language, to recount his military exploits, and to assail the monarchal tendencies of the government in Washington. In a year when the common man was arriving on the political scene, "Old Tip" seemed to be waiting with an outstretched hand. Whig strategists took full advantage of their cooperative candidate to stage mammoth celebrations, replete with replicas of log cabins and appropriate quantities of hard cider.

Administration supporters tried valiantly to counter these tactics. For every log cabin, they raised a hickory pole; for each Tippecanoe club, they formed a Rough Hewer's association. Jackson himself graciously consented to appear at a number of political rallies in his home state. Several prominent senators toured the hustings on Van Buren's behalf. Tennessee's Felix Grundy, Pennsylvania's James Buchanan, Missouri's Thomas Hart Benton, and New York's Silas Wright, each took a turn at partisan speechmaking.[43] For Wright, at least, this novel experience was less than satisfying. "Not having any peculiar attachment to the business when I entered upon it," he complained after one strenuous outing, "I cannot say that my relish has in any way improved."[44] Like the president, Wright found it difficult to play the demagogue. Both had risen to power by relying on organization and discipline, not by cultivating a colorful image. Richard M. Johnson, the controversial vice-presidential nominee, proved to be the most effective Democratic campaigner, making a widely publicized swing through New York, Pennsylvania, and Ohio.[45]

Despite these grassroots heroics, Democratic spirits lagged. The administration continued to view the Whig campaign with a mixture

---

[43] Gunderson, *The Log Cabin Campaign*, pp. 161–72, 231–47.
[44] Wright to Azariah C. Flagg, October 4, 1840, Flagg-Wright Papers.
[45] Van Buren to Jackson, July 16, 1840, Van Buren Papers; Leland W. Meyer, *The Life and Times of Colonel Richard M. Johnson of Kentucky* (New York, 1932), pp. 446–49.

of scorn and disbelief. In a statement that captured the prevailing mood in Washington, Levi Woodbury wrote, "The people are becoming tired of mere hard cider. What a reproach it would be to have such an imbecile triumph over a vigorous and sagacious statesman."[46]

In New York, meanwhile, remnants of the Regency made an eleventh-hour bid to deliver the state to Van Buren and halt the Whig advance. Acting on the president's suggestions, Azariah C. Flagg and John A. Dix issued a complete set of instructions, telling subordinates how to establish an effective county and district network. This document was an impressive, practical handbook, listing all the duties and procedures for each level of the hierarchy. That the Democrats saw the need to publish such a plan barely two months before the election indicates the attenuation of the party machine.[47]

Although caught up in the excitement of election eve preparations, Van Buren became increasingly despondent. He could not understand the reason for Whig success, but he knew that his own party was in trouble. While not admitting defeat, the president became more and more concerned about the problem of vote frauds. Each Whig gain seemed to prove the existence of a massive plot to assault the ballot boxes.[48] Van Buren wrote urgently to Jackson that unless state leaders took immediate precautions, "the mischief will be done before you are apprised of the danger."[49]

Not satisfied with appeals for election day surveillance, the president's New York supporters decided to provide the state and the nation with irrefutable proof of Whig chicanery. Former Attorney General Benjamin F. Butler, now a federal district attorney, spent the greater part of October trying to assemble evidence showing illegal procedures in former state elections.[50] Late in the month, Butler arrested James B. Glentworth, claiming that the Whigs had paid this state employee to import voters during the canvass of

---

[46] Woodbury to John Law, May 26, 1840, Woodbury Papers. See also statements by Jackson quoted in G. Harris to Jackson, June 13, 1840, Jackson Papers.

[47] Flagg-Dix, Circular, September 6, 1840, Woodbury Papers; Albany *Argus*, October 6, 1840. For comments on the use of this plan in Maryland see Benjamin C. Howard to Van Buren, October 11, 1840, Van Buren Papers.

[48] Smith Thompson Van Buren to Azariah Flagg, August 30, 1840, Flagg Papers, Columbia University Library.

[49] Van Buren to Jackson, September 5, 1840, Van Buren Papers.

[50] Butler to Van Buren, August 28, October 17, 1840, John W. Edmonds to Van Buren, October 18, 1840, John J. Bedient to Van Buren, October 21, 1840, Van Buren Papers; Edmonds to Azariah C. Flagg, October 18, 1840, Flagg Papers, New York Public Library.

1838.[51] The Albany *Argus* rushed into print with a front-page spread giving all the details of Glentworth's nefarious activities.[52] In Washington, Blair used this new evidence as the basis for a continuous barrage against the opposition.[53]

This last-minute act of desperation could not stem the Whig tide. Swept along by a massive rush to the polls, Harrison carried nineteen of twenty-six states and received 234 electoral votes to Van Buren's 60. The unprecedented outpouring actually swelled the president's popular vote by nearly 400,000 over the total in 1836. Still, the Whigs proved more adept at recruiting new voters and thus derived the greatest advantage from the sudden upsurge in national interest. Van Buren lost every Northern state save two, New Hampshire and Illinois. In the South, he fared better, winning Alabama, Arkansas, Missouri, and Virginia.[54] Although cheered by the return of the Old Dominion, the president had reason to regret that recovery had come so late.

Shocked at the outcome of the voting, Francis P. Blair set the tone for the subsequent parade of Democratic protests. "General Harrison, the standard bearer of the Federal and Abolition parties, has been elected, if the process by which the result has been brought about can be called an election."[55] Jackson warned that the nation would have to correct election abuses or submit forever to "the combined money power of England and the federalists of this Union."[56] Of all Van Buren's followers, Azariah C. Flagg came closest to grasping the true reason for the Democratic downfall. "Never in my experience of 27 years," he told the president, had he seen "the rank and file show so much spirit and zeal."[57]

Van Buren accepted defeat calmly. By November he had convinced himself that the battle was lost and therefore "scarcely felt the catastrophe when it occurred."[58] In his mind, there was only one explanation for the outcome; the Whigs had succeeded in their plans

[51] Butler to Van Buren, October 23, 1840, Van Buren Papers.

[52] Albany *Argus*, October 26, 1840; William L. Marcy to Van Buren, October 25, 1840, Van Buren Papers.

[53] Washington *Globe*, October 26, 27, 28, 30, 1840.

[54] Gunderson, *The Log Cabin Campaign*, pp. 251–56.

[55] Washington *Globe*, November 9, 1840.

[56] Jackson to Van Buren, November 24, 1840, Van Buren Papers. See also Edwin Croswell to Van Buren, November 9, 1840, John Dix to Van Buren, November 17, 1840, Van Buren Papers.

[57] Flagg to Van Buren, November 15, 1840, Van Buren Papers.

[58] Van Buren to James Buchanan, November 24, 1840, Buchanan Papers, The Historical Society of Pennsylvania. See also Van Buren to Hermanus Bleecker, January 27, 1841, in William Gorham Rice Papers, New York State Library.

to subvert the popular will.[59] Believing that the voters would soon come to their senses, the president looked forward to some future vindication. As he remarked to Andrew Jackson shortly after the election, "Time will unravel the means by which these results have been produced, & the people will then do justice to all."[60]

By wrapping himself in the mantle of injured innocence, the president avoided a painful look backward. He would soon retire to his country estate, leaving behind a national career of exhilarating achievement and bitter defeat. Martin Van Buren first came to Washington at a time when the nation had begun to admit the necessity of political parties. Applying the lessons of his New York experience, Van Buren helped create a new political alliance that drew its strength from the states and promised to end the factional bickering that had so disrupted the Washington community. He saw in the Jeffersonian concepts of state rights and limited government the means to form and maintain a truly national party.

During his long service in the Jackson administrations, Van Buren remained acutely aware of state problems. Repeatedly he counseled Jackson to proceed with care, lest the Democracy compromise its commitment to the Jeffersonian creed. In part Van Buren succeeded; he believed that his own election would usher in a new era of Democratic unity.

Chosen to preserve the Jacksonian legacy, Van Buren saw that heritage dissolve like a rope of sand. Financial catastrophe destroyed his hope for harmony. Badly shaken by the onslaught of the Panic, he tried to rally the party and avoid both political and economic disaster. Neither his practical training nor his ideological upbringing pointed the way. Like his predecessor, Van Buren discovered the cruel limitations of the Jeffersonian concept of government. In trying to assert strong leadership, Van Buren alienated his most important allies. He attempted to act for the nation, but found himself in conflict with the states. Lacking the popularity that had sustained Jackson, Van Buren never escaped this dilemma. In 1840, the political system that once seemed so attuned to a decentralized, competitive society, collapsed under the weight of its own contradictions. The president was left standing amid the ruin, bewildered and alone.

[59] Angelica Singleton Van Buren to Mrs. Richard Singleton, November 11, 1840, Angelica Singleton Van Buren Papers, Library of Congress.
[60] Van Buren to Jackson, November 10, 1840, Van Buren Papers.

Epilogue

A TWENTY-SIX GUN salute shattered the predawn stillness, signaling the commencement of a bright new day for the Whig party. Despite the threat of snow, thousands of visitors crowded the streets of Washington. At ten o'clock, the inaugural procession began to form at Fourth and Pennsylvania. The Potomac dragoons, decked out in full regalia, led the march, followed by the Columbia Artillerists, the National Grays, and the National Blues. Then came a group of combat veterans who had served with William Henry Harrison during the War of 1812. They carried a flag reportedly captured from the enemy at the Battle of the Thames.

The president-elect chose not to ride in the traditional carriage; instead he mounted a white charger for the one-mile trip to the Capitol. Surrounded by marshals and friends, the sixty-eight-year-old Harrison appeared dignified but tired. Strung out behind him, delegates from local Tippecanoe clubs lofted placards and shouted lustily, giving the parade the aura of a political rally. As the column proceeded along the avenue, ladies leaned from the windows, waving white handkerchiefs at the aged warrior. Whig journalists, jubilant over the end of the long political drought, let no detail pass without comment. "Here might be seen a little fellow of seven or eight, his chubby cheeks rosy with joy, his bright eyes sparkling with the bustle and gladness of so novel a scene, waving proudly over his head a little banner, purchased probably with the savings of his pocket money for several days." Harrison greeted each burst of applause with a slight bow.

Surrounding the eastern portico of the Capitol, an impatient crowd of 35,000 awaited the beginning of the ceremony. When the dignitaries appeared, the audience broke into sustained cheering, stopping only when Harrison stepped forward to speak. The president-elect wasted little time in announcing the end of Democratic rule. "The great danger to our institutions does not appear to me to be in a usurpation by the Government of power not granted by the people, but by the accumulation in one of the departments of that which was assigned to others." Harrison then went on to list the ways in which an executive might undermine the popular will. He spoke of misuse of the veto, centralized control of the economy, presidential interference with the legislature, the corrupting effects of federal patronage, and abusive restriction of the nation's press. Rarely had an incoming administration so totally rejected or distorted the record of the past.[1]

Martin Van Buren heard none of this. The day belonged to the victors, and he remained discreetly out of sight. A week after the conclusion of the inaugural festivities, the former president bade farewell to the city that for nearly two decades had been his political home. He left office a dejected, disillusioned man, looking forward to a day of reckoning that never came. Van Buren longed to start the race anew, but in 1844 the Democrats turned instead to Tennessee's James K. Polk. Rejected now by both party and nation, Van Buren engaged in a brief, disastrous flirtation with the Free Soil movement before abandoning the presidential arena in 1848. He began his last political crusade eight years before his death, when at the age of seventy-two he compiled his autobiography, intending to vindicate his administration.[2] Unfortunately, the long, rambling manuscript remains incomplete and only recounts Van Buren's prepresidential career.

Still, the anguish of 1840 frequently intrudes on the narrative. In one particularly revealing passage, Van Buren paused to reflect on the whims of the electorate. "When one is presented to them possessed of an ardent temperament who adopts their cause," he observed, "they return sympathy for sympathy with equal sincerity and are always ready to place the most favorable construction on his actions and slow to withdraw their confidence however exceptionable his conduct in many respects may be." Van Buren both envied and regretted this political phenomenon. During his long career he had often captured the public's attention, but had never fired its imagination. "When a politician fails to make this impression," the former president concluded, "when they on the contrary are led to regard

---

[1] *National Intelligencer*, March 5, 1841; Richardson, *Messages and Papers*, 4: 3–21.

[2] William A. Butler, A *Retrospect of Forty Years* (New York, 1911), p. 2.

him as one who only takes the popular side of public questions from motives of policy their hearts seem closed against him, they look upon his wisest measures with distrust, and are apt to give him up at the first adverse turn in his affairs."[3]

[3] Van Buren, *Autobiography*, p. 168. Although Van Buren was recalling the career of De Witt Clinton, these comments accurately reflect the former president's attitude toward the electorate.

Bibliographical Essay

THIS essay attempts to describe those sources most relevant to a study of the presidency of Martin Van Buren. It makes no effort to comment on all material cited in the footnotes, nor does it review the vast body of secondary literature on the Jacksonian period. Alfred A. Cave, *Jacksonian Democracy and the Historians* (Gainesville, Fla., 1964), Charles G. Sellers, Jr., "Andrew Jackson Versus the Historians," *Mississippi Valley Historical Review* 44 (1958): 615–34, and the bibliographical essay in Glyndon G. Van Deusen, *The Jacksonian Era, 1828–1848* (New York, 1959), make this task unnecessary.

The Van Buren Papers (Library of Congress) provide a wealth of information on all phases of domestic and political affairs. Although it consists largely of incoming correspondence, the collection contains a number of the president's outgoing letters. Examination of these documents for the years 1821–1841 does not substantiate the claim of Holmes Alexander in *The American Talleyrand: The Career and Contemporaries of Martin Van Buren* (New York, 1935) that the president systematically destroyed incriminating material before his death. By consulting both the Van Buren and Jackson Papers, one could, for instance, reconstruct almost all the dialogue between the White House and the Hermitage. This would not have been possible had Van Buren or his heirs embarked on a large-scale destruction of historical evidence. In addition to private communications, the Van Buren manuscripts contain the complete draft of the *Autobiography* and copies of state papers. *The Calendar of the Papers of Martin Van Buren*, ed. Elizabeth H. West (Washington, D.C., 1910), remains an accurate guide to the bulk of the Van Buren collection.

Although completely inadequate by modern editorial standards, James D. Richardson, ed., *A Compilation of the Messages and*

Papers of the Presidents, 1789–1897 (10 vols.; Washington, D.C., 1900) and its several supplements give Van Buren's annual reports and other key messages. These volumes are by no means complete. Inconsistent in his criteria for selection, Richardson chose only a portion of the available material. His random and haphazard methods make this compilation unreliable; one must consult the congressional "serial set" and the *Journal of the Executive Proceedings of the Senate* 1789–1948 (90 vols.; Washington, D.C., 1828–1948) to find all the president's communications to the legislature.

The papers of Van Buren's associates vary in quality. The voluminous Andrew Jackson Papers (Library of Congress) are not so revealing for the period 1837–1841 as for earlier years. Frequently ill and out of touch with Washington, Old Hickory no longer stood at the center of Democratic politics. Francis P. Blair's regular letters to Jackson offer some insight into developments in the nation's capital. Blair's papers themselves (Library of Congress, Princeton University) show less of Van Buren's presidency than of Jackson's. The same is true of the Andrew J. Donelson Papers (Library of Congress) and the Andrew Jackson-Amos Kendall Papers (Library of Congress).

More helpful are the letters of key cabinet officials. As secretary of the treasury, Levi Woodbury played an important role in planning fiscal strategy. The Woodbury Papers (Library of Congress) are more extensive than those of any other presidential adviser and are vital in determining Van Buren's course during the Panic. The Joel R. Poinsett Papers (two collections, The Historical Society of Pennsylvania) are less illuminating; poor health and overwork often prevented the secretary of war from writing to his numerous political acquaintances. Still, these collections contain important documents on the Panic and foreign affairs. The Benjamin F. Butler Papers (Princeton University, New York State Library) do little justice to the attorney general's influence in the administration. Both he and Amos Kendall supervised party machinery, and yet neither left behind any significant personal letters on Van Buren's term. Nor is there adequate detail on John Forsyth. Small collections of his papers (Library of Congress, Princeton University) make practically no reference to his service as secretary of state. The Henry D. Gilpin Papers (The Historical Society of Pennsylvania) are somewhat fuller but pertain only to the closing months of the administration when Gilpin joined the council. For a sketchy account of cabinet meetings from 1834 to 1838, see the manuscript diary of Mahlon Dickerson (New Jersey Historical Society). The official correspondence of the various executive departments (National Archives) largely concerns administrative routine. Occasionally, however, these records yield significant political information.

One might expect to find elaborate descriptions of congressional proceedings among the papers of Democratic legislative leaders. Unfortunately, this is not the case. James K. Polk, the quiet, efficient Speaker of the House, rarely commented on his colleagues' activities; the Polk Papers (Library of Congress) tell far too little about the administration's organization and tactics. If the Polk Papers are unenlightening, those of Silas Wright and Churchill C. Cambreleng are practically nonexistent. Each man wrote fully and freely to Van Buren, but these letters came during congressional recesses. There are a number of significant Wright letters in the Flagg-Wright Papers (New York Public Library). Of all Democratic spokesmen, Connecticut's Senator John Niles most consistently reported events in the legislature. His frequent communications with Gideon Welles (Welles Papers, Library of Congress) constitute a major source on Van Buren's relations with Congress. So, too, the James Buchanan Papers (The Historical Society of Pennsylvania, Library of Congress) serve as a guide to deliberations on both fiscal and foreign affairs. The Adams Family Papers (Massachusetts Historical Society), the Franklin Pierce Papers (New Hampshire Historical Society, Transcripts in the Library of Congress), the Henry Clay Papers (Library of Congress), and the Daniel Webster Papers (Library of Congress) contain occasional hints on legislative maneuvers.

No body of correspondence provides greater insight into Democratic politics at both the state and national level than the Papers of William C. Rives (Library of Congress). This voluminous collection includes letters from practically every major statesman of the Jackson era. It is especially valuable in tracing the Democratic defection in both Virginia and New York. Governor David Campbell's regular reports on the Old Dominion, coupled with Nathaniel P. Tallmadge's frequent suggestions about congressional strategy make the Rives Papers an indispensable index to the Conservative revolt. By contrast, the Tallmadge Papers (Wisconsin State Historical Society) are disappointing, as are the Thomas Ritchie Papers (Library of Congress).

Although by no means as extensive as the Rives collection, the William L. Marcy Papers (Library of Congress) clearly demonstrate the decline of Democratic solidarity in the Empire State. The embattled New York governor frequently bared his soul to his confidant, Prosper M. Wetmore; these exchanges are the essence of political frankness. The Simon Gratz Autograph Collection (The Historical Society of Pennsylvania) contains some additional Marcy-Wetmore letters, as well as other major items bearing on Van Buren's administration. On the Regency and its relations with the national party see the Azariah C. Flagg Papers (Columbia University, New York Public Library), the John A. Dix Papers (Columbia University), and the Thomas Olcott Papers (Columbia University). The Galloway-Maxcy-Markoe Papers (Library of Congress) and the James Hammond Papers (Library of Congress) are of some assistance in determining the South's reaction to Van Buren's programs.

An abundance of diplomatic correspondence makes it somewhat easier to document Van Buren's foreign policy. The dispatches of the British minister, Henry Fox (Public Records Office London, Photostats in the Library of Congress), show the president's relentless attempts to maintain neutrality during the Canadian rebellion and the Northeast Boundary controversy. Fox's own biting commentaries accompany each transmission and indicate many of the obstacles strewn in Van Buren's path. As American minister to the Court of St. James, Virginia's Andrew Stevenson drew the difficult assignment of presenting Van Buren's entreaties to the Palmerston government. The Stevenson Papers (Library of Congress) contain several reports that show how closely the president directed negotiations during the spring and summer of 1838. This collection also includes key information on Southern politics. On the actions of Maine's governor during the northeast boundary controversy, see the John Fairfield Papers (Library of Congress). The Caleb Cushing Papers (Library of Congress) allude to congressional action on Van Buren's foreign policy.

Most of the pertinent correspondence on Mexico and Texas appears in print. The State Department Diplomatic Despatches (National Archives) are devoid of particulars about Van Buren's handling of Texas annexation, since he delayed accrediting a representative until just before the opening of the special session. On Texan sentiment in 1837 and 1838, see the following collections in Barker Library, University of Texas: Sam Houston Papers, Robert A. Irion Papers, Memucan Hunt Papers, and the Ashbel Smith Papers.

The published writings of Van Buren's contemporaries furnish supplementary information. John Spencer Bassett and J. Franklin Jameson edited the *Correspondence of Andrew Jackson* (7 vols.; Washington, D.C., 1926–1935). While displaying thorough acquaintance with the era, they occasionally deleted crucial letters. When using the Jackson and Van Buren manuscripts, one soon realizes the shortcomings of the Bassett edition. *The Life and Correspondence of Rufus King*, ed. Charles R. King (6 vols.; New York, 1894–1900), is an excellent source on Van Buren's rise to national prominence. King's frequent observations on the state of the Union corroborate the most recent interpretations of politics in the Era of Good Feelings. Equally beneficial, though not nearly so numerous, are the "Unpublished Letters of Thomas Ritchie," edited by Charles H. Ambler and printed in the *John P. Branch Historical Papers of Randolph Macon College*, 3 (1911): 199–252, 4 (1916): 372–418. Both the *Papers of William A. Graham, 1825–1856*, ed. J. G. de Roulhac Hamilton (4 vols.; Raleigh, N.C., 1957–1961), and the *Papers of Willie P. Mangum*, ed. Henry T. Shanks (5 vols.; Raleigh, N.C., 1950–1956), elucidate Van Buren's involvement in Southern politics. Nearly a half century ago, Reginald C. McGrane sifted through the Nicholas Biddle Papers (Library of Congress), selecting those bearing on the national scene. The editor's judgment was by no means infallible, but the *Correspondence of Nicholas Biddle* (Chicago, 1919) remains a serviceable volume, especially for the years 1837–1841. During this period, Biddle gradually withdrew from national affairs; McGrane's edition is thus much more reliable for Van Buren's presidency than for the bank war.

Unfortunately, current projects for publishing the writings of John C. Calhoun and Henry Clay have not yet reached the 1830's. Until they do, the following collections must suffice: J. Franklin Jameson, ed., "Correspondence of John C. Calhoun," American Historical Association, *Annual Report for the Year 1899*, 2 (Washington, D.C., 1900); Chauncey S. Boucher and Robert P. Brooks, eds., "Correspondence Addressed to John C. Calhoun 1837–1849," American Historical Association, *Annual Report for the Year 1929*, 2 (Washington, D.C., 1930), 125–533; Calvin Colton, ed., *The Private Correspondence of Henry Clay* (Cincinnati, Ohio, 1856) and *The Works of Henry Clay* (10 vols.; New York, 1904). For additional material, one should peruse the writings of Daniel Webster, Millard Fillmore, Robert M. T. Hunter, John Tyler, Hugh Swinton Legaré, James Kirke Paulding, John Tipton, and Richard M. Johnson.

Published diplomatic correspondence is invaluable to a study of Van Buren's foreign policy. George P. Garrison's edition of the "Diplomatic Correspondence of the Republic of Texas," appears in the American Historical Association, *Annual Report for the Year 1907*, 2 (Washington, D.C., 1908) and contains the exchanges between the Houston regime and Texan representatives in Washington. A check of the Texas State Archives (Austin) indicates that

Garrison omitted little. Also thorough and painstaking are two superb collections by William R. Manning: *Diplomatic Correspondence of the United States: Canadian Relations, 1784–1860* (4 vols.; Washington, D.C., 1940–1945) and *Diplomatic Correspondence of the United States: Inter-American Affairs, 1831–1860* (12 vols.; Washington, D.C., 1932–1939). Charles R. Sanderson, ed., *The Arthur Papers* (3 vols.; Toronto, 1943–1959) casts new light on Canadian-American relations in 1837 and 1838. As lieutenant governor of Upper Canada, Sir George Arthur superintended Canadian defenses. His correspondence with Henry Fox clearly gives the British view of Van Buren's policies.

Autobiographies, diaries, and memoirs supply added depth and fresh perspective. Van Buren's "Autobiography," edited by John C. Fitzpatrick, is printed in the American Historical Association, *Annual Report for the Year 1918*, 2 (Washington, D.C., 1920). It is very useful in charting Van Buren's early career but concludes before his election and therefore makes only passing references to the presidency. None of Van Buren's cabinet members have left detailed recollections. *The Autobiography of Amos Kendall*, ed. William Stickney (2 vols.; Boston, 1872), barely mentions the Kentuckian's tenure as postmaster general. *The Reminiscences of James A. Hamilton* (Washington, D.C., 1874) prints crucial correspondence on Van Buren's career in the 1820's and his role in the Jackson administration, but it contains little on the period after 1836. The same may be said of Catharina V. R. Bonney's *Legacy of Historical Gleanings* (2 vols.; Albany, N.Y., 1875).

For an acidulous and sometimes witty commentary on proceedings in the House, see Charles Francis Adams, ed., *Memoirs of John Quincy Adams Comprising Portions of His Diary from 1795–1848* (12 vols.; Philadelphia, 1874–1877). In the Senate, Thomas Hart Benton was in an excellent position to report the intricacies of political maneuvering, yet his *Thirty Years View* (2 vols.; New York, 1854–1856) is mainly an unabashed magnification of the author's oratorical feats. Both the *Diary of Philip Hone*, ed. Bayard Tuckerman (2 vols.; New York, 1889) and the *Diary of George Templeton Strong 1835–1875*, ed. Allan Nevins and Milton Halsey Thomas (4 vols.; New York, 1952) register the distress wrought by the Panic. The diaries and memoirs of Roger B. Taney, William C. Preston, Robert M. T. Hunter, and Hugh Lawson White contain little on Van Buren's term.

Of the numerous travelers' accounts of the Jacksonian period, three are of particular importance. Alexis de Tocqueville, *Democracy in America,* trans. Henry Reeve, and ed. Phillips Bradley (2 vols.; New York, 1945) remains the most perceptive analysis of the United States during a period of rapid social and economic change. In *Retrospect of Western Travel* (2 vols.; London, 1838), Harriet Martineau drew some penetrating sketches of political life in the nation's capital. Frederick Marryat left his impressions of the Van Buren administration in A *Diary in America with Remarks on Its Institutions,* ed. Jules Zanger (new ed.; Bloomington, Ind., 1960).

In an age of limited communications, the press dispensed news and served a vital political function. Although the Washington *Globe* (Democrat) remained the official paper during Van Buren's administration, its editor, Francis P. Blair, frequently misrepresented the president's policies. The *Globe's* intolerance hindered efforts to reach a compromise on the sub-Treasury bill. The *National Intelligencer* (Whig) spoke for the opposition, while *The Madisonian* (Conservative) aided those Democrats who broke with the president during the Panic. The Albany *Argus* (Democrat) is a key source for a study of the Regency in the 1820's, Van Buren's views during the Jackson administration, and the impact of the depression on New York's Democracy. Croswell's editorial policy in 1837 dramatically shows the disaffection between Albany and Washington; Thomas Ritchie's Richmond *Enquirer* (Democrat) demonstrates the same phenomenon in the Old Dominion. Two contemporary periodicals commented on the partisan scene. *Niles National Register* (neutral) often provides the text of speeches unavailable in the *Congressional Globe,* and contains convenient summaries of newspaper opinion throughout the country. The *United States Magazine and Democratic Review* (Democrat) approached politics in a polished, stylized fashion, a fact that may explain why it did not immediately supplant the *Globe* as the leading Democratic organ.

Secondary works must fill the gaps left by primary materials. The biographies mentioned in this section are not limited to the best works but to those that devote the most attention to Van Buren's presidency. There is no adequate biography of Van Buren. Hopefully, Robert V. Remini will soon fill this void. His *Martin Van Buren and the Making of the Democratic Party* (New York, 1959) traces Van Buren's political career to 1829 and focuses on the creation of the Jacksonian alliance. Of existing Van Buren biographies, Edward M. Shepard, *Martin Van Buren* (Boston, 1888) gives the fullest account of the presidential years. Despite the recent historiographical furor over Jacksonian democracy, Old Hickory remains a relatively neglected figure. John Spencer Bassett, *The Life of Andrew*

Jackson (2 vols.; New York, 1911) is the most authoritative study of the seventh president.

Biographies of Van Buren's advisers are of limited value. In his work on *Silas Wright* (New York, 1949), John A. Garraty chronicles the New York senator's career, but occasionally distorts key events. Garraty seems unwilling to admit that during the Panic, Wright hesitated to support the sub-Treasury. The best treatments of cabinet members are J. Fred Rippy, *Joel Roberts Poinsett* (Durham, N.C., 1935), and Joseph H. Parks, *Felix Grundy* (Baton Rouge, La., 1940). Alvin Laroy Duckett, *John Forsyth* (Athens, Ga., 1962), is uninspired. William E. Smith, *The Francis Preston Blair Family in Politics* (2 vols.; New York, 1933), overestimates Blair's influence within the Van Buren administration. There are no biographies of Churchill C. Cambreleng, Benjamin F. Butler, Amos Kendall, or Levi Woodbury.

By far the most succinct and worthwhile account of a congressional leader is Charles Grier Sellers, Jr., *James K. Polk: Jacksonian, 1795–1843* (Princeton, N.J., 1957). A thorough mastery of relevant source material enables Sellers to strike an excellent balance between state and national developments. At the same time, he is not wont to inflate Polk's importance. No student of the 1830's can ignore Charles M. Wiltse, *John C. Calhoun* (3 vols.; Indianapolis, Ind., 1944–1951). Wiltse goes to great lengths in exploring the myriad political alignments of the day and examines congressional proceedings in minute detail. What emerges from this effort is a well-argued defense of the Nullifier's tortuous political career. Wiltse rarely questions Calhoun's motives and slights those sources that do. In interpreting the Panic of 1837, he feels bound to justify Calhoun's desertion of the Whigs and support of the sub-Treasury. He does so by claiming that the senator took advantage of the financial crisis to assume leadership of splintered Democratic forces. Wiltse's whole case rests on his assertion that Van Buren decided to press for passage of the divorce bill only when sure of Calhoun's backing; there is practically no evidence to prove this theory. It is much more likely that the threat of a protracted battle between bank and antibank forces left Calhoun nowhere to go but back into the Democratic ranks. For a more persuasive interpretation of Calhoun's machinations see Gerald M. Capers, *John C. Calhoun—Opportunist: A Reappraisal* (Gainesville, Fla., 1960). While Wiltse distorts major congressional issues of Van Buren's presidency, Samuel Flagg Bemis, *John Quincy Adams and the Union* (New York, 1956), tends to ignore them completely. Bemis, like Adams, involves himself entirely in the growing antislavery crusade of the 1830's. This preoccupation prevents the author from making mention of the other debates to which Adams was a party.

Studies of other congressional leaders include William N. Chambers, *Old Bullion Benton* (Boston, 1956); George Ticknor Curtis, *Daniel Webster* (2 vols.; New York, 1870); Robert J. Rayback, *Millard Fillmore* (Buffalo, N.Y., 1959); Glyndon G. Van Deusen, *The Life of Henry Clay* (Boston, 1937); Albert D. Kirwan, *John J. Crittenden* (Lexington, Ky., 1962); Linda Rhea, *Hugh Swinton Legaré* (Chapel Hill, N.C., 1934); James P. Shenton, *Robert John Walker* (New York, 1961); and Philip S. Klein, *President James Buchanan* (University Park, Pa., 1962).

To appreciate Van Buren's trials as president, one must investigate the effect of the sub-Treasury on local politics. For a vivid picture of the Regency's torment see Ivor D. Spencer, *The Victor and the Spoils: A Life of William L. Marcy* (Providence, R.I., 1959). Glyndon G. Van Deusen treats the undoing of the Regency in *Thurlow Weed: Wizard of the Lobby* (Boston, 1947). Less perceptive on response in the Old Dominion is Charles H. Ambler, *Thomas Ritchie* (Richmond, Va., 1913). Francis Fry Wayland, *Andrew Stevenson* (Philadelphia, 1949), adds little on the operations of the Richmond Junto, but does contain a useful summary of Stevenson's activities while minister to England. Thomas P. Govan, *Nicholas Biddle* (Chicago, 1959), skillfully combines an understanding of Pennsylvania politics with a detailed analysis of the battle between Biddle and Van Buren over the bank.

General works on the presidency are of little use in a study of Van Buren's administration. Too often they employ present models to evaluate the past. One new work that hints at the difference between the nineteenth- and twentieth-century executive is James Sterling Young, *The Washington Community, 1800–1828* (New York, 1966). Leonard D. White, *The Jacksonians: A Study in Administrative History, 1829–1861* (New York, 1954), contributes significant data on the routine conduct of national government.

Any analysis of Van Buren's administration must treat the financial crisis of the 1830's. For the workings of the national economy and a guide to other relevant studies see George Rogers Taylor, *The Transportation Revolution* (New York, 1951) and Douglass C. North, *The Economic Growth of the United States* (Englewood Cliffs, N.J., 1961). Few publications can match the scope of Bray Hammond's, *Banks and Politics in America from the Revolution to the Civil War* (Princeton, N.J., 1957). Hammond is extremely partial to Nicholas Biddle and quick to fault the Jacksonians for not anticipating modern banking practices. Frank Otto Gatell's "Sober Second Thoughts on Van Buren, the Albany Regency, and the Wall Street Conspiracy," *Journal of American History* 53 (1966): 19–40 effectively challenges Hammond's main thesis on the motives behind the bank war. On the conflicting economic theories of the age see Joseph Dorfman, *The Economic Mind in American Civilization* (3 vols.; New York, 1946–1949); Fritz Redlich, *The Molding of American Banking: Men and Ideas* (New York, 1947); Sister M. Grace Madeleine, *Monetary and Banking Theories of Jacksonian Democracy* (Philadelphia, 1943); and pertinent sections of Marvin Meyers, *The Jacksonian Persuasion: Politics and Belief* (Stanford, Calif., 1957). Peter Temin, *The Jacksonian Economy* (New York, 1969) came to hand while this book was in press.

Robert V. Remini's brief portrait of *Andrew Jackson and the Bank War* (New York, 1967) serves as a useful guide to this highly complex subject. In *Biddle's Bank: The Crucial Years* (New York, 1967), Jean A. Wilburn tries to indicate the sources of probank sentiment. Her cursory treatment adds little to our knowledge of the Jackson-Biddle duel. More informative are Ralph C. H. Catterall, *The Second Bank of the United States* (Chicago, 1903) and Walter B. Smith, *Economic Aspects of the Second Bank of the United States* (Cambridge, Mass., 1953). Several incisive articles treat various aspects of the struggle: Frank Otto Gatell, "Spoils of the Bank War: Political Bias in the Selection of Pet Banks," *American Historical Review* 70 (1964): 35–38, "Secretary Taney and the Baltimore Pets: A Study in Banking and Politics," *Business History Review* 39 (1965): 205–27; Richard H. Timberlake, Jr., "The Specie Circular and the Distribution of the Surplus," *Journal of Political Economy* 68 (1960): 109–17, "The Specie Standard and Central Banking in the United States before 1860," *Journal of Economic History* 21 (1961): 318–41; and Harry Schieber, "The Pet Banks in Jacksonian Politics and Finance, 1833–1841," *Journal of Economic History* 23 (1963): 196–214.

On the political and economic aftermath of the bank war see John M. McFaul, "The Politics of Jacksonian Finance" (Ph.D. diss., University of California, Berkeley, 1964). McFaul argues that after the removal of deposits both Jackson and Van Buren took strong steps to control the economy and that the sub-Treasury capped these efforts. This theory attributes too much logic to Democratic fiscal strategy. McFaul also tends to underestimate the importance of the Panic in prompting adoption of the independent treasury as an emergency expedient. James Roger Sharp, "Banking and Politics in the States: The Democratic Party after the Panic of 1837" (Ph.D. diss., University of California, Berkeley, 1966) surveys state reactions to the financial crisis, but does not discuss the policies of the federal government.

The only narrative dealing directly with the depression is Reginald C. McGrane, *The Panic of 1837* (Chicago, 1919). McGrane's economic and political judgments stand the test of time. Neither David Kinley, *The Independent Treasury of the United States and Its Relations to the Banks of the Country* (Washington, D.C., 1910) nor Esther R. Taus, *Central Banking Functions of the United States Treasury, 1789–1941* (New York, 1943) has much to say about the Van Buren administration. Of more assistance are Richard H. Timberlake, Jr., "The Independent Treasury and Monetary Policy before the Civil War," *Southern Economic Journal* 27 (1960): 92–103 and Edward G. Bourne, *History of the Surplus Revenue of 1837* (New York, 1885). None of these studies consider Van Buren's reasons for turning to the sub-Treasury or his efforts to secure its adoption.

Biographies and general surveys of the Jacksonian era tend to disregard foreign affairs. The standard interpretations of the Texas question and the Mexican claims dispute are Stanley Siegel, *A Political History of the Texas Republic* (Austin, Texas, 1956); Justin H. Smith, *The Annexation of Texas* (New York, 1911); George L. Rives, *The United States and Mexico* (2 vols.; New York, 1913); and Clayton C. Kohl, *Claims as a Cause of the War with Mexico* (New York, 1914). Rives alone considers the interaction of domestic politics and diplomacy. An inaccurate account of Van Buren's neutrality policy mars Albert D. Corey's otherwise helpful *The Crisis of 1830–1842 in Canadian-American Relations* (New Haven, Conn., 1941). There is no up-to-date, book-length discussion of the northeast boundary controversy. Thomas Le Duc, "The Maine Frontier and the Northeastern Boundary Controversy," *American Historical Review* 53 (1947): 30–41 and David Lowenthal, "The Maine Press and the Aroostook War," *Canadian Historical Review* 32 (1951): 315–36, are useful articles.

Richard P. McCormick's *The Second American Party System* (Chapel Hill, N.C., 1966) is a convenient synthesis of the numerous examinations of state politics in the early nineteenth century. McCormick persuasively restates a thesis advanced in earlier articles, namely, that by 1840 the United States had developed a genuine two-party system, explaining the sudden upsurge in voter participation during the log cabin campaign. In tracing this evolution in each state, McCormick often finds himself at the mercy of inferior scholarship. As a consequence, his survey is extremely uneven. McCormick argues that Van Buren's candidacy created discontent in the South; no doubt this was a factor in the collapse of 1840. Still, Jackson sowed the seeds of dissension long before Van Buren became the heir-apparent. McCormick also tends to disregard the impact of the Panic of 1837 on the electorate.

Most state studies tend to focus on the concept of Jacksonian democracy and, as a consequence, ignore Van Buren's term. Lee Benson's *The Concept of Jacksonian Democracy, New York as a Test Case* (Princeton, N.J., 1961) is the most provocative of recent works. He effectively challenges many of the observations of Arthur Schlesinger, Jr., *The Age of Jackson* (Boston, 1945). Still, Schlesinger comes closer than any other historian to capturing the spirit of the era. Furthermore, Benson's methods, taken too far, could preclude all but the most trivial generalizations about politics. For a recent challenge to Benson's socioeconomic analysis see Frank Otto Gatell, "Money and Party in Jacksonian America: A Quantitative Look at New York's Men of Quality," *Political Science Quarterly* 82 (1967): 235–52.

Both Jabez D. Hammond, *The History of Political Parties in the State of New York* (2 vols.; Albany, N.Y., 1842) and Dixon Ryan Fox, *The Decline of Aristocracy in the State of New York* (New York, 1919), help untangle the labyrinthian involvements of Bucktails and Clintonians. Robert V. Remini, "The Albany Regency," *New York History* 39 (1958): 341–55, analyzes the structure of the Van Buren machine. Despite poor organization, Alvin Kass, *Politics in New York State, 1800–1830* (Syracuse, N.Y., 1965), has some useful insights. Robert Shaw's *Erie Water West* (Lexington, Ky., 1966) gives a complete account of the Regency's duel with De Witt Clinton over the Erie Canal. On the turmoil in New York politics during the Van Buren administration see William Trimble, "Diverging Tendencies in New York Democracy during the Period of the Locofocos," *American Historical Review* 24 (1919): 396–421.

Richard H. Brown brilliantly examines conditions leading to formation of the Albany-Richmond axis in "The Missouri Crisis, Slavery, and the Politics of Jacksonianism," *South Atlantic Quarterly* 65 (1966): 55–72. Brown's account far surpasses Joseph H. Harrison, Jr., "Martin Van Buren and His Southern Supporters," *Journal of Southern History* 22 (1956): 438–58. Charles H. Ambler, *Sectionalism in Virginia from 1776–1851* (Chicago, 1910), does not provide an adequate interpretation of the Old Dominion in the 1830's. There is no separate study of the Richmond Junto, although Harry Ammon, "The Richmond Junto, 1800–1824," *Virginia Magazine of History and Biography* 61 (1953): 395–418, discusses its formation. Nor is there a work on the Conservative defection. Howard Braverman, "The Economic and Political Background of the Conservative Revolt in Virginia," *Virginia Magazine of History and Biography* 60 (1952): 266–87, glances at local responses to the sub-Treasury, but does not relate these to developments in Washington.

Perhaps the model treatment of state politics in the Jackson era is William W. Freehling, *Prelude to Civil War: The Nullification Controversy in South Carolina, 1816–1836* (New York, 1966). Freehling's judicious assessment of the Southern temperament is particularly relevant to an understanding of Van Buren's efforts to achieve sectional calm. William Hoffman's study of *Andrew Jackson and North Carolina Politics* (Chapel Hill, N.C., 1958), is also rewarding, but unfortunately does not carry the story beyond 1836. In his biography of James K. Polk, Charles Sellers makes the best political survey of Jackson's home state. The same author's "Banking and Politics in Jackson's Tennessee, 1817–1827," *Mississippi Valley Historical Review* 41 (1958): 615–34, is a thought-provoking article on political change in the Era of Good Feelings.

On Pennsylvania see Philip S. Klein, *Pennsylvania Politics, 1817–1832: A Game without Rules* (Philadelphia, 1940) and a complementary study by Charles M. Snyder, *The Jacksonian Heritage, Pennsylvania Politics, 1833–1838* (Harrisburg, Pa., 1958). Snyder's work points out the perils Van Buren faced in trying to distribute patronage among the warring factions in the Keystone State. The other notable state studies of the period, Edwin A. Miles, *Jacksonian Democracy in Mississippi* (Chapel Hill, N.C., 1960) and Paul Murray, *The Whig Party in Georgia, 1825–1853* (Chapel Hill, N.C., 1948) were of little use. William G. Carleton, "Political Aspects of the Van Buren Era, 1837–1841," *South Atlantic Quarterly* 50 (1951): 167–85 and Lawrence Hurst, "National Party Politics, 1837–1840," *Studies in American History Inscribed to James Albert Woodburn* (Bloomington, Ind., 1926), pp. 119–52, outline party maneuvering during Van Buren's presidency. For a colorful narrative of the election of 1840 see Robert Gray Gunderson, *The Log Cabin Campaign* (Lexington, Ky., 1957).

In addition to those cited above, several unpublished dissertations contributed to the preparation of this work. Richard H. Brown, "Southern Planters and Plain Republicans of the North: Martin Van Buren's Formula for the Democratic party" (Ph.D. diss., Yale University, 1955) discusses the formation of the Democratic party with particular emphasis on the construction of the North-South alliance. Brown's thoughtful insights into the latent sectional crisis of the 1820's invigorate his narrative. He does exaggerate Van Buren's importance during Jackson's first administration and concludes by sidestepping the nullification controversy. Not nearly so helpful, Leon W. Cone, Jr., "Martin Van Buren: The Architect of the Democratic Party, 1837–1840" (Ph.D. diss., University of Chicago, 1951) does not explore the available source material and tends to ignore both the cabinet and foreign affairs. Cone sketches the debate on the sub-Treasury but fails to analyze its impact on the party. Until a biography appears, Raymond C. Dingledine, "The Political Career of William C. Rives" (Ph.D. diss., University of Virginia, 1945) remains the only account of a crucial Jacksonian congressional figure.

Richard P. Longaker considers the Jackson administration in "Andrew Jackson and the Presidency" (Ph.D. diss., Cornell University, 1954). By divorcing the executive from his political base, Longaker misses a great deal of the significance of Jackson's term. For a convenient summary of Van Buren's public position on the sectional dilemma see Richard W. Smith, "The Career of Martin Van Buren in Connection with the Slavery Controversy through the Election of 1840" (Ph.D. diss., Ohio State University, 1959).

Index

abolitionism: Van Buren's actions concerning, 47–48, 202

Adams, John, 193

Adams, John Quincy: and election of 1824, 20–22; presidential policies of, 24, 27; and election of 1828, 25–26; and antislavery agitation in Congress, 117–18; and Texas annexation, 159, 169; and Mexican claims dispute, 166; mentioned, 24, 28, 30, 48, 59, 88, 99, 127, 189

Alabama: and election of 1840, 205

Albany, N.Y.: as terminus of Erie Canal, 9, 13; postmastership in, 15–16; communications with Washington, D.C., 115, 121; mentioned, 7–8, 92–93

Albany Argus: as Regency paper, 12; and abolitionism, 48; and election of 1836, 49; and specie circular, 68; and special session, 84, 92, 94, 109; and first annual message, 116–17; and election of 1840, 192, 205; and militia reform, 201; mentioned, 25, 38, 80, 135, 145

Albany Regency: creation of, 11–12; and battle over postmastership (1822), 15–16; and People's party, 20; removes Clinton from Canal Board, 21; and election of 1828, 25; and anti-Masonic party, 25–26; economic policies of, 33; relationship to Van Buren administration, 61, 120–21, 145; and bank suspensions, 74; disenchantment with special session program, 92; and elections in New York (1837), 113, (1838), 135–37; Van Buren's efforts to resurrect, 191–93; and election of 1840, 204–205; mentioned, 41, 48, 54, 55, 80, 87

Allen, Thomas: and founding of *The Madisonian,* 82–83; elected congressional printer, 96; mentioned, 91, 149

American Anti-Slavery Society, 47

anti-Masonic movement, 25–26, 190

antislavery: agitation in Congress concerning, 88, 117–19, 127

Argus of Western America, 58

Arkansas: and election of 1840, 205

Aroostook River, 183, 185

Aroostook War. *See* northeast boundary controversy

Augusta, Me., 185–86

Baltimore Convention (1832), 37–38; (1835), 46; (1840), 194, 196–97

Bangor, Me., 186

Bank of England: and Panic of 1837, 67

Bank of the United States (1816–1836): Jackson's attack on, 35–36, 38, 64–65, 114; removal of deposits from, 45–46, 52, 59, 65–66, 142; Biddle's efforts to resurrect, 72, 133–34; mentioned, viii, 101, 131

Bell, John, 88, 146

Benton, Nathaniel, 172–73

Benton, Thomas Hart: and Panic of 1837, 66–68; as Democratic stalwart in Senate, 87; and election of 1840, 203; mentioned, 5, 37, 123, 125

Biddle, Nicholas: and bank war, 35–37, 64; attempts to obtain recharter, 72, 133–34; attacked by Washington *Globe,* 112; and sub-Treasury bill, 131–32, 133; and bank suspensions (1839), 142–43; mentioned, 59, 71, 74, 81, 89, 101, 130, 135, 142

Blair, Francis P.: and election of 1836,

strength in Twenty-Sixth Congress,
145, 149; and speakership election
in 1839, 146; and passage of sub-
Treasury, 150–51; structure of,
189–90; and election of 1840, 189–
206; Van Buren's attitude toward,
193; celebrates Harrison's victory,
207–208; mentioned, x, 75, 81, 98,
148
White, Campbell P., 111–12
White, Hugh Lawson, 47, 49, 189
Whitney, Reuben, 83
Wise, Henry, 162
Woodbury, Levi: biographical sketch
of, 59; and specie circular, 70;
actions on the eve of the Panic of
1837, 71, 73; and sub-Treasury, 98,
122; and state banks, 141; mentioned, 56, 58, 68, 82, 97, 100,
111, 134, 140, 142, 175, 204

Wright, Silas: and nullification crisis,
41; as adviser to Van Buren, 61; and
possible repeal of specie circular, 68,
70; initial reactions to idea of an
independent Treasury, 78–79; agrees
to support Van Buren's proposals,
80–81; biographical sketch of, 87;
leads Senate fight for special session
program, 96–97; sponsors sub-
Treasury bill in Senate, 98, 103–
105, 132, 139, 140, 147; introduces
resolution against recharter, 101;
criticizes Washington *Globe*, 114;
and special deposit scheme, 121–23;
and state banks, 141; supports
Van Buren's Texas policy, 155;
works to secure Van Buren's reelection, 194, 203; mentioned, 79,
93, 99, 100, 102, 107, 117, 125,
126, 130, 143